Joanna Maxwell started her working life as a corporate lawyer, a career from which she has now fully recovered. Sydney-based, Joanna has been a guide, confidante and coach for people with career dilemmas for over 20 years, helping those in midlife and beyond to escape unhappy careers, to reinvent their working life and to flourish.

Other career highlights include writing on careers and creativity for *AFR BOSS* magazine, running a business start-up program for migrant women in Lakemba and working on two series of the Fairfax Digital radio show *The Road Next Travelled* with co-host Ray Martin AM.

In late 2017, Joanna joined the Australian Human Rights Commission as part of the Age Discrimination Team.

Further information about Joanna's work can be found at: joannamaxwell.com.au.

Praise for Joanna Maxwell

'Joanna's ideas and advice were key to my confidence when I started up my catering business. She wouldn't let me see my age as a barrier.'

Sahar Elsemary, 48, small business training

'Joanna has given me the tools and ideas to take away and work with once I give up my corporate career. I feel so much more excited about my future.'

Reg Jarvis, workshop participant

'Joanna is wise, in touch with your situation and no-nonsense. I took her ideas as opportunities to lift my thinking. After a while, I had to start doing the thinking by myself. As time went on, Joanna had me on my own two feet.'

Keren, 60 plus, coaching client

'So much focus is around the money that you have for your older age, but your course reminded me that it is all so much bigger and broader than that.'

Jan Dalton, 57, workshop participant

RETHINK
YOUR
CAREER

In your 40s,
50s and 60s

JOANNA MAXWELL

ABC
Books

Author's note

The case studies in this book are real but in some cases identifying details have been changed to protect people's privacy. While this book is intended as a general information resource, it does not take account of individual circumstances and is not in any way a substitute for financial or legal advice. Any views or opinions expressed in this book by the author are personal to her. The author and publisher cannot be held responsible for any claim or action that may arise from reliance on the information contained in this book.

 The ABC 'Wave' device is a trademark of the Australian Broadcasting Corporation and is used under licence by HarperCollins*Publishers* Australia.

First published in Australia in 2017
by HarperCollins*Publishers* Australia Pty Limited
ABN 36 009 913 517
harpercollins.com.au

Copyright © Work in Colour Pty Limited 2017

HarperCollins*Publishers*
Level 13, 201 Elizabeth Street, Sydney, NSW 2000, Australia
Unit D1, 63 Apollo Drive, Rosedale, Auckland 0632, New Zealand
A 53, Sector 57, Noida, UP, India
1 London Bridge Street, London, SE1 9GF, United Kingdom
2 Bloor Street East, 20th floor, Toronto, Ontario M4W 1A8, Canada
195 Broadway, New York, NY 10007

National Library of Australia Cataloguing-in-Publication entry (paperback):

Creator: Maxwell, Joanna, author.
Title: Rethink your career : in your 40s, 50s and 60s / Joanna Maxwell.
ISBN: 978 0 7333 3810 6 (paperback)
ISBN: 978 1 4607 0802 6 (ebook)
Notes: Includes index.
Subjects: Career changes.
Occupational mobility.
Career development--Handbooks, manuals, etc.

Cover design by HarperCollins Design Studio
Typeset in Sabon LT Std by Kirby Jones
Author photograph by Scarlett Vespa
Printed and bound in Australia by McPherson's Printing Group
The papers used by HarperCollins in the manufacture of this book are a natural, recyclable product made from wood grown in sustainable plantation forests. The fibre source and manufacturing processes meet recognised international environmental standards, and carry certification.

To all the people who generously shared their stories and helped me understand how things are now for people over 50.

And to my son, Joshua, who gives me hope
that the future is in good hands.

Contents

Foreword

I met Joanna Maxwell in 2015. I was hosting a couple of radio series for the Fairfax Network about retirement and she was hauled aboard to be the program's 'life coach'. We laughed a lot, and tried our best to come up with a better word than 'retirement' – which somehow seems to imply bowls and bingo and polished wooden boxes. (Not that there's anything wrong with TWO of those lifestyles!)

It's important to think about life and work as we age, because life expectancy in Australia has doubled since Federation. And people are not just living longer, they're healthier, too. And if they're lucky, they may have a few more dollars in their pockets than their parents did. They want to start a new chapter in life beyond just buying a caravan and hitting the road as grey nomads. (Not that there's anything wrong with that, it's just not for everybody.)

It's not about stopping, it's about having a go.

I once asked David Attenborough, who has just turned 90, 'What's the secret of success in later life?' He said, 'Within reason, you don't do anything you don't like, you don't do anything you like, you only do things that you love.' That's a great mantra.

I'm on that journey already. I've spent about 50 years as a journalist and I've loved it – writing stories and putting them on television. But I've also had a passion for taking photographs, almost on the quiet. Well, now I've come out, as they say. I've had a photographic book published and I've been part of a photographic exhibition. For me, rethinking my career has given me the chance to write some books and turn my hobby of photography into a bit of an obsession. It's allowed me to turn a dream into reality.

Whatever stage of life you're in, one of the things we know is that it's important to set some realistic goals and have a sense of purpose. Having a plan and being willing to take a few risks also help when you're rethinking your career.

In one sense we can say, 'I've got a lifetime of experience, I know what I can do and I can't do', but we also have to know that you *can* teach old dogs new tricks. Nearly 150,000 Australians un-retire every year and about one-third of those say they were just so bored that they went back to work.

People who get to a certain age have had a life – they've had jobs, they've had children and homes, they've succeeded or they've stumbled, they've really chalked up some victories. They have what it takes to do a new challenge, but they need courage, they need to be flexible. They need to avoid saying, 'I can't do that, I've tried that and it doesn't work.' To take a deep breath and say 'I am just going to have a go' is probably the toughest thing of all. Persistence is the key to success, really.

At the end of the day, you have to get out the front door and make it happen. This book will help you do that because Joanna has a way of cutting to the chase, identifying the problem and offering some colourful options. That's what you need when you're at a crossroads, I reckon. A lawyer in an earlier life – I suspect a very good one – Joanna chooses her words carefully, not given to rash generalisations. Or loose talk. So, if you are searching for some tips as you rethink your career, she's a wonderful mentor.

Joanna makes me smile. Sometimes even laugh. That's gotta be a good thing. She's calm and gently confident, easy-going, a listener – and not judgemental. She has the knack of quickly understanding a situation – no matter what the circumstances and oddities – and dispensing fresh ideas and solutions. It's a real skill.

If you're wondering whether you should buy *Rethink Your Career*, I suggest you do – for yourself, a parent or a friend. Joanna Maxwell is terrific value and her book is highly readable, illuminating and wise.

Ray Martin AM

Is this book for you?

I wrote this handbook for people who are looking to reinvent their working life so it can take them through their 50s, 60s and beyond. I wrote it for people who want to take charge of planning the coming decades, the next stage of their life.

If you:

- are 40 plus
- are unsure about what lies ahead but are interested in making the most of it
- want to change how you think about your working life
- are keen to access the latest thinking in this area
- have no ideas, some ideas or many ideas about your working life over the next decades
- keep being nudged by an old dream that won't go away
- or if you are just plain unhappy at work and want to find a better path

then this book is for you.

It's also for the partners, friends, parents, children or colleagues of the above. If you are suffering through the work crisis of a loved one, or the person in the next office, then do them a favour and give them this book.

This handbook is different from standard career guides, for several reasons.

Firstly, it is written specifically for people in their 50s and beyond (and people in their 40s looking towards that time). The interviews, advice and exercises are tailored to meet your needs and circumstances. And I am 59, and have lived, worked and researched this demographic. I get it.

This book is Australian, which most career guides are not, so the examples, interviews, case studies and expert tips are aimed squarely at Australians.

Every exercise in this book has been tried and tested – on me, and on hundreds of my clients over the last 20 years. This proven process is grounded in experience, backed up by research and case studies, and is versatile enough to suit many career issues.

It's solution-focused, and paced to give you a sense of progress and momentum. You get to take charge of your own process, with a structured toolkit of exercises, inspiration from experts and people who have successfully reinvented their working lives, and practical advice at every stage.

The techniques, tips and exercises in this book draw on logical, linear, analytical thinking, but also creative, 'possibility-thinking' ideas and paradigms. It will give you new ways of thinking, problem-solving and dealing with our changing world.

Most importantly, the reinvention process is based on my 'inside-out' philosophy of careers. Often when things aren't going well at work, we look outside ourselves for the answer – the job, the person, the course or the lucky charm that will fix us. I believe that we need to start by looking inside, by discovering our strengths, beliefs, values, dreams and desires. Only then can we find that perfect match in the world of work.

How does the book work?

This book is primarily a guidebook. Just as a travel guide to a foreign destination has a mix of information, tips, stories and local knowledge, this handbook is both a toolkit and a compass, with a good dose of inspiration and encouragement to keep you going.

The book is full of:
- topic discussions, ideas and stories
- exercises
- examples
- case studies
- interviews with people who have reinvented their careers
- tips from experts
- suggestions for experiments, research and other actions you can take.

If you follow the book, it will guide you every step of the way to rethink and reinvent your working life.

Introduction

The breeze at dawn has secrets to tell you. Don't go
back to sleep. You must ask for what you really want.
Don't go back to sleep. People are going back and
forth across the door sill where two worlds touch. The
door is round and open. Don't go back to sleep.

Rumi

Before the twentieth century, most people worked until they
dropped. Some in the leisured classes never really got the hang
of working at all, but for most, working life started early and
ended shortly before death. And for an Australian born in 1880,
death was likely to happen at around 50. So 'retirement' was a
meaningless concept for many and unaffordable to boot.

In the mid-twentieth century, the concept of the 'golden
years' of retirement was born. Think endless golf, world cruises,
special retirement communities, bingo and bridge – almost
a carefree second childhood. Many industry sectors had a
compulsory retirement age, and most Australians were encouraged
to retire early.

But things are changing. The pension age looks likely to rise
to 70, over time. Those who turn 50 in 2015 can expect to live
well into their 80s or beyond,[1] and are also likely to be healthy
for most of those years. That's a lot of bingo and golf. So, people
are starting to talk about adding a new stage of life between
adulthood and retirement. The discussion is new, and there's not

even consensus on what to call it – suggestions include third age, third act, next act, rewirement and phased retirement. There are less flattering terms, too, such as the grey tsunami or the not-yet-dead. Enough said about those.

Whatever label we give it, just think of the Australians you know in their 60s, 70s and 80s who are still working, learning, creating, helping or contributing in other ways. Some are famous, but many are working in local communities or workplaces. And that's because increasingly, people are deciding to postpone retirement, because they don't want to stop working or because they can't afford to – or both.

What do older Australians want from the world of work? The truth is that 'people over 50' are not a homogeneous group – they are just as varied in their characteristics, wants, needs and lifestyles as those under 50. And although the media often lumps all older Australians together, of course someone of 55 and someone of 85 will have significantly different outlooks and desires. Many women had interrupted working lives while raising children and often have less superannuation or savings, so for them this is a time to ramp up, not down. Levels of education and training vary widely and this can be a critical factor in the choices people have, and whether they remain in the workforce.

Maybe for you it's about changing the mix, shifting gears and establishing a new balance between work and other activities. Or seeking more flexibility in the times and location of work. Or restructuring things so you can change careers, activate an old dream to set up a business, give back, do some teaching or write that book. Maybe you want to work harder than ever before but in a cause that's meaningful to you. And maybe you feel you have been spat out by the system and just want a job, any job.

There are plenty of options. Are you ready to reinvent your working life?

Journey with maps: What we know

I love data. And I love research. And I love finding evidence-based stories to inform my work. But I understand that you may not share my passion, and that's fine. So, my full *Journeys Without Maps* special report is available as a free download from joannamaxwell.com.au. It's full of research and statistics about trends for this over-50 demographic. You'll enjoy reading it if you share my love of data.

This book is very focused on practical ways that you can reinvent your working life at a personal level, not on social trends and research data. But even if you just want to jump straight into the 'how-to' chapters that make up most of the rest of this book, it's important first to bust some common myths about older people, so you don't let yourself be limited by things that just aren't true. Here's a quick peek at some of those myths.

Myth: People over 50 are all the same

If you believe the newspaper stories or the common portrayal of older people on television, you might think that we are all similar, but it isn't so. One of the things we know about ageing is that people become more individual, not more alike, as they age.[2] So this is a time for creating your own pathway, for building a life that works for you. I know from my many clients and others that feelings about the future vary widely. Here are some of the things I hear:

- I want to work.
- I'm looking to retire as soon as possible.
- I'm excited by the possibilities in this stage of life.
- I'm going to change careers, activate a secret dream.
- I am frightened by the future.
- I see my future, and despair.
- I need to work.

- I want to give back to the community.
- I want freedom to travel and play.
- I want to work part-time so I can be with my grandchildren.
- I'm a successful professional seeking to reinvent myself.
- I've been made redundant and just want a job, any job.
- I'm a woman who spent years raising children – my time is now.
- I have retired but would love to work if I could find a job.
- I feel angry about changes in my retirement expectations.
- I want to start a business.
- I have so many projects I want to do.

How do you feel? What do you want to do?

Myth: The pension should fund a 30-year holiday

Did you know that more years were added to the average life expectancy in the twentieth century than all years added across all prior millennia of human evolution combined?[3]

In 1909, when the Commonwealth started paying age pensions to men at 65 years of age and to women at 60,[4] the average life expectancy for males was 55, and for women 59.[5] Only 4 per cent of Australians were 65 or over.[6] But now it's very different. Men aged 65 in 2013 can expect to live to 84.2 years and women to 87.1 years,[7] and this continues to rise[8] at the rate of about a month for every year we live. In 2014, nearly 15 per cent of Australians were over 65 and the percentage of us over 85 has doubled in the last 20 years.[9]

Because we are living longer, many more of us are becoming eligible to receive the age pension and for more years, so demands to increase pension entry age are understandable and inevitable.

Myth: Chronological age is everything

Research clearly shows chronological age is no longer a relevant marker for measuring health, mental capacity or motivation. Most of those extra years added to our lifespan are healthy years, and we have more energy than our forebears at the same age. We remain productive, mentally able and capable until at least well into our 80s. For example, a 2014 study showed that even at over 85, 56 per cent of people report no health-based limitations in work or housework.[10] Research also reveals that productivity doesn't fall away over the normal working age range, although of course younger and older people have different skills.[11]

Staying at work can be good for you. Older workers have lower rates of heart disease, diabetes, obesity and arthritis than their non-working peers, says the Australian Bureau of Statistics.[12] You might think this is because sufferers of these diseases opt out (or are forced out) of the workforce earlier, but controlled studies validate the statistics. And even those workers with a health condition feel more positive than non-workers.

Myth: Older workers aren't committed

It's sometimes said that older workers lack commitment because they are getting ready to retire, focused on other things and just marking time. But in fact, a 2009 Australian study showed workers 45 and over were 2.6 times less likely to have left their job in the last year than those under 45.[13] Also, people over 63 are the fastest growing segment of workers in Australia, numbering over half a million in July 2014, having doubled in the last 15 years.[14] And business start-ups by people 55 to 64 in Australia are the fastest growing segment of entrepreneurship.[15]

Myth: Older workers take jobs from younger ones

Sometimes people tell me that they feel they shouldn't keep working as they age, because they are taking a job that belongs to a younger person. The idea that older workers take jobs from the young is known by economists as the 'lump of labour' fallacy, and has been disproved by numerous reputable studies all over the world.[16] It's the same fallacy as was raised (and debunked) when women started to enter the workforce in larger numbers and is based on the idea that there are a set number (or 'lump') of available jobs, and every older person who keeps working is denying a space for their younger colleague. In fact, the number of jobs is not finite and there are considerable economic benefits in keeping people employed for longer. I am not an economist, and this is not a polemic, but if you are interested, a quick online search will bring up all the data you like on this topic.

You may be surprised to learn that Australia has a lower percentage of older people in the workforce than many other developed countries, including the United States, United Kingdom, Canada and New Zealand.[17] This concerns our government and many commentators, as it has implications for our economic stability and future prosperity. Deloitte Access Economics says there is a trend for more Australians in their 50s and 60s (and increasingly more women) to participate in the workforce, and shows an extra 3 per cent of participation by the over 55s would add $33 billion to GDP and a 5 per cent increase would add $48 billion.[18]

Myth: We get more stupid as we age

One of the most pervasive stereotypes is that our brains decay as we age, and many people assume that after 50, 'senior moments' increase and our capacity to think and our ability to contribute intellectually both decline markedly, with dementia almost inevitable.

Not so, according to research conducted by Monash University with the Australian Institute of Management in 2012.[19] Researchers found that older, more experienced managers recorded higher levels of 'crystallised' intelligence – a type of intelligence that relates strongly to wisdom gained through experience and also verbal reasoning, as a result of education and practice. In contrast, 'fluid' intelligence – the ability to solve novel problems using inherited basic reasoning ability – was slightly higher among younger managers.

Overall, the Monash study found no reason to justify distinguishing older workers based on intelligence, problem-solving or leadership ability. Older workers are just as valuable to economic and social growth in business as younger ones, bringing assets such as experience and psychological stability to the workplace.

Many other studies echo these results, including a German analysis which concluded that current assumptions about cognitive decline are seriously flawed and mostly formally invalid.[20] And Queensland Government research shows no sign of general cognitive decline until people are well into their 80s or even older.[21]

And there are many things older people can do to help 'age-proof' their brains, and preserve (even increase) all kinds of cognitive function throughout their life. Most are simple and are being adopted by people of all ages – including physical exercise, meditation, better diet choices, living a purposeful life, connecting with others and learning new skills. So, no more 'senior moment' excuses!

Myth: People over 65 should retire and buy a rocking chair

There are plenty of examples of individuals who have lived vibrant and interesting lives well into their 70s, 80s and 90s – such as Melbourne woman Millie Browne, who at 98 (in 2015) was the world's oldest iPhone App Store game developer.[22] Laura Ingalls Wilder became a journalist in her 40s, and was 65 when she started writing the *Little House on the Prairie* series.[23] British doctor Peter Mark Roget is best known for *Roget's Thesaurus*, which has never been out of print since it was published in 1852, when he was 73.[24]

And if you're interested in the less famous, check out the story of Vita Needle. Located in Massachusetts, Vita Needle employs about 35 production workers, 95 per cent of whom are part-time seniors. The oldest employee is 100 and the average age of its workforce is 74. The company has been the subject of documentaries and research studies in several countries – all indicating the employees are happy, properly paid and productive.[25]

In the United Kingdom, 33 per cent of Marks & Spencer employees are over 50, more than 4000 employees have over 25 years' service, and they have an employee who was recruited at 80. This has helped them: to have one of the lowest employee turnover rates in UK retail;[26] to retain highly effective staff; to increase loyalty of employees who value choice to work longer; and to use performance management in an identical way for workers of all ages.

Here in Australia, people often cite hardware chain Bunnings as a standout employer of older workers, and it's true, they do great things. But they are not alone:

- half of the workers at Taylors Wines in South Australia are aged 55 or more, and 70 per cent are 45 or more[27]
- 21 per cent of Woolworths' workforce is mature-aged, and they employed more than 700 people aged over 55 in 2014[28]
- 60 per cent of Dial an Angel's workforce is aged over 45.[29]

If you search you'll find plenty more stories like these.

The myths we have just busted are only a few of many.[30] We will dismantle others as they crop up through this book, such as that older people can't or don't want to learn new things (they can and they do) and that a sense of purpose is not important as we age (having one may help you live years longer). So when you are presented with a media story that suggests 'all older people' are like this or like that, don't just accept it as truth. Instead, double-check its claims. You may very well be surprised by what you discover.

Journey without maps: What we don't know

We have just seen that we know plenty of things about people over 50 and we have busted some pervasive but incorrect beliefs about this cohort. But we don't have a generation-wide role model, and we don't really know what this new stage of life will look like in the future, or what will shape its trajectory.

Marc Freedman, a pioneer of the 'encore' movement in the United States, often describes this age group as the 'population with no name'.[31] It has also been said that those in this demographic are embarking on a journey with no maps. However, this does not mean we are going nowhere and doing nothing. We are creating our own paths through this new stage, often with little outside encouragement.

This is exciting – and it's scary, too. I don't peddle fairy floss, and in this book I will tell it as it really is. But, actually, this new stage of life is likely to be characterised by possibilities and new adventures and may well be the most satisfying time of your life. Research consistently shows that older life is a much happier and less stressful time than midlife, let alone adolescence – so let's make the most of it.

A call to action

Those of us over 50 don't need to sit in our rocking chairs, waiting for someone to come along and fix it for us or tell us how we can live. We have plenty of choices. We can create interesting lives – or get on with the ones we already have. We can have new adventures, start that encore career, learn something completely different and create our own possibilities into our 70s and beyond.

We can get together and share our stories. We can speak up when someone treats us unfairly. We can lobby for workplace decisions to be based on ability, not age. We can talk to the media about the reality of our lives, good and bad. We can bust the stereotypes about all people over 50 being the same, or a burden on everyone else or going downhill fast.

Your best option right now is the one that gives you the most control. Taking what's called 'agency' over your life, creating choices, even in stressful or unhappy circumstances such as unemployment or a bad job, is essential. You'll be happier, you'll be more engaged and useful – and all the indications suggest you will live a longer and more productive life. Changing your life can bring up deep feelings. If so, you may find it helpful to seek support from a trained counsellor.

Only you can navigate your own path through this journey without maps, although this book is intended to be your guide. It won't necessarily be easy, and there are no guarantees, but it will show you how to create a pathway to rethink your own career. You'll be creating your own future, but also shining a light for others. In fact, as time goes on, that's how the more systemic change required will come about – because we took charge of our lives and demonstrated what is possible, for ourselves and those who will follow.

I'm thinking it's time I became a disrupter. Maybe you would like to join me?

SECTION 1

REIMAGINE

CHAPTER 1

Reimagining work for people over 50

The people who think the glass is half full and
the people who think the glass is half empty are
both missing the point, the glass is refillable.

2016 Facebook meme

The introduction to this book looked broadly at changing
demographics and shifts affecting people over 50, and smashed
some pervasive myths about what's possible as we age. This chapter
zooms in closer to look at reimagining work in this new stage of life.

I am often asked, 'How old is too old' when it comes to
reinventing your working life. I don't think there is an arbitrary
cut-off for this – some people have always planned that they would
retire at 55 (or earlier), others can't imagine ever fully giving up
work. As long as you have an interest in a new direction, some
enthusiasm and a realistic idea of what's involved, why not?

Late bloomers are more common than you might think. My
oldest career-change client (so far) was in his 70s, and there are
plenty of well-known stories of people who don't find their groove
in their first career and go on to successfully reinvent themselves
much later. Harland Sanders started his KFC empire in his 60s,[1]
Frank McCourt won a Pulitzer Prize for *Angela's Ashes* when
he was 66,[2] Julia Child wrote her first cookbook at 50[3] and Paul
Cézanne was 56 when he had his first one-man show.[4]

And there is a body of evidence that suggests that people who have careers that don't really run out, such as artists, architects, professors and nuns, are less likely to retire, may well do their best work as they age, and are more likely to live for longer.[5]

The new life course

The life course was once thought to have a predictable trajectory up to a high point in midlife then a slow decline through retirement to a wooden box in the local cemetery. Personal growth was not expected later in life (or thought possible) and your world was anticipated to shrink year by year.

This traditional view of the lifespan was very linear – first you did your learning, then you did your working, then you did your resting. You married at a certain stage, and had 2.2 children, aged steadily and finally died. Many other aspects of life were lived out within a fairly prescribed and narrow cultural context. Mostly it was all one way, no repeats or twists. It looked like this:

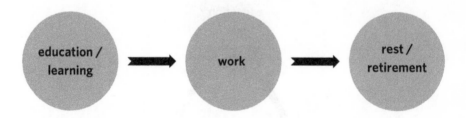

This picture has been crumbling at the edges for quite a while now, and it's time to stop struggling with our largely unsuccessful attempts to shore it up. We need to rethink it altogether in the light of changes in society as well as longer and healthier lifespans. We don't need to ditch the concepts of 'family' or 'work' or 'community', but we must reshape them where necessary to create the best possible 21st-century futures for ourselves and our children.

When it first became clear in the mid-twentieth century that more and more years were being added to the average lifespan, the first idea was to tack them on to retirement. Remember the trend towards early retirement, leisure communities and endless tennis and cruises? It turned out to be a clumsy idea, as people couldn't afford (and largely didn't want) a 30-year holiday.

In fact, the life-course trajectory often now continues to rise until well into our 80s and maybe more, with research showing that 80 is the average peak age for life happiness.[6] The potential for growth, adventure and achievement is ongoing, and for many people the later years are the most satisfying life stage of all. These days, although the major elements are much the same, it's not as linear – many people move back and forth through the phases of work and private life, mix them up, leave one out, delay another, revisit some ...

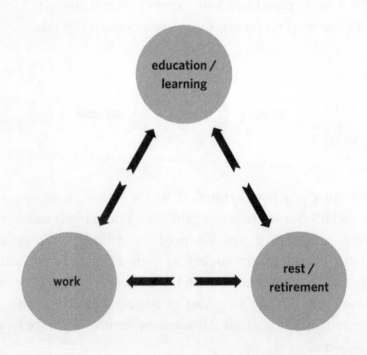

This can be challenging, and we will talk about that in this book. But it is also exciting, and gives you many more opportunities to find a future that you absolutely want to live.

Redefining life and work stages

It's easy to forget that retirement is a human invention, originally created so that people could rest for a few short years before an early (by today's standards) death. The added years we have now are a wonderful thing, but by tacking them on at the end of life we stretched retirement way beyond its intended purpose.

Professor of psychology Laura Carstensen's book, *A Long Bright Future*,[7] reminds us that retirement is a social construct and so, if some of the original concepts are no longer working properly we can and should change them. We can and should apply some creativity to imagine work lives that are more satisfying, sustainable and enjoyable than is the case for many people today. Rather than clinging to old ways, or tinkering at the margins, let's reinvent work.

Carstensen's core idea is that we should spend more of the early years of life easing into work, deciding what we want to do and learning how to do it. In the middle years, there should also be far wider use of part-time work and time off for other things, such as travel and raising children. Only once you turn 50 would career become the central focus of your life, perhaps for the next 30 years. Or perhaps for more than 30 years – Carstensen talks about a 50:50 split, where you would spend 50 years shaping yourself and then 50 years giving back to your community.

She stresses that this needs to be a choice, and that some people won't be able or willing to continue their first career, or to work at all, in this new phase. She talks of the changes needed in workplace practices and the challenges posed by the gap in life circumstances between different sections of our society.

I find this 50:50 suggestion quite fascinating, and I believe it is the right direction for us, in terms of government policy, pension reform and individual career and life planning. I have seen predictions that babies born in 2016 have somewhere between a 30 per cent and a 50 per cent chance of living to 105, so it is not as crazy as it might seem. If you find the idea interesting, do read Carstensen's excellent book.

Those of us already in our 40s, 50s or beyond can't turn back the clock to reinvent our past and retrospectively restructure our work span. However, we can take a much more creative look at our working future – and we should. There's a new shape of work coming and it will to a significant extent be found through our individual and collective redefinitions of what it is 'to work' and 'to be a worker'. It's time for all of us to step up and speak up.

What does this mean for you? What can you do, and where should you start? The answers to that last question are 'something' and 'somewhere'; the important thing is to start. Leaving aside the broader changes in society for now, you could begin by looking at the three core elements of learning, working and resting, and see how best to arrange them to suit you in this next stage of life. Perhaps you would like to go back to university or college and expand your skills or retrain for a new career? Or take an adult gap year so you can travel the world or stay at home and explore new possibilities? Is it time to start your dream business or focus more on grandchildren or other volunteering?

If you need further proof that the life stages are not necessarily one way or linear, then look at these statistics about 'unretirement'. In Australia in 2008–2009, 144,000 people 55 years and over came out of retirement and returned to the workforce. Why? For 34 per cent, it was because they were bored. An interesting opportunity came up for 13 per cent and around one-third returned to work for financial reasons.[8] This trend is growing and will continue to do so as the boundaries between 'work' and 'not work' become increasingly fluid.

A 2014 survey in the United States found that almost three out of five retirees go into a new line of work[9] and an Australian Government report says many older people seek to start new careers to add variety to their current work by engaging their untapped talent.[10]

This is a rosy picture, but for some Australians it may look like a pipe dream. There's no doubt that different life circumstances place constraints on our choices in later life. If you're still struggling to pay off your mortgage, or are exhausted from a lifetime of hard yakka, then suggesting that you take a gap year, or embark on expensive and demanding university studies, may sound ridiculous.

It's clear that there are a number of factors here. For example, there is evidence that many try to start a business because they need money and cannot get a job.[11] For women in particular, some more mainstream pathways may be closed to them because of lack of education or complex life circumstances – and we need more programs such as Money for Jam (a Melbourne-based initiative from Per Capita) that offer encouraging new pathways to earning money and finding community engagement.[12] And an Australian study suggests that the more educated choose to stay in work because they are well paid and satisfied with their jobs, whereas less educated workers need to work longer to maintain their living standards as they have less money saved.[13]

Whatever your life circumstances, it is well worth spending some time thinking about optimising your future. There are always steps you can take to improve your quality of life, and many more choices available than we tend to see from inside our own small world. Give it a go, and you may be amazed by the results. Promise.

Sylvia, 52

Sylvia had a couple of unsatisfying careers before deciding that nothing was more important than working in an area that she loved. At 51, she changed her life by leaving her job to open a yoga studio and her only regret now is that she didn't do it earlier.

When I started working 30 years ago, I was an aerobics instructor and then I travelled all over Europe for a leading sports brand teaching people how to use their products. I did a lot of aerobics in my younger years, but then my body started to suffer.

I got into law when I was close to 30 because I started working for my lawyer boyfriend in Melbourne. I didn't love the law, but it paid well. So I spent 15 to 20 years working as either a legal secretary or a paralegal and always teaching yoga on the side, but I could never really make a living doing what I loved to do.

I was always apprehensive about making a switch because I was scared of not being able to pay the bills. I was so afraid of failing. But I just hit the wall when I was 51, having a miserable existence, not wanting to get out of bed in the morning, and I decided that life is too short to be doing a job that eats your entire soul and all your energy. I realised that I'd rather just try to figure out the finance side than have a job that pays well but is making me emotionally and physically sick.

On a particularly bad day at the office, I knew that this was it, I knew that I had to make a change. I jumped off the cliff and now, a year later, I've opened up a yoga studio. I'm on the right road, teaching yoga to the public and to other teachers. I just wish I'd done it sooner.

When I made the change, I had to sell a lot of my furniture and move into a small apartment. I had to switch around everything in my life so that I could survive financially, as I didn't have much money coming in. I went to classes to learn to write a business plan, how to operate a business and how to build a website. And it helped a lot. My legal background has also helped me, because many yoga teachers don't really have much business sense, and I can think through things as well and organise myself more effectively.

I wake up every day and I'm excited, but I still have a feeling in my stomach that it's scary. I wouldn't be honest if I didn't say that. I'll know I'm successful when I can pay my bills and feel comfortable and have a bit extra to just do whatever I wanted to and not worry. I don't have to be rich. For me, success means waking up every day and knowing that everything is on the right track, I have enough money and my business is solid.

I'm focusing so much on making this business work that I just don't think as much about my personal life. And so that's suffering. I'm single and I want to meet somebody, but I just don't have enough hours in the day for dating.

I often say to other people my age, 'What's your passion, what would make you happy in your life? Is it what you're doing right now?' And if they say, 'No', I'll say they should just go for it, figure out a way that it can happen. But it's important to strategise, don't just jump in. I strategised for a good year before I actually made the leap and left my job. I figured out how to get most of my bills paid off, and find a way to live on a really small amount of money.

Every day now I feel like it's a brand-new day and it's not the same old sad feeling anymore. I don't know what the day will bring, and it's a great feeling that something wonderful could happen.

The dangers of stereotyping

Many of my clients are apprehensive that they will encounter age stereotyping and discrimination as they start their work reinvention. This is indeed possible, perhaps even likely, but there are steps you can take to minimise its impact on you.

Numerous reports by government and others[14] make it clear that workplace stereotyping of and discrimination against older Australians are rife. A 2013 Productive Ageing Centre report found that 36 per cent of people who have looked for a job in the past five years experienced age-related exclusion from the job-hunting process,[15] and within the workplace itself it's just as much of a problem.

Although it's illegal to discriminate against someone on the basis of age, it's also hard to pin down. It may manifest in vague statements at job interviews such as, 'You have too much experience', 'We need someone who is more dynamic' or 'You wouldn't fit in with our current team'. A disturbing recent report suggests employers in the United States are masking age discrimination by using phrases such as, 'We are seeking a digital native',[16] as in someone born since the internet became commonplace.

Just like religious or race discrimination, age discrimination results from stereotypes based on assumed characteristics or behaviours and disregarding an individual's actual capacities. A 2013 report from the Australian Human Rights Commission found that age-related discrimination was perceived as less important than other forms of discrimination.[17] In other words, it's fine to make jokes about old people but not jokes based on race. This has particular implications in the workplace, as it subtly reinforces and normalises the age stereotypes.

One challenge is that people often do not realise they are being ageist – they believe the stereotype is a simple truth. That's why it's important to remember the myth busting we did in the introduction, and to challenge stereotypes wherever possible.

I spoke to Susan Ryan AO, who was the Age Discrimination Commissioner from 2011–2016, about ageism and work. She said that people who lose their job in their 50s face the most challenges in getting re-hired. 'It's financially devastating, but it's also psychologically devastating. In my view, the number of older people drawing the disability pension is directly linked to age discrimination.'

The gender gap is also a worrying trend. 'Women in their 50s and 60s generally need to work even more than men, particularly if they're living without a partner,' Ryan said. 'We've got a burgeoning problem of homelessness amongst older women, those just sucked into poverty because they can't get employment and they have nowhere to live.'

Ryan sees that changing employer attitudes is a big challenge. 'I think Australian society is very ageist, and I link that to the commercial promotion of youth. Employers in general are very conservative, they're low risk and accept the common prejudices.' The concept of creating intergenerational teams is essential – it's not about choosing older workers to the detriment of younger people. 'The biggest thing is to get them to take off their blinkers and say, "I want the person who can do the job".'

This book is not a social activism manual, so if you want to read more on this topic, I will leave you to download my special report from my website or read Ashton Applewhite's terrific book, *This Chair Rocks: A Manifesto Against Ageism*.[18]

One thing you can do is to make sure you don't buy into these negative stereotypes yourself. Say you read that older people aren't good at technology and you believe it, so you decide not to enrol in a digital marketing course. Or you're told that you're 'too old' for a new exercise program at your gym, so you don't even give it a go. This is known as 'stereotype threat' and can have real consequences for your confidence and actions.

Older adults in a study who were reminded of negative age descriptors (such as 'confused' or 'decrepit') showed poorer memory and reduced walking ability immediately afterwards compared to those who were reminded of positive stereotypes (such as 'guide' or 'wise').[19] Even small suggestions such as these have an impact, and if you buy into the stereotype over time, it can have a significant cumulative negative effect.

Research from 2012 suggests many older workers retire around the age of 65 because social norms say that's the right age to retire.[20] They assume that's what they're supposed to do without necessarily considering their personal desires or capacities. And just over half of non-employed older people say that discrimination in the job-search process affects their desire to work.[21] They become what are described as 'discouraged workers' and may take themselves off job-seeker lists, despite still wanting to work.

Even those who don't believe the stereotyping may worry that they are being judged and found wanting. This has a measurable impact on job satisfaction, commitment, engagement and retirement intentions – and will inevitably impact their productivity.

The answer is obviously the promotion of accurate, more positive ideas about older workers, ideas that focus on their experience, wisdom, dependability and commitment. There are signs that the media are starting to portray more realistic pictures and stories about older people, at least some of the time. And more employers are beginning to appreciate the value of their older workers.

But don't wait for our culture to change – decide right now that you will look beyond stereotypes, that you will seek out stories about positive role models, and that you will create your own map to a future that excites you. And in Chapter 12 we will cover some practical strategies you can use in interviews and other workplace situations to deal with this issue.

How old is 'old'?

To some extent at least, we can act as if age is a mindset. Do you know about Ellen Langer's brilliant experiment in the 1970s where she took a group in their 70s to a converted monastery in New Hampshire, in the United States? The whole environment was set up to mimic their lives 20 years earlier, and for a week they lived in a time warp – food, activities and television were all one big blast from the past. They were treated as people in their 50s who were living in the 1950s and encouraged to act as such.

And when they left the converted monastery a week later, guess what? Their blood pressure, physical mobility, appearance, in fact most of the biomarkers of ageing, had all changed for the better, in real and measurable ways.

In 2010, Michael Mosley, the BBC medical and science expert, joined with Langer to repeat the experiment in the United Kingdom and film it as a TV series (*The Young Ones*). The results were similar and follow-ups with participants three months later suggested the effects had continued.

Langer has done other ground-breaking work on the impact of positive or negative mindsets on ageing. For example, she conducted research in a nursing home, where some residents were given the power to decide who visited them and when; they were also given a house plant and told they were responsible for its care. The control group had no say over visitors and they were given a house plant but told that a nurse would take care of it for them. Eighteen months later, less than half as many of the more engaged group had died than had those in the control group. Langer concluded that the small changes she implemented had changed the residents' mindsets and given them a sense of control over their lives.[22]

Studies like these illustrate the importance of your own attitude to ageing and to your sense of what's possible for you. We are not talking miracles, but there's no doubt that 'mind over matter' is part of the picture.

50 is the new 50

I am pretty enthusiastic about the benefits that can come from adopting a positive mindset about ageing – or even from refusing to buy into negative, gloomy stereotypes. But let's be very clear: I make a significant distinction between determining your own sense of your age, irrespective of society's norms and stereotypes (which I think is a GOOD thing), and buying into notions of eternal youth or the need to appear always vibrant, bouncy and up for anything (which I think is a BAD thing, and pretty futile, too).

To say that 60 is the new 50 or even 40 is to say that we value youth over experience, that being young is better than being old, and that we are happy to wipe out 10 or even 20 years of our lives just to seem younger than our chronological age. Our prevalent cult of youth has seduced many older people, whether through fear of ageing or yearning for eternal, wrinkle-free youth. But this comes at a great cost. In the case of cosmetic wrinkle treatments and the like, it's a monetary cost, but in all cases it requires us to deny the benefits and experience that age has brought us.

Professor Molly Andrews talks of the 'seductiveness of agelessness', and the self-hatred that lies underneath this willingness to masquerade as younger versions of ourselves.[23] She says the fantasy that old age is not real or that we can somehow just avoid it carries the high price of taking away our own future. In fact, it is our lifetime of experiences that give our lives meaning and allow us to develop wisdom, and the trivialising of that passage of time and experience suggests that we think there is something wrong with getting older.

Several older female workers have told me that they have been asked to dye their hair or wear different clothes in order to pass as younger than their chronological age; others pre-emptively made this decision themselves. And many people fudge the dates of key life events or refuse to have a birthday cake at work in case it raises questions about their exact age. I think this is very sad. If you want to colour your hair, wear bright colours or obscure your age, go for it, but to feel pressured to do so by your boss or by society is just wrong.

Think of it this way: when autumn arrives and leaves turn red and orange, we don't weep and wail, or rush around with cans of green spray paint trying to stop the hideous changes. We celebrate the beauty in every season of the year, and equally, old age needs to be valued, embraced and enjoyed, not recoiled from or denied.

If we consider this as it relates to older workers, then instead of hiding our age, we should parade it as evidence of our experience and ability to contribute to our workplaces. Older workers have accumulated experience, knowledge and skills. They can be highly reliable, productive and motivated. And as a bonus, their insights are essential to any organisation looking to engage with customers over 50 – described by the Australian Institute of Management as the 'diversity dividend'.[24]

There are some positive signs that attitudes to older workers are changing. The Australian Human Rights Commission's excellent 2016 *Willing to Work* report drilled into the reasons that underlie age discrimination in the workplace, and made some useful recommendations. One of the most interesting was that we should install a Minister for Longevity to address employment discrimination, explain the economic dimensions of longevity and drive the increase in labour-force participation of older Australians. Who knows if it will ever happen, but it's a good sign and a great idea.[25]

In the introduction I talked about employers like Taylors Wines, Vita Needle and Marks & Spencers, all great examples of employers actively recruiting older workers. And I was delighted to see recent ads for bus drivers in New South Wales that featured older men and women, grey hair, wrinkles and all.

So take heart, be brave, and flaunt your age wherever possible.

David, 70

David had very clear ideas about what felt appropriate for him at different ages. Once his children were grown, he moved countries to start a TV station at 55. Now aged 70, he continues to work in media, although the role of work in his life has again shifted.

At the age of 53, I finished about 25 years with public television in Israel and I was at a point of exhaustion, which I think many 50-year-olds reach, especially those who are 25 years at one workplace. I was trying to look for a way out and a way to do things differently. I was encouraged by a friend of mine to just get out of my job first, then think what I can do. Some people say, 'Oh, until I know what I'm going to do I won't get out', but I think in many cases you have to get out and then start figuring what your roadmap is.

I felt totally in the wilderness. My generation felt that you always had to have tenure, a fixed place where you take care of yourself, your family, and don't move before you've got that part of your life sorted. So I was wondering what I could do, and that took about seven or eight months to figure out.

I had a relationship with an American non-profit media group and I pushed them to create a new TV channel, and I moved there to do it. It was a risk to start in a new country, and a whole new venture where there's no profit assured. It was just a vision to tell Americans about the world, broadcasting about cultures and political trends and social trends in the world, as a counter-narrative to commercial TV.

I think age is very relevant to these decisions, because until your kids grow up you feel responsible to maintain them, including financial, social and learning stability. Then they are on their own and you are on your own. I don't think I would have gone to America if I had a young family.

All of us were journalists, producers and people who had quite a few decades in the broadcasting environment but were always told what to do, what not to do or censored and so on. We decided to be not only the international channel, but the uncensored one. We were our own masters and at 54, 55 or 60, we all were highly motivated. I was there 10 years and the channel is still going now.

My wife was a Bondi Beach girl and so my children have Australian passports. They visited Australia and they liked it and built families here, so by 2010 I had four grandchildren in Australia and they asked me, 'How many more grandchildren do you need to be convinced to come here?' So I came. It is difficult at the age of 65 to come as a foreigner to a country and say, 'Hi, I can tell you this idea or that idea.' I think this combination of age and being a foreigner didn't work for me in Australian media, but I have no regrets. I have continued with media work reporting to an American-based website.

I went through two major careers but in the one ecosystem that I know, the media ecosystem of visual information. It's only in the last three years that I went into writing for the web, which was for me a new way of expressing myself and was very interesting, but I didn't see it as a major career change.

Now work is for me important but not a priority. Until the age of 65, work was the number-one priority for me financially, but also for keeping myself busy and expressing my whole field of knowledge and personality and so on. At this age of 70, I'm not sure I can or should reinvent myself, I'm just looking at different options now of trying to create something new, but it's definitely not the same conviction and energy level that I had. Some people at the age of 55 called me 'David Turbo'. I don't think I can be called that anymore.

Late bloomers

You often see articles in the press about finding success later in life. Apart from the common, rather strange assumption that age 40 or even 30 constitutes 'later in life', they usually have some inspirational examples and useful tips.

They remind me of something Malcolm Gladwell wrote about in his book *What the Dog Saw*,[26] in a chapter called 'Late bloomers: why do we equate genius with precocity?' He argues that while some people 'get' their career direction and their talent very early on, many people do not. Gladwell says that we assume genius is obvious from an early age, but the truth is that it can come to fruition at any stage. Gladwell (relying on research by a bloke called Galenson) distinguishes between two types:
  - 'conceptual' talents – people who have a very clear idea from the start and just jump in and execute it with total confidence; and

- 'experimental' talents – people who have a much more organic approach, with imprecise goals, incremental progress, and often a great deal of self-doubt.

They're not better or worse than each other, just different styles.

As a decidedly late bloomer, I love this distinction. Gladwell tells stories about a number of people who came into full flower later in life, and whose work was the better for it. People who stumbled towards a finish line they couldn't see or define, who let each project shape and define the next, people who changed careers or even their sense of self more than once. Experimental types often feel a lack of progress or even failure because they don't get it together in their 20s (or even 30s or 40s). The thing that distinguishes the late successes from the never-successes is of course persistence – and, I think, the willingness to try new things, to learn and change and slowly accumulate people who believe in you.

However, you don't need unshakable self-belief, which is a really important point. I have long thought that the doubting stories we tell ourselves are only problematic if they stop us doing the things we want to do. I see clients like this quite often. They come to me almost in despair, as if I am their last staging post before giving up entirely. Occasionally, they seem to be daring me not to believe in the possibility of late blooming, of true satisfaction, even worldly success in middle age (or any age, for that matter). They seem to want me to tell them it's too hard, not possible, that there's no hope. To let them give up their dream and justify a life of quiet desperation.

But I always have hope. I always believe. I always hold the possibility of finding your abilities or talents or potential and turning it into something tangible in the world. I hold the possibility because I've done it and many of my clients have done it. And I frequently find (and post on social media) examples of everyday people who are also blooming into their 80s, 90s and even beyond.

Maybe you can do it, too. Do you have an unlived dream, or even a vague sense of unfulfilled potential? Then keep inching towards the light, and never say die!

Exercise: Reflections

This is the first practical exercise in this book, but it will not be the last. You might like to dedicate a notebook to your answers to these exercises, to your reflections and to all the ideas that come to you as you read and think and explore your possibilities.

Think about these questions, write about them, talk to trusted friends and family about them, really examine your feelings about them. You may find it useful to revisit these questions from time to time as you go through this book, as your answers become clearer to you. As you build on these initial exercises, the importance of different questions to you may also change, or may be affected by other aspects of your reinvention process. This is all as it should be.

- How would you describe your working identity? How much of your sense of 'who you are' is tied up in this identity?
- How do you feel about working until you are 80?
- What are the advantages of working longer? The disadvantages?
- Think about the three life arenas of learning, working and resting/relaxing. What have you done so far in your life in each of these arenas? What would you still like to do? How could you arrange things to suit you in this next stage of life?
- How old are you in chronological years? How old do you feel?
- Who is in charge of your tomorrow? How can you maintain or reclaim a sense of control or agency over your life?

Is retirement dead?

Such are the changes to the life course that some commentators are starting to say that retirement is dying, if not dead. I think there will always be people who wish to stop working completely at some point in their lives and never return to it, as well as people who for whatever reason cannot continue in paid work. But how many, and at what age?

Let's agree for now that retirement is changing, leading some to try to find a replacement word for 'retirement', with its connotations of withdrawing from the world. The *Collins Dictionary*, for example, defines it as 'the act of retiring from one's work, office, etcetera; the period of being retired from work; seclusion from the world; privacy; the act of going away or retreating'.[27] As we have seen, this one-way, line-in-the-sand approach is not the experience of everyone today, and is likely to be even less so in the future. Even more importantly, it does not leave room for the many different approaches to the next stage of life.

Although recent research suggests there may be an upper limit[28] to our maximum age (perhaps 125, which most will never get close to reaching), for the moment humans are still adding a month to our lifespan every year – so if you are 50 now, by the time you are 80 you may expect to live 30 months longer than a person who is currently 80. And who knows what retirement will look like by then.

On the assumption you are reading this book because you do not want to permanently stop working (or at least not yet), let's turn our attention now to five types of work you might want to consider.

CHAPTER 2

The 'big five' types of work

Choose a job you love, and you will never
have to work a day in your life.

Confucius

Just like the 'big five' animals in Africa, I have come up with a big five of different types of work to consider. As you read through each one, let yourself be curious, ask yourself, 'Is this something that might interest me?'

Don't worry about practicalities yet. Section 2 will help you work out where your strengths lie and Section 3 encourages you to experiment as well as offering practical tips once you get closer to a decision. But for now just think about the kinds of work that might appeal to you.

Encore careers

Have you ever dreamed of changing careers? Do you hang up half your personality with your jacket when you get to work? Feel like jumping ship but not sure where the exit is? Take heart: no matter where you are in your career, or how old you are, you can find an alternative career path that inspires you, instead of reluctantly dragging yourself out of bed every morning.

In the United States, 'encore careers' has a specific connotation of later-life work that has a social impact. It could mean volunteering, or working for a good cause at a reduced salary.

Typically, this involves retired professionals or senior executives who can afford to transition in this way.

However, in Australia it is developing a different meaning. Here, encore careers can mean paid work that results from exploring new directions, new experiences and self-reflection. Consultant on ageing and writer Jane Figgis has done some excellent research in this area. She concludes that an Australian encore career needs to be flexible and allow for a sense of autonomy; it needs to start around typical retirement age and take you in fresh directions.[1]

Figgis says that if it is work that becomes central to your identity, it's an encore career.[2] This tallies well with other research on the encore urge that often happens at midlife and beyond, and the interconnection between work and other areas of life at this stage.

Career reinvention is at the heart of encore careers. Those who succeed generally have access to support and resources to make it happen, and you often need some creative thinking to realise the possibilities. But if you do the hard yards and rethink your work properly, it can transform your later working life into an extraordinary time.

An encore career generally offers flexibility and to some extent you can control the time you spend on it. But if you're going to make it work, it will involve a significant commitment of time and energy, at least in the beginning. It may be your big chance to live out a secret career dream, to take a path you've dreamed of for years but didn't feel able to take – until now. As we've seen, you may not discover what you really want to do with your life, or where your talents and strengths lie, until well past middle age. Being open to new experiences as you age, and taking some time to reflect on your sense of purpose, can open the door to a new direction.

And importantly, an encore career gives you the same sense of identity that your earlier career provided. With planning, it will keep you connected with others, provide you with income, interesting and meaningful experiences, and give a renewed sense of possibilities. An encore career may or may not involve as much financial remuneration as you received previously, so those who are better financially prepared for retirement may have more options at this stage.

Let yourself imagine what it might be like to reinvent your career. What would you like to do? What are the essential things to include? What are the intolerable things, what couldn't you put up with?

Alexander, 74

Alexander's story illustrates the encore career type well, as he has pivoted from one career to the next more than once, each time building on his experience and contacts. And at 74, he is contemplating yet another change so he can stay engaged and work to his strengths.

I was 53 and I'd been a law partner for over 20 years in the corporate and commercial area when I got interested in a new niche area, but I had very blank looks from people when I started to talk about it. I thought it was a new, coming thing and if I couldn't interest the firm in it I wouldn't forgive myself if I didn't have a crack at it, so that's why I decided to leave.

I went to the States to talk to the movers and shakers in the area and then set up shop offering analytic services, with two partners who were also thinking of something similar.

I actually thought it would be much easier than it was and one thing that it taught me was the value of goodwill, because it took a long time to get established. But then for about 10 years we became pretty well-known in the market. We brought in a few more local principals and then expanded internationally. Eventually, we became part of an international group.

I was in my late 60s then, and I wanted to step back from the hard yakka of day-to-day operations, and focus on succession planning the Australian business for its international owner.

I was a house husband for a while, but it didn't suit me, so I had a stint on an international board and did a couple of local projects to revive my name and as a good springboard to a third career in the industry. Now I'm offering high-level advice and liaison services to the corporate sector.

I never really contemplated fully retiring. I think intellectually it doesn't appeal and I suppose I think if you retire that's the beginning of the end in a sense. Plus, my wife is 10 years younger and working full-time. It's very important that I keep my mind engaged because her mind is certainly engaged and I think one of the essential things in a relationship is you have to have a good balance of power. And we are two fairly feisty people, so I want to keep going for that reason.

But I also want to do it because it's very interesting and over a period of 20 years or so I've met some marvellous people. And I actually know what works and what doesn't work and what's needed and I've got the contacts.

Financially, I couldn't retire early. Divorce and all those sorts of things don't help, and I didn't come into life with a big bit of capital behind me, I've had to make it all myself. I think 20 years as a partner in a major law firm is probably enough, I think you'd be terribly boring if you did that all the time. So you need to do something else. I don't think I ever would have retired in my 50s, I would have done something. Financially I couldn't afford to retire, but psychologically I don't think I could have stood it.

I want to stay engaged. As I see it, what I contribute are my contacts, my ability to see very clearly what's needed, but I need a bit of horsepower to help me do it, which is why I'm talking with a company for my third career. I don't want to have to do the hard nitty-gritty grunt because I think at 74 I can't do that, but also it's a bit of a waste of what I can do.

I think career satisfaction is being able to think, 'Well actually, I've done what I wanted to do and my latter careers have also been socially useful.' That's one reason why I went into this field, because I saw things that ought to be changed. I can look back and say, 'I've basically done what I wanted to do and I think I've achieved something in doing it.'

Same–same but different

You may be happy in your current career, and intend to plan your next decades within that context, but as you age your priorities naturally change, so you may start to want greater flexibility.

This may involve working part-time as a transition to retirement, like the 40 per cent of Australian full-time workers who say they intend to switch to part-time for a few years before they retire.[3] Or you may want to cut back on a stressful commute by starting later and finishing earlier on certain days, or working from home sometimes. You may also want to take additional unpaid leave to travel, or to care for older relatives or pick up grandchildren from school. (Of course, these issues don't only relate to people over 50. The story may be different for young parents or millennials wanting to travel, but the desire for flexible conditions is clear across age groups.)

You may want to keep using your hard-won experience and knowledge, but in a different role. If you've been a tradie all your life, maybe it's time to teach, or to bring a younger worker on board to mentor and train? My plumbers are a father and son team, and it's a joy to watch them sharing the load – you can read Ross's story below.

It's not for everyone, of course. For some, the 50s and 60s are a time to ramp up their career, not wind it down. Women who have interrupted careers to raise children or care for others may see this period as a chance to achieve longstanding career aspirations, such as promotion or board roles – and to accumulate superannuation. There is also a significant sub-group of women (and men) who are financially less well off than expected due to divorce and may need to reactivate career ideas for that reason.

Is it too hard for employers to meet us halfway? Maybe not. A few years ago, managers at BMW realised that with Germany's greying population the average age of their workers would jump from 41 to 46 by 2017. So they decided to be proactive, and in 2007 they set up an experimental assembly line with older employees, with hoists to spare ageing backs, adjustable-height work benches, and wooden floors instead of rubber to help hips swivel during repetitive tasks. The verdict: not only could they keep up, the older workers did a better job than younger staffers on another line at the same factory. Today, many of the changes are being implemented at plants across the company.[4]

This BMW case study could be a good story to have with you when you meet your boss to discuss a flexible workplace; after all, chances are the adjustments needed to retain you won't involve anything as complicated as bringing in hoists or changing the floors.

Many workers say they are frightened to raise requests for flexibility, but it's important to have an honest conversation with your employer – you may be surprised by the ideas that come from such a meeting, such as new mentoring roles, further training or flexible hours. Employers know how disruptive it can be to lose good staff and they will hopefully be interested in keeping you motivated and contributing productively. You may even find you can tap into government policies (such as under the *Fair Work Act*) that encourage workplace flexible arrangements.

Does a same–same-but-different approach appeal to you? What would you like to change in your current work situation? What are the essential things to include? What couldn't you put up with?

Ross, 63

Ross has always been a plumber, but has modified the balance between work and play as he aged. He teaches at TAFE to pass on his considerable experience to the next generation and has brought his son into the business to continue the family tradition. He's the boss so he can make changes without needing anyone's permission – though he still must ensure it works for his business as a whole.

I was born and bred into plumbing. My grandfather was the first plumber in Five Dock, in 1903. My father was a plumber, and I was his apprentice. I employed my nephew, then my two sons. When you come from a long line of plumbers, it's pretty hard to break the links in the chain.

Over the years, things have changed for me. I've gone from working six or seven days a week when I was 18 or 19 years old, to when I had a family and I always had all the school holidays off. I would work longer hours so there was enough money to take time off in the holidays. Then when I was 49, I went back to five days a week and started teaching at TAFE one day a week. Now I've handed some of the work in the business to my son Rob, so I teach two days a week and I only want to work for two other days a week maximum.

I still do a lot of quoting, because elderly people like to deal with elderly people. We talk the same lingo. The younger generation are all on iPads and the rest, whereas I go in with a notepad and draw it all up on a bit of paper and say, 'This is what you want and this is what it's gonna cost you.' I have no interest in technology, I like to be face to face.

I'm 63 and in good health. I still do the long hours, I was up at half past five this morning and by the time I get home tonight it will probably be six o'clock – hard work's not the problem. But in my day, we had to do everything with earthenware pipes and now I pull up with a truck with six lengths of plastic pipe on the roof and it's enough to do your whole house. So, physically it's much easier now.

I try to teach my TAFE students that yes, I'm the old fart, but I'm the old fart that's got this up here [touches his head] that you don't have yet. You haven't got those skills yet, it comes with experience. You've gotta learn to improvise. I tell my students it's not as though you can go and buy it at a hardware shop – you're gonna be out the back of Cobar somewhere and you've got to make it work. You have to be able to adapt.

I never get up in the morning and think, 'Oh shit, I have to go to work today.' Every day's a different challenge. Over the next five or ten years, my work will be the same, just a bit reduced. I might say instead of working five days this week I'm only going to work two or three days, and then I'll go fishing, or we'll just get in the car and hook up the caravan and take off for a couple of weeks.

Family comes first, that's the be-all and end-all. Everything else is after that. My philosophy of life is that you go to work to put bread and butter on the table, to live. You've gotta have money, but you can't make your whole life about money. People are just too money hungry today, they're just too greedy. Money causes more problems than it solves.

My life satisfaction is when I walk away from every job knowing that we've done the best we can to resolve that problem. It's been the same since I started work. I still enjoy every job we do because they're all different.

I'll probably die with a spanner in my hand. That's the truth of it, because I love my work.

Starting a business

Have you ever wanted to start your own business? Do you have a secret dream to become an entrepreneur, or are you seeing a business start-up as a way to create a job for yourself as you age?

Older people starting businesses (sometimes called 'seniorpreneurs') may start a solo enterprise, work as consultants, brokers, agents or freelancers, or team up with a few partners to create a new business venture. Some may even sow the seeds of a new global empire, like Arianna Huffington, who was 54 when she founded the *Huffington Post*, and 11 years later in 2016 started a new wellbeing business.

Forget the myth that successful start-ups belong to the young. In fact, the networks, resources and expertise you've built up over decades of work will be an advantage. Starting a business takes a good idea, some self-belief and perhaps some financial backing. There are risks, such as loss of capital, failure to master the diverse skill set needed to run a business, and heavy demands on time and energy, so you need to think carefully whether it's for you. But the rewards can be very real.

Older people are the fastest growing category of entrepreneur in Australia. The activity of entrepreneurs aged 50 to 65 is growing more rapidly than those aged 20 to 34, and there is some evidence that success rates are higher in the older demographic.[5] This trend towards older people starting their own businesses is widely predicted to increase even more.

Australian research in 2015[6] showed that 34 per cent of new businesses in Australia are led by older people, with an average age of 57. Older entrepreneurs had more industry experience than younger entrepreneurs, invested more in their business and earned greater profits.

Some start a business because they can't find a job, and see this as a practical alternative (often called 'necessity entrepreneurship'). If you're made redundant in your 50s and are finding it hard to break through age discrimination to find another job, running your own business may feel like the only way to secure an income. Others wish to monetise a hobby or create a socially useful paid project ('opportunity entrepreneurship'). Some are looking for a small supplement to their income, others are risking all to activate an old dream. Many want to achieve a desired lifestyle for themselves, or discover a new way of working on their own terms, rather than building a business to sell for a profit.[7]

The 2015 research also indicated that older entrepreneurs are more open to taking (measured) risks, and have experience, solid networks and greater resources.[8] They are also highly motivated – they appreciate the flexibility and autonomy of running their own show and have a clear sense of what they enjoy doing and where their strengths lie.

American expert on the over 50s Elizabeth Isele is recognised globally for her work in senior entrepreneurship programs, policy, funding and research. She believes that senior entrepreneurs are the new engines driving economic revitalisation throughout the world.[9] Isele emphasises the importance of developing the mindset of an entrepreneur, drawing upon who you are, what you know, who you know, and what resources you already have at hand.

What do you think, does starting a business appeal as an idea? What might be the pros and cons of a business start-up for you?

Jan, 57

Jan is very honest about her decision to start her own business. She left her corporate job on an impulse and had to learn on the run about the challenges of becoming an entrepreneur. She is now thriving – and shaping her business to suit her particular goals.

I certainly didn't expect to run my own business. I started as a secretary and worked my way up the corporate ladder to become a director of a leading merchant bank. It was a long climb, I'd do three years in an organisation and if I didn't get promoted then I'd leave. I created my career path, with some luck along the way.

In 2001 the bank moved me from London to Sydney. My now-husband joined me. I had a ball, I absolutely loved it. It was 14 to 16 hours a day and travelling, but I was in my element. Then they wanted to move me again and I didn't want to leave.

We're living in Wahroonga, it's a Sunday afternoon, pouring rain, and my husband, Steve, says, 'This is miserable, let's get a bottle of wine and a couple of magazines and just chill.' I opened the magazine and there was an advert that said, 'We work long hours' and I thought, 'Yes we do.' 'We don't have enough time for our family and friends' and I thought, 'No we don't.' 'Believe it or not, there's a better way' and I thought, 'There is? I want to know about it.' I rang the number and it was a network marketing company in the health and wellness arena. Initially I said, 'No way.' And a friend said,

'You're going to get healthy, that's the worst thing that could happen. And supposing it works, supposing you actually can quit your job and you can sustain yourself here in Australia, how would that be?'

So I jumped in, not knowing the stigma of network marketing. And of course all the doors slammed shut in my face, but I was determined and I said to my husband, 'I think if I could go full-time, I reckon I could make this business work.' I was 49 and I had three months' long service leave, so I took it.

Two weeks later a friend said to my husband, 'You need your head examined. You've let her out of the bank for three months, you'll never get her to go back.' Steve said, 'If I thought we could afford for her not to go back to work I'd let her resign immediately because this is the woman I fell in love with' and I said, 'Oh, darling, we'd better talk.' We had a chat and then I rang up my boss in Chicago and told him I wasn't coming back.

I really struggled in the beginning. I was disciplined, but I didn't find it easy. As a director of a large company I'd say, 'Jump' and everyone would say, 'How high?' and suddenly that was all gone. You can create a business plan, a marketing plan, but then you're out there.

I got a business coach, I did online courses and webinars, joined mentoring groups, but you've got to put yourself out there. I felt that I needed some training in coaching skills. I got my coaching diploma and settled on the niche of executive wellness, wellbeing and performance coaching. I really liked it, I started getting clients and ended up shifting into the coaching business.

Being in my 50s is a huge positive. People are more comfortable coming to me because they feel I've got life experience. I understand, I can be empathetic, but I can also kick them up the butt if they need it.

I want to work three days a week, just enough to keep the brain cells going, but having four days a week with my husband to do the things we want to do, like travelling. We met later in life so we didn't have the courtship when we were younger, so I want to do it now.

When I was younger, success meant climbing the corporate ladder and the title and the pay that went with it. Now it's having quality time with my family and my husband, my friends, and it's the autonomy to be able to run my business the way I want to do it and to see the money coming into the bank account.

Before I left the bank, my husband would say, 'You'll never leave, it'll be nine o'clock on a Friday night, you'll be 90 years of age and I'm going to have to drag you kicking and screaming to get you out of work.' But the minute I left, it was as though the corporate blinkers came off, I saw the whole world for what it really was and I thought, 'Oh my God, aren't I lucky? I nearly missed out on life.'

Giving back

I like to think that the urge to give back is hardwired into most people. Some do volunteer work throughout their lives, and others think, 'When I retire I will build houses in Cambodia, or do a regular shift at a refuge, or mentor kids who need a helping hand.' Either way, the later decades present many opportunities if you do want to give back.

It doesn't have to be a formal thing; you might take the grandchildren one day a week, or help a neighbour get to her appointments, or provide meals in times of crisis. I will never forget an old friend of my mother's who cooked and froze numerous meals for me when my son was born. It wasn't a crisis exactly, but much appreciated all the same.

You don't need my help to work out how to bring soup to a sick friend or agree to take your grandchildren to school, but if you do want to structure your giving back, here are two broad strands of community contribution.

Volunteering

Volunteering has demonstrable benefits to physical and mental wellbeing and it's a brilliant source of personal satisfaction – you tend to get at least as much as you give in a feel-good sense.

It's also great for learning new skills, and doing less intensive work.[10] People over 60 may be drawn to volunteering to make friends or have social contact.[11]

According to Volunteering Australia, 43 per cent of adults aged 45 to 54, and 31 per cent of those over 65, do some kind of formal volunteering, with older volunteers giving more hours.[12]

Valerie Hoogstad, Chairperson of The Centre for Volunteering in New South Wales, confirms that older people volunteer in big numbers, and for a variety of reasons. 'I think in their mind most of them do it to give back. But there are both physical and mental health benefits – they feel better about themselves, they can forget their health troubles and woes, and mentally it keeps them alert. The friendships they form are very, very valuable. We've had people who've been coming for 12 or 15 years, some longer, and if they come on Tuesdays then they're friends with other volunteers in the Tuesday group.'

Hoogstad sees two types. 'There are people who want to use their skills to volunteer to help people, such as in mentoring, coaching or financial help. They might teach migrant women if they're teachers. If they're bankers, they'll be helping with finance. Then there are those who say, "I definitely don't want to be involved in finance. I'm sick of it. I've done banking all my life and I want to do gardening or bird watching." They want to do something they've had an interest in and not been able to develop. The other day I had a fairly senior finance guy just retiring, passionate about animals all his life and he wanted to work with Taronga Zoo. He said, "I don't care what I do at the zoo, I can brush the pavements. If I can be around animals I'll be very happy."'

There may be less ageism and stereotyping in the volunteer sector, so if you are jaded or bruised by the world of work, volunteering could be an excellent way to regain confidence and get work experience.

Social entrepreneurship

The other trend in giving back is social enterprise, an interesting fusion of entrepreneurship and volunteering – using business strategies to achieve social improvement through innovative approaches to entrenched community problems. It's about clever businesses that give back.

A significant number of social entrepreneurs are over 50. Some are caring for family members, such as parents or children, and think there must be a better way of delivering a service to their mother, or whoever. Others have paid off some of their mortgage, want to get out of the corporate world, and think now is the time to do that thing they've always wanted to do. Either way, older social entrepreneurs have had time to think it through.

Would you like to give back in some way? Consider whether it appeals, and if so, what area might be your choice?

Michael, 78

Michael had a long career as a financial planner before finding a way to give back to the community in his 70s. He chose to build on his work experience and adapt it to a new area by adding some new skills so he could volunteer in a specialised area.

In 1971 I started a financial services advisory business. My daughter joined the business in 2004. She brought a breath of fresh air, new ways of doing things. She basically took over the business.

In 2014 she said, 'This is ridiculous, you're not doing anything, it's time you retired.' I knew it was coming. My wife said, 'When you're retired there's no way you're going to sit around the house doing nothing but watch football all day. You've got to find something to do.' I thought about this and that and the other, all different things I felt I was qualified and experienced to do, going back to my early days as a photographer, or becoming an insurance-fraud investigator.

Then my daughter said, 'Have you thought about financial counselling?' and I looked into it and found I had to have a Diploma of Community Service in Financial Counselling. So I started this diploma. Of course, I was by far the oldest student because by this time I was 77. It was all very interesting and very difficult. I was worried about the level of knowledge and work that I'd have to do. I've finished the course except for the last practical sessions with a financial counsellor doing interviews with real clients. I'm trying to arrange all that now.

I was looking at jobs for financial counsellors, but they were in places like Walgett and Dubbo, and I only want to work in Chatswood. I'm not a bushy, I'm a city man. I got onto the Salvation Army coordinator for a program that arranges no-interest loans for 12 months in order to purchase things like fridges and washing machines; they lend on average $800 to $1600. It's not like payday lenders, because they're crooks. This one's a terrific scheme, it's fantastic for poor people. There was nobody running the scheme in the Chatswood area, so I said, 'I'll volunteer one day a week and I'll set it up and keep it going.'

That's one day a week and then I want to do a couple of other days. And somebody said to me, 'Look, there's a mob called Jewish Care that is based in Bondi, but they don't have anybody on the North Shore.' So I thought maybe I'll get in touch with them and maybe I'll do a day a week for them.

I've never given a thought about retiring. I still don't want to retire. Look, when I was working for a big company, back then you had a job for life. You started as an apprentice when you were 12 or 14 or 16 and you were with them for the rest of your working life, then when you reached retirement age they gave you your gold watch. And year in and year out people who had been at the company all their working lives came to retirement and we'd say cheerio and within 12 months they'd died.

Some of them didn't even last to retire – 63, 64 years old, boom, kaput, dropped off the twig. I think that scared me from ever retiring. I thought once you retire you're dead.

I don't feel old and according to most people I don't look my age, and I certainly don't act it. I've got a routine. I still go to the gym three nights a week like I've been doing for the last 22 years just to keep fit. You've also got to keep your mind active and so I do the cryptic crossword every day in the *Herald*. I like to do the other puzzles as well, there're a few number puzzles, Sudoku and all those things.

And then, of course, you've got to find something to do apart from all that. You can't basically sit around being idle because then you just vegetate and that's no good, and there are plenty of things for people to do to give a bit back to the community. There are so many organisations that need people.

Land that job

Maybe you're reading this chapter thinking that it's okay for some, being able to choose between changing careers, setting up a dream business, giving back or putting more flexibility into your work. Maybe for you it's just about getting a job, any job. If so, you're not alone.

Some Australians over 50 have plenty of options and resources for their next step, so their biggest challenge is deciding which direction to take. But nearly two million Australians aged 55 and over are outside the workforce but willing to work. Estimates suggest that not using the skills and experience of older Australians costs our economy $10.8 billion a year.[13]

Older workers may find themselves made redundant in a declining industry. Or they may be exhausted from several decades of physical or demanding work and need to think about new avenues, including upskilling or re-skilling in new areas.

As we saw in Chapter 1, age discrimination certainly plays a role, with five in six older job seekers saying they experienced age discrimination during their job search.[14] Michael O'Neill, former National Seniors Australia CEO, says it takes someone aged 55 or older an average of 94 weeks to find work in New South Wales – compared with 45 weeks for a younger job seeker.[15]

But no matter your age, with persistence and a bit of creativity and savvy, you can land that job. Truly. Before you start answering job ads and making interview times with local recruitment agencies, take a step back and think about how you'd really like to spend the next years of your working life. This may be your big chance to pivot your current career, or to reinvent yourself entirely.

If you decide to stay in your current field, treat looking for a job as a job itself, where you need to turn up every day, and if you keep hitting a brick wall rethink your strategy. The most important thing is to realise that the world of work has changed a great deal, so you'll need to activate some 21st-century practical strategies, like the ones in Chapter 12 for job hunting, résumé writing and acing the interview.

Leanne, 52

Leanne assumed it would be easy to change jobs in her early 50s. She soon realised it wasn't as quick or simple as she'd thought, but she developed a solid and creative strategy that led to her success at landing a job.

I've always been an EA. My last position before I was unemployed was EA to the CEO of a private company for eight-and-a-half years. Eighteen months ago, I decided to leave because there were things happening in the company and the dynamics between myself and the CEO had changed substantially.

I'd had a bit of a glance around and it looked like there were plenty of positions, so I wasn't in any rush. I thought it'll probably take me a month, and I was totally shocked. I had interviews with the reputable, top-end-of-the-market agencies. And I started to find that when you did the phone interview they were very enthusiastic and even talked about positions that were available. But when you go there you have to give proof of identity, and of course it's got your date of birth. I'm extremely well dressed, extremely well presented, but it doesn't matter how great you look, instantly you're in that over-50s category.

I went for one interview at an agency and she was very enthusiastic, but her tone changed as soon as she photocopied my birth certificate. And then she reneged on the job that she had told me about, saying, 'Oh no, the job really wasn't a definite.' And it was funny because it was with a really small company, three or four people, and she said, 'They've promoted within' and that just didn't ring true.

But it didn't defeat me and I applied for a lot of jobs and I was meticulous about the way I applied. Many people send off automatic replies to online job ads just because the ad might mention the word 'administration'. I never did that. I read every job, I would think a lot about it and I always wrote a covering letter pertaining to that actual position. And I would always tweak my résumé, not as in being dishonest, but if I sounded too overqualified I would take out the really beefy part so they didn't automatically discount me.

I did all that and I really was not having any luck and I was getting very disheartened. The EA role is slowly dying so that limited my choices. And then I got two months' temp work.

In the middle of June I got another temp role as a PA for a CFO. While I was there a casual position came up as an admin assistant in retail sales, 30 hours a week. I've been in that position for 10 months; it's been a learning curve for me because it's like nothing I've done before.

I am so thankful I have a job, I am so thankful I work for a lovely company. I must admit at 52 it has been very nice working part-time; it's the very first time I've ever worked part-time.

I was so determined to get a job that I never gave up. I have a mortgage so it wasn't a choice. And my husband was extremely supportive.

Years ago, you would go to an agency and you would have an interview and whatever and they would think about you for jobs. These days, I suppose because there are so many people looking for a job, they're not interested in seeing you and, in essence, wasting their time unless there's a position that you've applied for.

Age is a barrier but it's just the way things are now, so you just have to take job hunting really seriously. Don't give up, treat it like a job that every day you're going to do. I felt it was harder looking for a job than having a job. I did get disheartened, but there was never a day that I said, 'Damn it, I'm not gonna do it today' because my attitude always was that will be the day when a fantastic position will come up.

[And since our interview, Leanne has changed jobs once more. She reactivated her job-search strategies to secure what she describes as a 'fantastic' full-time job as the personal assistant to the CEO of a disability company.]

Portfolios

A final word on our 'big five'. You don't have to choose just one and ditch the rest forever. It's quite likely that you might do two or three of them in a serial fashion, or even simultaneously. Portfolio work, where you do more than one type of work in your week, is becoming quite a trend. Maybe you will get some flexibility in your current job, so you can care for grandchildren or do community work. Or start a business while volunteering at your local soup kitchen. Or …

There are plenty of possibilities here, that's the great thing about this journey without maps. You get to be in charge of your future, to create something that works for you. Just don't try setting up a business and changing careers and committing to volunteer work all in the same week. That would be quite silly.

CHAPTER 3

Creative ways to look at your future

Fear not for the future, weep not for the past.
Percy Bysshe Shelley

Numerous academic and popular books were published in the twentieth century dealing with the changes in life themes, interests and psychological development that occur in childhood, adolescence, and in our 20s, 30s and 40s. Typically, these were written when the lifespan was much shorter than it is now and tracked that old life course we looked at earlier with the one-way linear trajectory from birth to death.

The teens were all about individuation, the 20s about settling down and having children, and the 30s about balancing intimacy and achievement, for example. The idea of the midlife crisis in your 40s became popular through books like these and research about each stage has added a great deal to our understanding of adult psychological and social development.

Traditionally, relatively little attention was paid to changes in our 50s and beyond. Many writers assumed that we don't continue to change and grow after 50, or even that our lives start to shrink as we accumulate loss after loss. It was somehow taken as given that we drift from midlife to a nursing home, without much change or adventure along the way. 'Nothing to see here' appeared to be the motto of adult-development writers, if indeed they gave much thought to the over 50s at all.

As we began to live and work for longer, researchers started turning their attention to these later decades, and seeing this time as one of potential for ongoing personal growth and life experience. New themes are appearing around consolidation of experience and identity, spiritual learning, reflecting on life and thinking about legacy.

Sometimes this discussion divides people over 50 into sub-categories (usually decade by decade) and it often looks something like this list, adapted from Frederic Hudson's excellent work on the adult years: [1]

- 50s: interdependence, enjoying nature, spiritual awareness, post-parental roles, travel, preparing for losses
- 60s: redesigning life and work, racing against time, sharing knowledge, being a grandparent, searching for meaning
- 70s: contributing, celebrating the fullness of life, searching for meaning, managing physical decline
- 80s: legacy, simplifying, managing physical decline, gratitude, caring for favourite causes
- 90s: turning inward, embracing mortality, generosity, summing up.

I expect these themes may shift to later timeframes as we continue to add years to our lifespans, and new ones may emerge, but it's interesting to think about what is important to *you* now and in the future, particularly as this new life course is not a rigid, one-size-fits-all prescription. It's important to think about what things like 'success' and 'life satisfaction' mean to you.

What does success mean to you?

I've long been a travel tragic, and my life highlights include climbing Mount Kilimanjaro, trekking the Himalayas, and making journeys through the Middle East, India, Africa, Borneo, Burma and Tibet.

Wherever I go, I enjoy visiting historic places and hearing the stories of people who lived and died there over the centuries. Each time it strikes me what a huge role external circumstances can play in a career. You might be the best, most skilled or most experienced cardinal, stonemason, farmer, warrior or queen, but if the French Revolution intervened, or your country was invaded, or plague arrived, or your boss (or worse, husband) was Henry VIII, it may all come to naught in a pretty sudden and dramatic fashion.

It's not just about famous types like Anne Boleyn, Aung San Suu Kyi or His Holiness the Dalai Lama, or even about big dramatic events like the two world wars or the colonisation of India. None of us ever has total control over our careers (or anything else, really). So, relying on the external world to bring you success could well prove to be a tricky strategy.

One of my favourite writers and thinkers, Robert Fritz, works with these ideas when he talks about the dangers, even futility, of having goals based on the desire for success.

Fritz says that we should stop obsessing about external markers of success, which are generally about our identity or ego (in the sense of 'being' a success or having 'arrived'), and focus instead on thinking about what we want to create in the world and how we can take steps towards making it real.

I love this distinction because it's values driven and about what you can create – and not who you want to become. As Fritz says, it is generative and not reactive. It may need a bit of reflection to see the difference, but it's time worth spending.

Whatever our external circumstances, we can still have internal markers of success, we can still be creative, we can still get excited and make stuff. (Okay, maybe not if your external circumstances include having your head chopped off, but for most of us, that's not our biggest worry.)

This internal model of success or satisfaction becomes easier as we age. As we mature, we see the world and ourselves differently and our ideas about what 'success' means to us also change. We become less hooked on society's definitions or markers such as money or promotions, or even the values we absorbed from parents or peers. We begin to realise that happiness is far more likely if we focus on what we enjoy, even if that is not necessarily going to bring vast external rewards. This is quite liberating and opens up many more possibilities.

One of my friends, Christina, who is now 65, has had experience with this. She started off studying Asian studies, Japanese and politics, combined with a law degree. She was very interested in Japan, but it was also a career choice much promoted by her family. When that didn't work out, she finished law and worked in a large law firm, where she was pretty unhappy. Various roles followed in financial services and investment banking, some of which were interesting, but all soul-destroying. Although they were ultimately lucrative, this world was populated by people whose values she didn't share.

Over time, Christina did a lot of deep reflection about what was important to her (rather than to her family or colleagues) in her working life and concluded that a not-for-profit or public sector role was better aligned to her values. She now works in that sector in a job that matches her values and allows her to draw on her people skills.

When we talked about this recently, she said that at the start of her career she picked up opportunities as they came along and tended to follow the expectations of other people, rather than sitting down and thinking through what was important for her. Her legal career was very much a function of societal expectations and those of friends and family.

As she says, 'It's interesting to look back and think, "Why didn't I stand up for what I knew was important for me earlier than I did?" I don't quite know the answer to that. I earned a lot of money, but money's no compensation for your peace of mind, really. You get a lot of social status from your professional status, but I don't quite know why I felt that that was important or valuable. Now that sort of thing is really not valuable to me at all.'

As Christina found, it's important to know what you really value in life, so you can make much better choices about what's right for you. Part of that is letting go of the expectations of other people and that's not easy. Even in your 50s and 60s you're often surrounded by people who expect you to behave in the same ways and keep doing the things that you've done in the past. In order to find your internal definition of success, what it is that will make *you* happy, you have to be ready to let go of those expectations and sometimes stand against them.

Christina sums it up very well, 'It's very difficult, but I think you have to be prepared to do that. It's vital for the integrity of the soul really, isn't it?' I couldn't agree more.

David, 51

David always loved music and his first job was working with audio equipment. However, this evolved into an IT career that took him away from music. Many years later he remodelled his internal definition of success and found a way to return to his first love. He is now happily selling musical instruments and developing creative side projects.

I studied as far as high school, but I loved music and started working in an audio company, doing installation of audio equipment, also building speaker boxes and that kind of stuff. Music doesn't pay well, you're in it for the love of it, so I thought I should find out what this computer world is all about, and I went back to college and did an Electronics Associate Diploma.

I started using my electronics skills in a computing environment and that was my career for the next 27 years. I did a few years in a real hands-on role, workbench technician type of work. It turned out I was pretty good with people, so I ventured into customer support and then moved to a customer-facing role, where I would be paired up with a salesperson, and visit a customer to work out a technical solution.

I've only ever joined three companies in my life. I've moved from being a hands-on worker to a knowledge worker, but I still really love doing things with my hands – I'm a musician as well, I play a lot of instruments, so that's my outlet. I've never been one to push myself into anything, I've always been at the right place at the right time and I've had good managers. I find it hard to say no, so when someone says here's an opportunity I think, 'Okay.'

Being a yes guy is sometimes a good trait, but you often say yes to things that you're not sure about: 'Can I really do this, am I pushing the boundaries of my skill set?' And during the end of my tenure with my last company I was starting to get quite stressed out. It was quite demanding, I wasn't even having quality time on the weekends, I was thinking about work. I have a general anxiety disorder, so I went on some medication to control it. It meant that I had to be careful about what positions and situations I put myself into.

I managed it for as long as I could, but when a redundancy came along I thought, here's my chance now to say, 'I've got to get off the fence and make a decision. I've had enough and it's time to go.' It wasn't just about a payout, it was the fact that at this stage of my life I'm 51, my life in general was fantastic though I was no longer doing any music and I thought, 'It's time for a change though I don't know what that change is going to be.' It scared the hell out of me.

My extremely supportive wife knows I love music and she saw this job online. It was a retail position working in a music store selling musical instruments. She said, 'You would love this, why don't you do it?' We've been building up a bit of a nest egg, and we're in a position now where I could take a bit of a back seat in terms of earning money and do something that I am passionate about. I'm on a minimum wage, but I don't care. When I clock off, the job stays there and I come home happy as Larry, my relationship's better for it, life is better for it.

I was really hesitant about this retail role, but I love dealing with people, having conversations, I find it exciting meeting new people. So being in retail really awakened that thing that I used to have back in the 1980s when I was working in the music industry. There are all different types of weird and wonderful characters, you know, good customers and bad ones. And I just love that interaction when mum or dad comes in with a little child saying, 'They want to play saxophone, I know nothing about it, I'm musically challenged, can you help me?' And I help them leave with whatever it is they need.

I had a call from a friend about a month ago about a music project so now I am composing music for children, which is something I've never thought of. Music's starting to be a big part of my life again. Not only am I working in the industry, I'm also being creative again with my music. It's like I've done a 360-degree turn back to where I started.

I lost my father two years ago and it really made me realise that the stress that I was under at work is not worth it. I'm alive once, as far as I know you only get one go at it, and there are more important things in life than a pay cheque. Of course, you need it at some level, but being happy, being healthy, being part of a family is a lot more important. I don't regret leaving the corporate train. It's the best thing I've ever done.

It's all one pond

This book is about your work, but work only makes sense when you know where it fits into your life – and I'm not sure whether the idea of splitting ourselves into 'work' and 'life' sections is even useful these days.

While on a Buddhist retreat a few years ago at the Nan Tien Temple near Wollongong, I had a chat to a Buddhist nun I know, Venerable Miao You. She is the director of the Nan Tien Institute and a most practical and also inspired teacher. She is also very amusing, which I like.

We were talking about fitting meditation and reflection into a busy life, and she mentioned that she saw it all as 'just one pond'. Just one pond. Not divvying up time between this compartment or that, finishing 'work' so you can move on to 'life'. Just one pond.

On any day you can move fluidly from one area into another, and back again. You can follow your sense of what needs to happen next, or what suits your frame of mind. For me, some days it's all about developing a new program, and on others the focus is on clients, or cooking risotto. But there's no trying to find that (mythical?) balance – whatever needs to happen on a given day, happens.

It's not always easy, and some days it may seem totally out of reach. And if you neglect one part of your pond for too long, it will stagnate, even develop scum. So, you need to have an eye on the different parts of your life, over time. But it is a great deal more flexible than striving for a daily balance, which can quickly degenerate into a frantic, unsuccessful juggling act.

Just one pond. It works for me.

Exercise: Your 'satisfying life' mind map

Having started to think about your internal definition of success, this next exercise lets you work with that in a creative way, and to expand it to include all the elements of a happy (or satisfying, or meaningful, or complete) life.

Think about the elements of your satisfying life – work, family, community, friends, travel, finances, health, purpose, whatever it is for you. There's no right or wrong, but it's worth spending a bit of time thinking about the pieces you want to have in place, even if some of them haven't happened yet.

It might sound corny, but it can help to imagine that you are at your own eightieth birthday party. Someone close to you is making a speech – what will they highlight about you?

You can also think of this in connection with your values. For example, which of these would give you most satisfaction:

- making $1 million from your work
- receiving an Order of Australia award
- becoming famous or a celebrity
- becoming an expert
- gaining the respect of your peers or community.

As you move through this book, it is a good idea to keep these questions in mind, so your new work plans resonate with your overall life aims and values. If you're up for it, you can even add in the biggest question of all: what is the purpose of your life?

A good way to work with these questions is by doing a mind map of the elements of your happy, successful life. Mind mapping is a deceptively simple, very elegant and creative tool. It allows you to tap into your left and right brains – to use images and association, logic and intuition, big picture and fine detail all at once. It's a bit like making a street map to your destination.

And it's fun.

Have a look at the mind map on page 65, which I've created as a typical client map, although it would usually be hand-drawn, in colour and include some drawings or other embellishments. I have shown only some generic branches to start you off – it is not meant to indicate all the areas or even the most import for you. Just use it as a guide to mind mapping, not a template for your map.

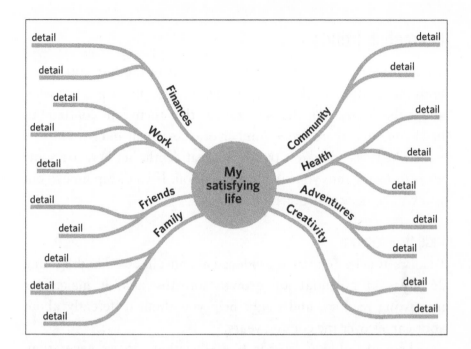

Your map

In this exercise, you will draw yourself a mind map of what a satisfying life would look like to you. Here's how:

- Put an image in the centre for the main idea – add a few words that will give your map a focus ('My happy life', 'My meaningful life', 'My successful life').
- Use colour to draw a branch line out from the centre, adding a word or two that relates to an aspect of your life ('Family', 'Finances' and so on).
- Have one idea per branch and make sure each branch is connected to the central image.
- Add sub-branches with further detail.
- Draw pictures or symbols to bring your map alive.

As you develop your ideas, check them against your map to make sure that your plans will allow you to flourish in every part of your life.

Interesting trends

We all understand that work has changed in the last 100 years, both the kinds of work we do and how we go about it – but what about the future? All that's certain is that there will continue to be change, but there are a number of clues about likely trends. A book like this can't cover trends in great depth, but here are some ideas to factor into your work reinvention. If you keep an eye out you will come across others, too.

Industry sectors

Deloitte Touche Tohmatsu produced a report in 2014[2] highlighting 25 areas of potential job growth for Australia. It makes for interesting reading, and might help you think differently about your career over the coming years.

There are obvious trends like education, power generation, tourism and health, as well as retirement living, medical research and even parcel delivery. In some sectors like personal services and parts of the media, there's a trend towards smaller, more nimble companies. But in other areas companies continue to grow and to offer more things to more people in more countries – think Amazon, Westfield and the big banks.

Flexible workforces

There's already a trend towards fewer permanent full-time jobs and increasing numbers of casual employees. This applies to workers of all ages, but there is a particular note of caution about older workers. On a research trip to the United States in 2014, I was able to meet with Joe Carbone, president of The WorkPlace in Connecticut and a noted commentator. The WorkPlace develops workforce strategies, helps job seekers and contributes to discussion about workforce trends, and Carbone spoke to me at length about older workers being given casual, low-paid and less secure jobs. He connects this 'casualisation' of the US workforce to the growing exodus of older people downwards from the middle class and warns of long-term damaging effects if the trend is not reversed. This needs to be watched in the Australian context.

In recent times, we have also seen the rise of what is being called the 'gig economy', often in areas of digital disruption like transport (Uber) and accommodation (Airbnb). These offer booking platforms but do not own the assets needed for the business, such as cars and apartments. It is the workers who provide the equipment and assume much of the risk.

The benefits of gig work include easy entry, flexibility, no minimum time commitment and the ability to do other things such as study or start a small business. However, gig workers are usually classified as independent contractors rather than employees, which means no guaranteed pay, no workers compensation and fewer rights in a dispute. Many platforms restrict gig contractors from working for competitors and from building their own network of clients or contacts for future work. When things go wrong, there are often issues around who is liable and whether it's covered by insurance. Australian courts and governments are currently wrestling with how best to regulate these disruptive business models and protect their workers.

These new businesses may offer excellent opportunities for some older workers – provided you do your research first and understand the nature of the arrangement.

The knowledge economy

With the decline of manufacturing and other traditional industries in Australia, and the rise of automation and new technology replacing human input in some areas, we are moving rapidly towards a knowledge-based economy. I'll leave you to read the many tomes written by economics professors on this subject, and instead single out a couple of features of this new world that you may find useful.

Lifelong learning is vital, either in or out of formal studies. Whether you love learning new things or not, if you want to stay relevant in a changing world, upskilling and re-skilling are not optional. You will also need flexibility, creativity, discernment and an openness to new experiences. The emphasis is likely to be in areas in which humans have the thinking edge over machines, including creative ways of looking at problems. Transportable skills (that move with you to a new job or even a new career) are highly valuable. A spin-off that may favour older workers is the growing value placed on interpersonal skills.

One big question is whether the generalist or the specialist will fare better in the new economy. Some favour generalists with their added flexibility in changing times and difficult job markets. Several writers believe we need more 'deep generalists' or 'generalised specialists' or 'specialised generalists', which seems a bit like hedging bets (though I suspect I might be a specialised generalist myself).

On the other hand, Professor of Management Practice at London Business School Lynda Gratton has coined the phrase 'serial mastery', saying that we need to give up on the generalist in favour of deep expertise, coupled with the need to reinvent ourselves over time as specialists in more than one field.[3] This may be a tall order for some, but as an overall trend it makes good sense. To people who started their working lives in the twentieth century, it may feel odd to imagine a life with more than one career, but for those now in their 20s, it's quite normal to plan for three or more careers.

A 2016 *Sydney Morning Herald* article suggests that we are rapidly switching from routine jobs (like retail or bookkeeping) and physical jobs (think tradies and drivers) to becoming increasingly specialised knowledge workers.[4] However, I believe we will always also need generalists and 'boundary spanners' (people who sit on the edge of their organisation or industry and look outwards to connect with others) to fill in gaps between specialist silos and to see the broader picture.

Portfolio careers

Portfolio careers happen when you split your work between two part-time jobs, or have a business on the side, or in some other way work in more than one field at the same time. I have had portfolio careers most of my working life, as I have a broad range of interests and love variety. This has allowed me to stay in touch with one area (such as writing) while also working in another (such as teaching or community work). For others, it may be a way to combine something you love that doesn't pay so well with a more prosaic income earner; many people with artistic leanings end up doing this. It may also be the only way to leverage the opportunities that are around you. I have a friend my age who would love a permanent full-time position – and keeps looking – but at the moment is making the most of a variety of contract and part-time work.

Digital nomads

One of the benefits of technology is the ability to live far from your work, or to travel from place to place, using email, cloud computing and Skype to connect with clients who may not even know you are on the road. I think it adds a nice option for older workers, who may want to leverage the flexibility it offers – just make sure you can access the internet wherever you go.

Intergenerational collaboration

I've been reading quite a bit lately about older and younger people working together on projects, whether it's setting up businesses or creating high-performance teams in large companies, or in community-service projects. Research demonstrates many benefits of intergenerational workplaces, including two-person teams with one older and one younger worker, sending an older and younger worker out together on all calls to clients, arranging for older workers to pass on skills formally and informally, and reverse mentoring where younger workers teach older ones, especially in technological areas.[5] Maybe you can team up with others in this way, and maximise the power of the different strengths and skills contributed by all generations.

Adult gap year

I have fantasised about taking a year out ever since I watched Stefan Sagmeister's inspiring TED talk on the power of time off.[6] His idea is that instead of taking retirement as a long continuous chunk at the end of life, we could break it up and have a year in every seven as a sabbatical. I was immediately taken with this, though I have yet to actually do it.

For older workers at a crossroads, this might shape itself as an adult gap year, where you stop, rest, explore and reset for the next phase. I think it sounds brilliant if you can find a way to make it work, even three or six months could do the trick.

Heather and Brian, both 57

Heather and Brian decided to take an adult gap year, as Brian needed a refresher from his long teaching career and Heather was exploring an interest in visual arts. Having time out has allowed them both to take a look at new possibilities and experiment in ways they would never have thought of previously. The result? Renewed energy, new directions and great enthusiasm for the next stage of their lives.

Brian: I've been teaching in the Blue Mountains for 32 years, from my first year out of uni, so I've had a very institutional life from school to uni to school again. I'm only two-and-a-half years out from retirement, but I got to the point over the last five years where I wasn't giving the optimum and I was fairly burnt out because of the increasing demands of the job. It was a difficult decision to step off the treadmill, but necessary.

By using my accumulated long service leave at half-pay I could take a year off work. That seemed a good idea – keeping my options open without making a massive change, but at least taking a break from the job to think and breathe, recuperate and regenerate.

I knew I had to leave the mountains, so we're living in Surry Hills. I did think about travel, but as the year has gone on I've had less and less inclination to do that.

Because teaching is fairly all-consuming, this gave me space to think about what I am interested in, how I see my life, what things motivate me, what things shape the way I'm looking at the world when it's completely divorced from what I've been doing for the last 32 years.

I actually took a bit of convincing to do it and stepping out from my comfort zone was a bit of a challenge, a bit of a risk. I didn't really know what to expect, I didn't go in with a lot of preconceptions and I was happy just to let it unfold. I knew I didn't want to just sleep in all year and watch television. I had a few ideas, but no definite plans, I wanted to make it up as I went along and let it emerge. That's been an enjoyable and different way of experiencing life for me.

Heather: I'd been encouraging Brian for a long time to do something different because he's been pretty unhappy in his job. A couple of our kids had gap years and for years we talked about it, and Brian said, 'I never had a gap year.' He was worried about money so I said, 'Look, you make the decision and I'll make it work.' One day he said, 'Right, I'm having a year off' and I thought, 'I've got to make it work!' I discovered that I could retire and take my super, and we managed to reorganise finances, rent out part of our house, a few things like that.

I'd been an artist and looked after my children, but when I got divorced I worked in a fruit shop and then as a real estate agent, then I came to Sydney and worked as an education officer, then I went back to nursing but I wasn't happy.

My 28-year-old son said, 'Mum, I'm really worried about you. What do you want to do? What do you want to be?' and I said, 'I want to be a professional artist.' I enrolled in a visual arts degree in Sydney and was commuting from the mountains, so we figured if Brian was going to have a gap year, maybe it was a good time.

Brian: Over the year, I've learned that there is life beyond school and that I'm looking forward to that. It's helped reinvigorate me but it's also made me more impatient and anxious to experience more, because in this year I've discovered a future career path in photography. I'll spend the next two-and-a-half years thinking and planning a new career in fine-art photography and curating and supporting emerging artists, so when I do walk out of those school gates for the last time I will definitely have something in place that I'll be walking into.

Heather: I've learned from our gap year that I want to be in the city. I was a bit funny about leaving our house, but actually I'm loving it. I'm loving being in a smaller place – when you're a creative person, a lot of your creativity gets drained by managing a house.

We're already having a conversation that maybe we don't go back to our house. When Brian goes back to work in November he's going to commute and if that works then we'll look at it.

Brian: I've fallen into this new way of living and new environment much more easily than I thought I would. I needed shaking up because too long in the one place doing the same thing narrows your perspective, narrows the possibilities. At the start I was anxious, but I needed to do something or I was just going to wither and die.

I've spent time taking care of myself, which is very foreign for me, a bit uncomfortable but necessary. There are more self-care things I need to build into my life, and this has been a good opportunity to explore that.

Heather: Once we'd actually made the decision, things just opened up. I would say to Brian, 'Now don't think about what's going to stop us, think about what you want to do. Let's just focus on what do you want' and at the beginning it looked like it was going to be hard, but things just kept opening up for us. When you do the same old thing you have the same old thoughts.

You get a new environment and all of a sudden you're thinking differently about stuff.

When I think about all the angsting we did, when we actually started it really wasn't as onerous or as difficult as we thought it was going to be.

Brian: In my previous life, it was all about connecting with people and making them do things and encouraging, inspiring them. Down here I feel more disconnected from the life around me and it's turned me into a bit of an observer. It's actually unleashed some of my own creativity that was bound before within very strict parameters. It's given me freedom to think and to explore more and released a lot of interesting ideas and thoughts into my head just by observing the world around me and capturing some of it with the camera.

One of our ideas is to have a base somewhere, but to regularly spend six months, a year maybe, renting in different cities, having a much more transitory life. I think the decade between 60 and 70 is pretty crucial because you've still got a sense of youthfulness about yourself, hopefully you've still got physical capacity, and I think it could shape up, if you handle it properly, as a bit of a golden decade of your life.

CHAPTER 4

Creative ways to look at your past

The unexamined life is not worth living.

Socrates (via Plato in *Apology*)

A few years ago, I was offered a new teaching gig in an organisation where I had trained two decades earlier. The guy who handed the course over to me was a friend, and while we were chatting, he told me that he became a teacher partly because of something I said to him all those years ago about my own life.

I had told him that I'd decided to leave the law after thinking about the Shakespeare quote, 'All the world's a stage.' If so, I figured (not the first person to do so, I know) that we could potentially play many roles – lead, chorus, set design, understudy, dresser or whatever. At that time, I had the deep sense that I was participating in the wrong play altogether, and it was time I took a lead role in my own story.

Apparently, this prompted my friend to wonder whether he was playing too small in his management career, and should step up to become a teacher himself – a dream he had long held but felt unable to reach. He decided to make the switch and became a much-loved educator.

As you work your way through this book, maybe it's time to ask yourself: what role do you want? Do you need to change plays as I did, or is it a matter of auditioning for a bigger part in the same production? Or do you need to celebrate the fact that you are already playing exactly the right part for you? Are you occupying centre stage?

Yumiko, 55

Originally from Japan, Yumiko married an Australian and settled here. When she had her son, he came first, but once he was older she retrained in accounting and financial planning to take centre stage in her life and new career.

Before I married my Aussie husband, I had come to Australia from Japan to work in the travel industry. And then I married Ron and my son came along, and suddenly I'm thinking, 'How can I work?' because we don't have family here to help. It was difficult to get a job and there was nobody to ask to help with child care and so I didn't work until he finished primary school.

Towards the end of his primary school I started to think about a job. Financially, having two incomes is much better security, as Ron is working for himself and so his income is always not sure, not a certain figure coming in and I am a person who likes certainty! I like to budget the amount that is coming in, so I was thinking what can I do? I am not a native of Australia and so I have some disadvantage there, too. When my son was in Year 4 or Year 5, I actually tried to get a job and I sent a lot of résumés for so many things, from service industry to administration kinds of things, but it was really difficult. If I use my language skills I can sometimes have a bit more pull, but still when I'm showing up for the interview I have a kid, a family situation to explain, so most of the Japanese companies are not interested. I can read most things and I don't think I am stupid, but compared with native Australian girls maybe in their 20s it is a bit difficult.

I'm actually quite good at numbers so then I thought about accounting. I did an Advanced Diploma of Accounting at TAFE and I qualified two years ago, but I started working before that. First of all, I got an administration job, including some accounting tasks. Once I brought my numbers skills into the picture, it was much easier to get a job. And my first job was with a

French company and so they had a capacity to accept not only Australian people, and the boss was dealing with quite a lot of Asian companies so he thought that maybe he could use Japanese skills. I was there for one year, and during that year I was thinking that administration is something I can do, but it's not really my piece of cake.

So I got an accounting job [working from home], but my boss was horrible. I worked for him for three years, and I did administration and also number crunching, and because he specialised in self-managed super-fund auditing, I learned auditing skills. I thought that auditing is not exactly for me, but I like this super-fund thing. I thought maybe I should go to a self-managed super fund or a super-fund-related job, but in a customer-related area. So I did a Diploma of Financial Planning and now I work for a financial adviser and my title is Portfolio Administrator, Superannuation.

My son is not a child anymore and my life has changed, it has actually shifted. From when I was 35 to 45, my life was all for my son, he was the first priority. But now he has finished school he is just the backbone. My job is important because it is financially important, that's the first thing, and Ron is semi-retired. I still want income for another 10 years so we don't use up our assets too much. That's important, but also I like it, talking to clients is quite interesting, and also it's self-satisfaction, isn't it? You learn that you can do things. Once you've got your first job, and then you get your second job, your work direction starts to be decided. Before, I never thought that I would work with superannuation funds, but now it's so interesting.

The value of stories

Stories provide an excellent way to take a fresh look at our work and life history. Storytelling is at least as old as language; until relatively recently it was the usual way to pass on shared knowledge, experiences and beliefs about our world. Even in the 21st century, our lives are held together by the stories we tell ourselves.

One of my favourite quotes is from twentieth-century American poet Muriel Rukeyser, who says, 'The world is made of stories, not of atoms.' I don't want to get into an argument with the scientists, but for most of us stories are the threads that link our life events, make sense of our days and allow us to find meaning in our lives. Logic and science are undeniably useful, but as psychologist Jerome Bruner points out, this analytic 'paradigmatic' way of thinking needs to be complemented with a 'narrative' mode through which we can think about the more ambiguous arenas of human needs, wants and goals.[1]

Storytelling offers a way to see that our lives are full of possibilities, perspectives and potential we may otherwise never uncover. We can use stories to effect real change, to realise we are not one identity or one story, but many and changing ones.

Storytelling can also be used to find meaning during confusing or overwhelming life events. It's particularly powerful when we are at a crossroads, looking to create a new pathway. For people in their 50s and beyond, the world may no longer be telling us who we are and how we should live, so we need to work this out for ourselves. A number of writers[2] have linked this to creating (and re-creating) your personal myth, which is a useful construct for some people. Even if you can't see yourself as a modern-day Ulysses or Athena, the exercises on your story in this chapter will be helpful.

In the past, you may have let yourself be limited by the stories you tell (or have been told) about your life. This may affect how you feel about change, about growing older and about what is possible for you. By working with your own story, you can experience other ways of seeing your life, bringing liberation and lasting change. Storytelling allows you to access different points of view and reinterpret the 'facts' of your life. It helps you to change how you see yourself and your possibilities and also helps others understand who you are, where you have come from and what you offer.

Professor Molly Andrews is co-director of the Centre for Narrative Research, University of East London. She believes narrative reflection is pivotal in our quest to understand ourselves, because looking back from the present into our past gives us fresh perspectives and creates new understandings about our lives, understandings that are only possible with hindsight.[3] She also says that age allows us to see that the meaning we've given to our life experiences is only one way of understanding our lives, and lets us appreciate the lives we didn't live.[4]

So, as you work with your story through the exercises in this chapter, it may be useful to be curious about your lives not yet lived, and about how you might introduce elements of these into your own future.

Life stories have several common elements:

- They are authentic. They bring in your past, the lessons you've learned, the obstacles you've faced and the struggle it took to overcome them (or are still taking).

- They are coloured by your background, your culture and the society in which you grew up and in which you now live. It's useful to consider the impact of your family of origin on your beliefs and your actions, the different perspective you may have as a woman, an immigrant or a gay man, and the social and cultural trends that affect how you see your world.

- They're ideally powered by agency, where you're in control and not the victim in your story, seen from the perspective of a realist who is basically optimistic about the present and future. Of course, your present feelings will affect your perspective and it can be very useful to just write it all out. However, if after reflection you still struggle to move away from feeling like a victim, you might read a book about narrative therapy[5] or talk to a counsellor.

- They help you answer questions: What are the threads in my working life? How did I get to where I am now? Where to from here? What do I love to do? What achievements make me most proud?

- They use elements of fiction such as plot, setting and characters. The more you bring a story alive by making a coherent and meaningful tale, the more useful it will be.

Exercise: Your story

Although the whole point of this book is that your story is not over, it is good to think about what you have learned along the way and how your life themes have developed. From our late 40s we tend to focus more on essentials and not dwell on things we can't change or which don't interest us. And as we age we also generally become more positive about things, which can result in new perspectives on our previous life and work history.

This exercise is about telling your own story, to yourself. You may be surprised at the patterns, the memories and the conclusions you find. It's not about making up stories or changing your past; your impressions may be recast over time, but the core must be authentic. The purpose is to start connecting the past and present together, so you can see where you could go in the future.

We'll look at three different ways of playing with your story – you can pick one or forge a story by combining elements from different techniques that appeal to you. I recommend the timeline as the easiest place to start, especially if you're not experienced at narrative writing.

Your timeline

In a timeline, you draw a map of your jobs, education, training, talents, skills, passions and interests, from childhood to the present day. While the point is to draw out clues about your career history, you may also want to include elements from across your broader life as they often point to key themes that resonate in your work. I do this exercise with all my clients, and it is often a core part of their process.

For example, Sally is a 60-plus divorced woman who needed to continue working because she had no financial support. She came to me after being made redundant, wanting to understand what she could learn from the experience, and how to identify and leverage her skills going forward. As she said, 'My favourite task was setting out my life story on an A3 page, using drawing and writing. I created an aerial view of myself and identified how I've reached where I am and the things that have influenced me. I got a sense of it being one coherent story and all things – even those I had thought were not so great when they were happening – were all aspects of myself. It was a great experience.'

Setting out the key understandings, achievements and lessons of your life in a chronological progression has many benefits – you see positive and negative experiences in a bigger context, you start to see patterns and themes and to notice connections between events, people and perspectives. You may be able to track both useful and limiting beliefs across the decades, spot the triggers for some of your behaviours, clarify your values and make sense of the big themes of your life.

Storyworks founder Bridget Brandon is a great fan of timelines. She works with people in their 40s or 50s who are beginning to realise, 'Oh my God, life's passing me by, what have I created?' and also people who are significantly older and who want to reflect on their lives. She sees the timeline as a 'fantastic tool' to give people stepping stones to be able to tap into what have been the major things, the pivotal moments, the moments of change in their lives.

She says, 'I often get people to draw symbolically, to use colour on their timelines. We do a timeline for a decade and use themes like "work". So it's to talk about their pivotal moments in work and who have been their main mentors and basically remembering your key moments. I think by looking at your own story you start appreciating your uniqueness, which quite often gets hidden when there's a lot of pressure outside for conformity. And it also is important in terms of appreciating that there is an unfolding of your story and you can only see that pattern when you start looking at your whole story.' Brandon comments that the pace of our lives, the fact that we just rush through our days, makes it difficult to find space for reflection and contemplation about what you've created and what you're wanting to create.

As she says, 'If you don't create your own story, if you don't understand your own story, then there's a whole part of you that's unlived. You have to have a lot of courage to make a transition and you really have to trust the creative process and be willing to sit with the discomfort of the voyage. And sit with not knowing and just letting yourself be with that discomfort and trusting that it will start making sense, what's the right next step, but if you try to abort that process you'll end up re-creating what you had before.'

Now it's time for you to get started on your timeline.

- First, draw a road or path as a timeline to represent your life from birth to the present. Mark off the years by drawing, say, five-year milestones at the side of the path. You can also mark it out by stages such as 'high school', 'first job', 'working overseas' or whatever.
- Next, moving along the path, draw symbols or pictures or jot down words to represent the emergence of a particular skill, passion or interest. Put down the key events in your life. Record your jobs, education, training. Find a way to mark changes in direction (a fork in the road, maybe?) and any 'aha' moments or other significant events.
- For each milestone, jot down the age you were as close as you can – if you don't know exactly when it first emerged, make a guess.
- Think about your values, your beliefs and the roles you played at various times in your life. If you like, you can

isolate different arenas of life such as work, play, love or health by using a grid with a line for each, or using different colours to represent each arena.

- Take your time, maybe do it over a couple of sessions, and don't worry about it looking messy – all that matters is capturing the information and making some connections from it.

If you prefer, you can do this on your computer using images from your photo library and other digital stuff. And if you want to be really fancy, there is software that lets you add pictures, video and more. However, at least at the beginning there is a real benefit to hand-drawing and writing your timeline – it's not meant to be a polished work of art, and many people find the act of writing and drawing helps them make connections and develop insights.

Narrative
If you keep a journal, or enjoy free-form creative writing, you can try telling your career story as a narrative, either a first-person ('I') story, or as if it was a tale told by another person (using 'she/he'). Are you a hero or heroine, an adventurer or a hapless traveller on storm-tossed seas? You can tell it in a particular style, such as melodrama, comedy, philosophical rave, whatever seems right. Start when you were young and move chronologically through your life, or write a series of episodes focusing on milestones or turning points.

Your other hand
Psychologically, it seems the non-dominant hand (your left hand if you are right-handed, and vice versa) may carry a lot of the disowned, buried, rejected, vulnerable parts of us. This 'other hand' expresses things that you may have judged as 'wrong' – awkward, child-like, vulnerable, raw emotions perhaps. It often expresses what you really feel and think, not what the 'socialised'

you thinks you feel. It can be a great relief, as well as extremely liberating, to explore these things.

Find a quiet place and some uninterrupted time. Grab some paper and pens (or textas, crayons, pencils) and play with writing or drawing with your non-dominant hand. Once you have tried that, ask yourself about the story of your working life, and write what comes, using your non-dominant hand. You can also do the journalling narrative in the section above in your other hand. Or do it in your usual hand, then comment on it while writing with the non-dominant hand.

Reflections

Whether you did this exercise as a timeline or something else, it's very useful to spend time reflecting on the process. Think about your impressions, observations and discoveries:

- Notice patterns or life themes – you may have had a recurring impulse towards a particular arena, such as teaching or a creative pursuit. Did you follow this, or knock it on the head every time it popped up? Why?
- Look for turning points, and notice charged or busy times – what was going on?
- Were some times more positive or negative?
- What strategies did you use to make decisions? Did they work for you?
- What were your beliefs about work at various times in your life? Were they about hard work, or getting ahead, or particular kinds of work being better than others? Have your beliefs changed? Is it time they did?
- What doors opened, what opportunities presented themselves? Did you follow them? Why or why not?
- Are there consistent values underlying your choices? What are they?

- What have you left out? What do you wish you could change?
- If this is your story so far, what might be next? Will it be similar to the past, or is it time for a new plot twist?

This can be a powerful exercise, so take care of yourself as you do it and as you reflect.

Exercise: Decoding your story

After you've done your career timeline or story, you can use this next exercise to drill deeper and decode it some more. This decoding process is also useful if you are uncomfortable with the story-reflection exercise, or find it difficult to access some of the answers. I use this exercise in my workshops, and participants often comment that it allowed them to see their attributes and achievements in a new light, and to value aspects of themselves they have previously taken for granted.

Step 1

List five or more work or life accomplishments, using a table like the one on page 85. These might have brought you fame or love or money (or not), but will be things you are:

- proud to have done
- enjoyed doing
- did well.

They may not be achievements that the world would recognise, but which made you feel really satisfied inside. As an introvert, I often have to summon reserves of determination and courage to walk into a room full of strangers, though most people no longer see my inner fear. For many years I would just not go to events, but over time, I developed a method that works for me – and I definitely class the overcoming of this obstacle as one of my biggest accomplishments.

Achievement or accomplishment	Contributing elements
Year:	Knowledge: Skills/Strengths: Relationships: Other?
Year:	Knowledge: Skills/Strengths: Relationships: Other?
Year:	Knowledge: Skills/Strengths: Relationships: Other?
Year:	Knowledge: Skills/Strengths: Relationships: Other?
Year:	Knowledge: Skills/Strengths: Relationships: Other?

Step 2

For each accomplishment, use the table to list the elements or factors that led to your achievement – what knowledge, skills, strengths, relationships and other things contributed?

Step 3

Review your completed table and your story timeline from the last exercise. Look for patterns, themes, common values or challenges.

- Did you rely on similar strengths or skills more than once?
- Did the achievements satisfy similar values or interests?
- Were there other times when you nearly got there but stopped short for some reason?
- Did you notice standout strengths or skills?
- What have you learned about yourself so far?

These patterns and themes are part of discovering the toolkit of skills, knowledge, relationships and other things that will help you pivot into your next stage.

Robyn, 59

Robyn has always been drawn to helping others. This theme has remained constant in her career, though she has given it life in a range of roles that look quite different on the surface, including running a dance school, becoming a nurse and having a successful career in hospitality. She then mined her own story, returning to nursing to start a baby-care agency.

As a young person I was always drawn to babies and kids, it was all about helping people, a highly maternal nurturing instinct I inherited from my mother.

When I left school I was unsure, but my mum and dad allowed me a gap year during which I set up a ballet school and I worked at a local kindergarten and at a chemist. Once that year came to an end, I put my hand up for the next intake into mothercraft nursing, so that was my first passion, which was all about mums and babies and helping and supporting and coaching.

I was recruited to the Crown Street Women's Hospital and I was there for about three years, but in my early 20s there was a total absence of glamour doing night duty in a hospital for weeks on end. I got bored in a nursery of 40 newborn babies and I wasn't meeting anyone, going anywhere.

So I put my pearls on and put my CV under my arm and off I went to the different airlines to look for a job, because I decided it was really glamorous working at the airport. I was really wrong about that. I was there for three years, both the domestic and international terminals, then moved on to the tourism industry in sales and marketing.

By then I thought that perhaps the whole marriage, white picket fence and five babies weren't going to happen, so I got very serious about a career. I studied tourism and put my mind to it, then I started to achieve some real success. I love sales and marketing, the dynamics, leading and managing a team.

I identified the five-star-hotel industry as a place I could make my mark in a senior capacity as a woman. I was there for 10 years and progressed through two hotel groups to a very senior role in hospitality as a director of sales and marketing, which I adored.

I think I hit the wall and burned out a bit at the age of 40, when one does great reflection on where you're at in career and personally. I set up a small executive search business after that, feeding back into the hotel sales and marketing business. The GFC hit, recruitment was tough, particularly as a small niche operator, and I decided to go back to nursing. I'd always remained registered, so I went back to hands-on nursing, working through an agency until my early 50s when I decided that maybe I could do it better.

I still had a passion for supporting new parents and being around babies and coaching parents on how to enjoy parenting more, but in setting up this new business I could also draw on my skills from sales and marketing, and from recruiting.

There was no grand plan, I was never one for five-year plans, but I've certainly had a common theme in the service industry for 40 years now. Even when I first left school I loved to coach or teach and help people, so that's why the ballet school and working in the kindergarten. I've always done something around that. I knew from a very early age that I was never going to university, because I found the whole idea of study abhorrent, and I was very fortunate that I had practical and sensible parents who did not push me.

I need to be useful and to support other people, and it gives me great joy to help others. I think it's really important to have a sense of purpose every day and it gives me focus to continue to help and coach people and make a difference in terms of new parents and babies. I'm sure I could find other things to deliver the same sense of satisfaction and joy, but I'm driven by the financial practicalities.

As you get older, if you want to change your career I think it's difficult to find what gives you a buzz out of your work life and will pay you enough money to have a reasonably comfortable life. It's an old adage, but if you can find what you love and put that into a job you will always succeed.

I suppose I'm an example of someone who's never done a whole heap of forward planning and I don't think that's entirely necessary, because with the support of my parents early on, who understood me well, encouraged me in whatever I did to make sure I gave my best, I worked on the premise that if I found what I loved to do then I would be successful. And that's how it worked out for me.

SECTION 2

REVIEW

CHAPTER 5

Know yourself

Knowing others is intelligence; knowing yourself is true wisdom.
Lao Tzu, *Tao Te Ching*

This is a very practical chapter, continuing our process of getting clear on *you*. And that's because in order to make good decisions about your future, you first have to understand yourself and what is important to you. Only then can you match that to something that the world values and will pay you to deliver.

As you start to think about your future life, it's a good idea to take a snapshot of the important themes or elements that are in your life right now. This is a useful exercise from time to time (I do it once a year) and it's vital before embarking on life changes.

When you reach your 50s and beyond, new themes or elements sometimes slip into your life for the first time. Clients often mention such things as a new awareness of health, a changing sense of what is possible for them and a desire to give back or leave a legacy, but it's a very personal thing. By doing the 'life and work snapshot' exercise below, you can recognise these themes, take steps to foster the ones you want more of and work with those that are less welcome.

Exercise: Life and work snapshot

Step 1
Using the following list as a starting point, select your top eight to ten current areas of focus or importance. Please change the

wording to reflect your thinking, and add any areas that aren't on the list. They might be large or small aspects of life, it doesn't matter, all that counts is that they are important to you right now.

- ✓Work
- ✓Family
- ✓Partner
- Friends
- Social life
- ✓Finances
- ✓Health
- ✓Physical environment
- ✓Sense of identity
- ✓Feeling useful
- Creativity
- Engagement versus boredom
- Structured versus unstructured time
- Hobbies, fun, recreation
- Learning and adventures
- Spiritual life
- Community
- Giving back, service
- ✓The future, what lies ahead
- Dealing with change
- ✓Shrinking or growing sense of what's possible
- Legacy
- Other?

Step 2

Transfer each of the top areas you have just identified into a separate box down the left-hand side of the table on page 92. Then, rate your current level of satisfaction with each area of focus. This is entirely personal, and based on your sense of fulfilment or contentment with that area. For example, two individuals may be single, and one is 'fully satisfied' with that, and the other 'very unsatisfied'.

Area of focus	Fully satisfied	Mostly satisfied	Okay	Somewhat unsatisfied	Very unsatisfied
	❑	❑	❑	❑	❑
	❑	❑	❑	❑	❑
	❑	❑	❑	❑	❑
	❑	❑	❑	❑	❑
	❑	❑	❑	❑	❑
	❑	❑	❑	❑	❑
	❑	❑	❑	❑	❑
	❑	❑	❑	❑	❑
	❑	❑	❑	❑	❑
	❑	❑	❑	❑	❑

If this exercise is a snapshot, think about which parts of the picture you would like to change. Which elements would you most like to improve? These are good questions to think about as you move through the rest of this book.

Exercise: Some initial questions

One of the essential elements of any search is curiosity, and curiosity means asking lots of questions. For now, our search is about you, so our questions will also be about you. Spend a bit of time thinking about these initial questions – and don't worry if some answers seem hard to find, just see where it takes you.

- What have been your three best work experiences (be specific – what project, team, role, activities)?
- What have been your three worst work experiences (again, be specific)?

- What skills, talents, pursuits would you like to develop?
- What would you do if you knew you couldn't fail?
- What is stopping you from having your ideal work situation? What's in the way?
- List 12 experiences or jobs that you'd like to have in this lifetime.
- What four to six things do you value most? Why?
- List three or four times in your life when you have felt very passionate about something, whether work-related or not.
- List 12 things you are good at doing.
- List four or five people you hold in great admiration, living or dead, real or fictional. (Qualities we admire in other people often tell us something about qualities we would like to express more ourselves.)

These questions will help prime your 'career curiosity' pump, and start you thinking about the parts of your personality that need to have expression in your work.

Helen, 53

Helen always had a strong artistic core, but reassessed what was important to her in her work at several crucial stages in her life. She explored different avenues for making money from her art and has now come to realise that taking risks with her work and backing herself as she ages may be the best strategy of all.

Even before going to school I loved putting marks on paper. Then at school there was recognition of my affinity for drawing and that I was 'an arty person'. I was already teaching at university by the time I finished my first post-graduate work. Then I opened a studio and started designing and making ceramic tiles and taking commissions on plates and glassware, so I had a small business doing that.

When I married, there was a compelling need to make a wage, so I went into the retail industry for about 10 years full-time. I worked selling glassware, china and social photography and I didn't have an active artistic practice, except for dabbling at home. That was a real hiatus for me.

When my child was young, I devised a method of working with glass as a material at home, weaving vessels and different sculptures with beads on wire, and I exhibited a body of work in Sydney and I started shipping to the States and exhibiting around the world. I was so driven, the work came so easily, but also I had all the necessary skills because I'd been in marketing and sales in the corporate world and I'd had exhibition-design training. I had a whole range of skills and I just put them into action.

It was a compromise doing the retail work and I did it in the most creative and energetic way that I could, but there was something missing. I had walked away from my core identity. Once I went back to it, and I was lucky to have some success at it, I realised I was always an artist and I would never not be an artist again, that was going to be part of my identity for the rest of my life. I knew how important it was for my contentment. I went back to art school and started sitting in classes just to rejoin that critical environment, and then fell into a teaching career.

I had this idea that people have six jobs over their life, different careers, but also that most craftspeople have multiple income streams. I taught at a university for 17 years, but now that's coming to an end, and so I might move back towards making and selling my work. I am also thinking about how I can take the institutional teaching of creativity and segue that and develop it into working with other communities like corporate and manufacturing that are fascinated by creativity, who know they need it, but sometimes the A to B of how they get there is challenging for them. It's not challenging for me.

I'm encouraging myself to embrace change because it's actually great for artists to do that. It will bring wonderful new perspectives on my practice. If I could be of use to another creative institution I'd be more than happy to put that into my mix, but not full-time.

How I see 'success' seems to have come full circle, back to the days when you graduate art school and money's not really a big factor. Some funds are necessary, but beyond that the satisfaction comes from making my work, sharing my work with other people, sharing what I've learned. That's why people are happy to live in the bush and do stuff in a very minimal way, because their needs have shifted towards different things, it's not so much about possessions.

I think in some ways the most challenging thing has been having a really healthy wage for so many years. I had a really unhealthy wage for many years and I was really happy and now I've had a large wage for many years and I was happy, but I have enough experience of that former life to know I was okay then.

I wonder if there is a matrix of 'risk plus age'. Is it really a big deal, your age, or should you just be using the same mindsets as when you were young? I think if the risk is calculated enough then you should just go for it. I also get the feeling that in the past when success has come it's because I've completely backed myself, that I've taken a risk. Whenever I've been successful it's when I've completely shot for the stars and backed myself a hundred per cent.

So dialling it down or being safe just because of my age, I don't think that's going to be a winning strategy. If anything, I've got more skills now, so why wouldn't I be making more bold moves because I've got more in my kitbag? I think up to the end of your 60s there's so much energy and potential. I don't know about beyond that, but I'm going to give it a red-hot go.

Essential information

We will be taking a good look at your strengths, talents and skills in the next chapter because they are critical to your work-reinvention process. But before we zoom in, it's important to consider some wider aspects of what you need in relation to work. There's little point in securing your dream job from the point of view of your skill set and interests if it involves frequent travel and you have a regular commitment with grandchildren, or if it's in an industry you regard as unethical, or it requires you to be the public spokesperson of the organisation and you are a decidedly back-room type.

Last year I worked with Peter, a lawyer in his late 50s. Peter wasn't sure whether he needed a complete career pivot, but he knew he was unhappy as a corporate law partner in his mid-sized city legal firm. We talked about the type of work he was doing, the clients he enjoyed working with (and those he didn't) and the fast-paced, competitive environment of his firm. Over a few sessions, it became clear that Peter still loved legal work, solving problems for others and having a team of like-minded people around him. But he was tired of the emphasis on meeting increasingly demanding budgets, working round the clock – and the feeling that he was being managed away from the more interesting clients because of his age.

Once we had zeroed in on the need to change the context of his work, it quickly became clear that there were two new areas related to the law that Peter was interested in exploring – one was directorships and the other was the community arena. Within a few months, he had secured his first board role, and had negotiated with his firm to start up a new division working with not-for-profit organisations. His five-year plan includes exploring a move to a position in a community organisation, once he has more experience in this area.

Peter's story illustrates the importance of looking at the essentials in the context of your work, the things you MUST have in order to be happy at work. They may be about your colleagues, or the type of industry, or location, size of company or flexibility of working hours. And what about the 'no-ways', the things you couldn't tolerate, even if the rest of the job was absolutely perfect? These might be about breach of ethics, treating staff badly or not allowing staff to contribute – or maybe it would be extensive travel, or having to move overseas. And as we age, other things may enter the mix, such as a need for flexibility in work hours, or a desire to give back.

Some of your essentials and no-ways remain fixed for life; ethical issues are often a good example of this. But, as it was for Peter, some also change over time. Now that my son is an adult, I am much freer to attend evening events, to run workshops on weekends and to travel when it suits me (which is frequently). So, as you do this next exercise, make sure to test your initial ideas – is this something eternally true, or was this once the case but not so much these days?

Exercise: Some questions to think about

- What are the essential elements of any job? What can't you do without?
- What can't you put up with in a job? What are the real no-ways?
- What are the essential elements of any work environment? What can't you do without?
- What can't you put up with in a work environment? What are the real no-ways?
- What are your core values?
- What essential elements of your personality, identity or values must be let out to play at work?
- What about ethics? Are there industries you could not work in?
- What are your beliefs about work and career? Are they really true?
- Is status important to you?
- Do you need acknowledgement, praise, public recognition?
- What else is important in your life – family, hobbies, travel, friends, time out?

- What are your financial needs from work? Now? In five or ten years?
- Do you intend to retire? If so, when?

Interests and firelighters

There are plenty of clues in your current life about the kind of work that will make you happy. For example, we generally develop hobbies or side interests because something about them fascinates us or gives us pleasure, and so these activities tell us a great deal about our core life themes. I've had clients who have built their entire career change around an interest in riding motorbikes (John's story in Chapter 9), or a passion for helping refugees find a place to belong in their new country, or a longstanding love of jewellery (Jan's story in Chapter 7). And even if that's not the case for you, your interests will inevitably reflect aspects of your personality that may be useful to include in your career picture.

Exercise: What interests you?

- What are your interests and hobbies? If life is too busy at the moment, what did you do in the past to relax?
- What fires you up, makes you feel excited or gets you hot under the collar – where are your passions?
- How did you spend last weekend? Did you enjoy it?
- What kind of holidays do you enjoy?
- If you had a spare week suddenly, no commitments, no obligations, what would you do?
- What catches your attention in the papers?
- What cause would entice you to a public rally?
- What would stir you up enough to write a letter to the editor?
- If you volunteer, or would if you had time, in what area?

If you can't find your passion, are you doomed?

What if you don't have that 'one thing', the thing you are utterly passionate about, the thing that's just waiting to be turned into your dream career? Can you still have a satisfying working life?

Of course you can. In fact, you may have a greater chance of a happy and successful life if you can develop passion (or even just enthusiasm) from *within* your job. I've had career-change clients who worry that they cannot make a successful career transition because they don't know what they are passionate about. Rubbish to that.

Unless you are Mozart or Marie Curie, chances are you are interested in many things, and your enthusiasm waxes and wanes with time and circumstances. It's a lovely fantasy to think that there is one career for every person, and that somewhere in heaven is a fortune cookie with the name of your one true vocation inside it. But, like most fantasies, it just isn't so. For a very few, there may indeed be a calling that is always clear and never doubted, but most of us have to put in some hard yards and create our life and work satisfaction piece by little piece.

What to do if that single passion eludes you? Start by working out your strengths, abilities and skills, look at what interests you, what fires you up, what you care about. Follow the exercises and suggestions in this book. Then, create a list of possible occupations that might allow you to utilise these strengths and interests. Run some experiments, talk to people in that field, shadow a practitioner, read about what's involved, get some adult work experience. Apply for some jobs, see what you think.

It's not rocket science (unless that's your new field). It will take commitment and courage, hard work and reflection. You'll need to take risks. It's not nearly as alluring as lying around, waiting for your one true passion to fall like manna from heaven, but it's a great deal more practical and achievable.

And it's a great deal more likely to result in long-term satisfaction and success. Have you ever fallen for someone, absolutely known they were perfect for you, and then fallen out of love just as quickly? So it is with many of our career enthusiasms. We may fall out of love with our desire to be a nurse or a fireman. Or your dream occupation may disappear – think of papyrus scroll makers, telex operators, horse-and-carriage drivers.

But if you base your decision on research and a sound knowledge of yourself, coupled with enthusiasm for the field you're interested in, you may well find yourself falling in love with your work from the inside. You do it, you learn more, you find your feet, you engage your strengths … *et voilà*, you're in love!

Passion (or at least enthusiasm) is vital for long-term career satisfaction, it's just the expecting-it-to-descend-from-heaven-all-wrapped-up-and-ready-to-open bit that's problematic.

Purpose

Passion is not the same as purpose, but they are connected. If passion is 'I love doing my work', then purpose is 'I have a sense of direction and meaning, and I feel that life is worth living.' There is plenty of research linking a sense of purpose to psychological health and wellbeing, and to demonstrable[1] increases in lifespan – one reputable study even put a pretty precise number on it, saying you could live 7.5 years longer.[2]

And some 2015 research also shows that having a sense of purpose may lower your risk of heart disease and stroke.[3] This analysis found that a high sense of purpose is associated with a 23 per cent reduction in death from all causes and a 19 per cent reduced risk of heart attack, stroke, or the need for coronary artery bypass surgery.[4] I find the specificity of these statistics simultaneously a bit odd and strangely reassuring, but even if we can't guarantee a precise 23 per cent reduction in the likelihood of premature death, there's little doubt that a sense of meaning and purpose is good for you.

Of course, you can get a sense of life purpose from sources other than work, but if you can find meaning in your work it will pay off in many ways, as I discussed with Judith Claire, a Los Angeles career counsellor I met on a trip to the States.

Claire works mainly with entertainment industry professionals, creative thinkers and spiritual people who are looking to realise their true potential. If they're in a job or a career that doesn't fulfil either their creative or spiritual drive, she says (and I agree) they often become desperate to find something that does – and then work out how to make that career a reality.

Claire says that the most important thing she does with every person is to look at his or her purposes, using these questions:

- Why did you come into this life?
- What are the things you're here to do?
- What have you always wanted to do since you were a little kid?

As she says, 'accomplishing your purposes is what motivates you to get out of bed in the morning. It drives you and enables you to stick to what you're doing with determination and to overcome the inevitable conflicts and difficulties. It gives your life meaning.'

I have long thought that it is very important to distinguish goals from purposes. Our purposes are large and can be accomplished in many ways. We saw in Robyn's story in Chapter 4, for example, that her purpose of helping others remained unchanged, but she found a number of different avenues to express this purpose, from teaching dance to nursing to working in hotels.

Claire also agrees that purpose goes way beyond job ideas, suggesting that examples of purposes for creatives would be 'to communicate, to connect, to express yourself, to have fun. I had one client say "to sparkle". I love that. Purposes for entrepreneurs might include "to make something new, to build something by myself".'

There is an important caveat here: although finances matter to everyone, making money isn't a purpose. I have had a number of clients who have told me all they care about is making a fortune, but when you drill down by asking 'why?', the underlying purpose, although it may be deeply buried, is often about feeling safe or independent, or as Claire says, 'It might be to be secure, to take care of myself or to have the freedom to do what I want to do.'

People usually have some sense, however dim, of what would be fulfilling for them to do, says Claire. 'Often they have secret dreams, but they're too scared to actually do them, don't believe they're realistic or don't have any idea of how to go about doing them. Often parents or others have told them what they really want to do isn't practical or they're not good enough. Sometimes they've tried but had bad experiences and gave up. But purposes are ageless. You've had them since being a kid and you'll have them to the day you die. You don't stop wanting to find fulfilment when you're 50 plus.'

Claire tells a great story about a client who always adored horses. They fulfilled her drives for deep bonding, for being part of nature, and being healthy. She was a veterinary technician, but this didn't pay well and the upkeep of her horse was expensive, so she worried about how she'd take care of herself as she aged. She needed a career change, to something that involved horses, was well-paid and gave her time to ride. It was a long and winding road, but eventually she became a bookkeeper and accountant who specialises in people who own horses, have stables or teach riding. As Claire says, 'now she works less hours, has a good hourly rate for the bookkeeping and earns even more for the accounting. And the reason she could arrive at all this was she knew and was working from her purposes. It's the seed. It all starts there.'

My story

I've had numerous clients who are clear on their sense of purpose before we start our work together, but I also have a great deal of empathy with those who take a while to figure it out. Like I did.

When I was a small child I was convinced that I was an alien. I spent hours in our backyard at Terrigal on the NSW Central Coast, scanning the night sky for the planet where my real family lived. I just knew that one day they would magically arrive and take me back home with them. I also watched and re-watched every episode of *Star Trek*, in the hope I would find a clue to my real species. Gradually, it dawned on me that I was, in fact, a human and already had a loving family here on earth. And after a somewhat brutal adjustment period, I accepted my fate.

But it took me many years to truly fit in on this planet, to find my tribe and to develop a sense of belonging, let alone an understanding of my purpose. At university, I mourned being too young for the Vietnam protests, searched for a cause, wondered about feminism, contemplated a stint abroad as a volunteer. But I actually did very little about any of these things, drifting from class to class, idea to idea. Not a clue, really.

Then in my working life, I meandered from a legal career, through academic teaching, journalism, film writing, training as a therapist and working as a coach and consultant. In between jobs, I travelled to Tibet, the Middle East, India, Bhutan, Tanzania and more, seeking the place where I could belong and the contribution I could make.

In my 30s, I worked with people who also grappled with belonging. I volunteered at Redfern Legal Centre, I worked with kids at The Factory Community Centre, also in Redfern, and I visited refugees in Villawood Detention Centre. As a freelance journalist, I wrote about adopted children and refugee resettlement programs. There was no sudden epiphany, but gradually I came to realise that, whatever my childhood imaginings, I did belong. I had some great relationships, became a mother, did some interesting work projects. I was connected to my world, had a place called home and a satisfying work identity. My sense of purpose and direction was becoming clear.

In my early 40s, I founded my own business. I ran career-change programs (a role for which I was clearly well qualified) so I could help other people whose first career was not the right fit for them. I used creative thinking to teach people to think differently. And I kept on writing. I'd found my tribe, I loved my work and I was thriving.

Into my 50s, and I took my business in some new directions, worked with some fascinating people, did well and had fun. I have run a business start-up program for migrant women in Lakemba for five years now. Increasingly, I work to help Australians of all ages and backgrounds feel they belong and have a way to contribute, and to flourish. I run programs for people over 50, and I work with employers to help them appreciate and integrate the several generations in their workforces.

I have realised, like our expert Judith Claire, that purpose is not in the nitty-gritty of *this* task or *that* field. The projects I am involved in are different expressions of my overall purpose, which is helping people feel a sense of belonging so that they can flourish.

The fact that purpose can be expressed in many different areas is important for all of us. It means there are many potential jobs, directions and fields that will satisfy our purpose. Over the life course, we may have jobs that look quite different on the surface (as I have had) but are in fact tied together by a unifying theme.

Think about your own working life. Can you tease out any common links or deeper themes? If so, how might you use them in a new field in the future?

CHAPTER 6

Taking stock

Where your talents and the needs of the
world cross; there lies your vocation.

Aristotle

Identifying your talents, skills and strengths is essential for reinventing your working life. Over your life (in work and beyond), you have developed an inventory of things you can do well and this will serve you in the future, whether you want to change your work or keep doing what you've always done for another decade or more. This experience from decades on the job is a big selling point for older workers.

There are a number of ways to look at talents, skills and strengths, but here are some rough definitions I often use:

- Talents – the abilities or characteristics or quirks you are born with – are hardwired. Talents don't change.
- Skills come from applying knowledge (whether from book learning or formal training or on-the-job practice) and practising it. Deep skills must be built over a reasonable period. Although your top skills will be built on talents, it is possible to develop skills without an underlying strong ability, at least to a certain level of competence.
- Strengths are the things you love to do, the things that make you feel strong, even lose track of time. There are a number of views about whether you need to be skilled

at something before it becomes a strength; I would call anything you love to do a strength from the beginning, but strengths get deeper and more satisfying as you reach new levels of mastery.

Don't fret about over-categorising these, the main thing is to find a list of stuff you love doing and can potentially do well.

Let's get started by looking at your talents.

What are your talents?

Talents are the gifts, passions, interests and natural aptitudes we are born with. They start to reveal themselves in early childhood, though some may stay dormant until life throws you a chance to bring them out to play.

If you want a career that provides long-term satisfaction and success, it's helpful to identify your talents (and your non-talents). Start by listing all the things that come easily to you, the areas where you just 'get it', where you are a 'natural'. No matter how big or small, whether work-related or not, all these talents have a place.

The talents we are looking for here are not necessarily the same as the limited range of abilities that are praised at school or the things you might traditionally list on a résumé. Maybe you are known in your family for your ability to put together flatpack furniture, or for your lovely singing voice or your way with animals. Are you the one at work who everyone relies on to soothe a disgruntled client, organise the Christmas party or wrestle with a problem until it is solved? Or maybe your claim to fame (though this one mystifies me) is adding up a column of numbers and getting the same answer twice.

Don't include things at which you are competent but which don't thrill you – if you have become a good cook through having to prepare family meals for decades, but it's not something you would do on your own just for the pleasure of it, then leave it off your list. Although it is a skill, it's not one founded on a talent. In my legal career, I developed a number of skills that were not based on natural ability. Even though I was quite competent in these areas, I didn't enjoy using those skills and I found it exhausting to do so. This lack of enjoyment and exhaustion are both good clues for spotting skills that are not based on talents, as is the sense that you are an imposter who will one day be found out …

Exercise: Your talents

Start by writing down as many talents as you can, and perhaps also ask your friends and family. The more you really think about it, the more useful your list will be.

And if you have a little voice inside your head saying, 'I don't have any talents', don't worry. I've had numerous clients over the years who have struggled with the word 'talent'. In one case, a client had been forced to perform at amateur talent nights by his proud parents, and this had left him shuddering at the mere mention of the word. Another client had believed her father when he repeatedly told her that she had no talents. If you can relate to these stories, use another word, like abilities, or just think of it as a list of things that come easily to you. And remember that we all have talents, whatever your nearest and dearest may have tried to make you believe when you were young.

Spend some time answering the following questions:
- What are your top talents?
- Which talents would you like to develop further?

What are your strengths?

It used to be thought desirable to be an all-rounder – your strengths were the easy bit, and it was your weaknesses you had to shore up.

In school reports, in workplace appraisals, in our own assessment of our performance, weaknesses were emphasised.

In the last 10 or 15 years, there has been a shift. Writers like Marcus Buckingham[1] and Martin Seligman[2] have done excellent work suggesting we should emphasise strengths not weaknesses, and some serious scientific studies show that life satisfaction has a lot more to do with playing to your strengths than compensating for your weaknesses.

Strengths are the things you love to do. Literally, strengths make you feel strong inside, uplift you and energise you. You look forward to activities that rely on your strengths, and feel engaged with them. Even when I run a training session that is less than perfect (or not even close), or am maladroit in a coaching session, I still know that I am in the right place, that I am prepared to do whatever it takes to polish my talents and to shine in those arenas to the best of my ability. That's because I am using my strengths, which leads to the development of deep skills, and to that wonderful state known as flow,[3] where you lose track of time doing an activity you love.

Strengths are different from skills, which look purely at competence. As I mentioned earlier, I was a competent lawyer, but it gave me no thrills because much of my work was not built on talents or strengths. Skills have a place in your inventory, as we will see, but it is your strengths that will guide you to satisfying and sustainable work. We saw how Yumiko in Chapter 4 used her strength with numbers as the basis to retrain, develop new skills and establish a fresh career path for herself once her son entered high school.

Exercise: Your strengths

1. Thinking about the last week or two, what activities did you do that left you feeling strong, energised and positive? Be specific, what precise activities were they? What were the activities you looked forward to? Enjoyed, focused easily on, got you into the

zone, felt in flow with? What activities drew you in to the point where you lost track of time? (Work activities are great, but there may be clues outside your core working life, too, especially if you're not happy in your current job.)

2. Here's another list of strengths from a different angle. Circle the ones that resonate.

STRENGTHS TABLE			
Accessible	Driving force	Hospitable	Playful
Accommodating	Dynamic	Idealistic	Practical
Achiever	Effervescent	Imaginative	Problem solver
Adaptable	Empathetic	Impulsive	Reliable
Alternative	Enterprising	Independent	Resilient
Approachable	Enthusiastic	Industrious	Resolute
Articulate	Ethical	Intuitive	Responsible
Assertive	Exploring	Joyful	Romantic
Attentive	Fair-minded	Laid-back	Sensitive
Capable	Far-sighted	Listener	Sociable
Caring	Feisty	Logical	Spiritual
Cautious	Focused	Loving	Stoic
Communicative	Forgiving	Loyal	Straight-talker
Compassionate	Friendly	Mediator	Supportive
Confident	Funny	Multitasker	Tactful
Content	Generous	Musical	Talkative
Courteous	Gentle	Nurturing	Tenacious
Creative	Genuine	Open-minded	Trailblazer
Curious	Grateful	Optimistic	Understanding
Decisive	Grounded	Organised	Unflustered
Deep-thinking	Hard-working	Passionate	Warm
Down-to-earth	Helpful	Patient	
Dreamer	Honest	Perceptive	

3. Now, look back over the last two exercises and list your top five to ten strengths.
   - What do you do differently than other people?
   - What's a strength you'd like to be able to use more often?
   - What's your favourite strength? What strength makes you lose track of time?
   - List at least three ways you could use some of your top strengths next week.

Nathalie, 40 plus

Nathalie has been my dentist for many years and it has always struck me how suited she is to that profession and how happy she seems. When I interviewed her, I saw that she has been very clear about some of her strengths from a very young age, but that she also needed to rethink how she used some strengths and to develop others in order to become a successful dentist.

From about age eight I used to mix talcum powder and water, because in those days when you went to the dentist they hand-mixed everything. And my memory of going to the dentist was them mixing what I thought was talcum powder and water, so I used to play that way. I always thought, 'This is going to be a great job' because I like making a mess. As a kid I liked hands in the dirt, playing, crafting, moulding – if it wasn't going to be dentistry then I loved cooking.

As I grew up I used to say to my mother, 'I'm going to be a chef' and she encouraged me in a very gentle way to think of dentistry, because she felt that it would be a good job. So, when I did my HSC I aimed to get into dentistry because my mother would say to me, 'Even if you don't get in, it's good to know that you could get in.' And I did.

I loved first year, but in second year the medical sciences were really, really hard and I was enjoying partying a bit more than I should have, because that's what you do when you're that age. And so I blitzed all the practical subjects and failed all the theory subjects. So I re-did the whole year, and I thought, 'I really have to learn this' and now I really, really love that stuff – biochemistry, immunology, basic physiology, all the anatomy – because it's the basics that put everything together.

I love being a dentist, but I remember I had a career crisis when I didn't feel that I was getting the message across to my patients. I remember a colleague saying, 'It's not them, it's you – you have to realise what you're not listening to that's making them react that way.' And I started doing things like recording myself in the surgery, writing everything that happened after a patient consultation, and I realised that I was trying to take them to a place that they didn't want to go and it was very ineffectual.

I learned to think that I had to really be of service and listen to what someone wanted, and accept their choices. Some patients were happy with teeth that weren't in the best health, when I knew something else was possible for them. It was very tough for me.

I didn't have an understanding that maybe someone's teeth are not their total priority at that point in time. I said stupid things to mothers, like, 'Floss your four-year-old's teeth.' I wasn't a mother at the time so I didn't know how stupid this was, but in hindsight, I'm lucky if I can get a toothbrush in my four-year-old's mouth. What was I thinking?

Now I see it's not just about strengths and skill, it's about life experience and maturity and understanding. And growing. And so I love my job. I love doing things with my hands, I've got good technical skills, but I had to work very hard. If I have any advantage it's the fact that I have common sense. That helps me through difficult situations. And when something isn't working for you, you have to look at yourself first.

I love the opportunity to make a change in somebody's life, like sometimes the kids haven't been brushing their teeth and I'm always optimistic, I think, 'They didn't brush their teeth for the six months before they came here, but they showed up now. They're present, I've got an opportunity to make a change even in that small space of time.' And you can't judge them. You should never judge them.

When we rebranded my practice, it took six months for me to come up with three words: 'Love your teeth.' That's what we do, that's it. We love teeth. It's that simple.

Overusing strengths and ignoring relevant weaknesses

Strengths are the foundation of your inventory, and your guide to happiness at work and in life. But there are a couple of things to watch out for.

Overusing strengths

Are you completely immersed in your deep and narrow field of expertise? Or are you that person who always rushes to help in a crisis, whatever the circumstances? Because our strengths are by definition the things we love, there is a real temptation to delve further and further into the strength and to rely on it in an increasing range of situations. We saw in Nathalie's story that she allowed her core strengths to blind her to the reality of her patients' lives, until she stepped back and rethought her approach. In the process, she brought out other strengths and developed them to create a cluster that now serve her very well.

Relying on one strength is not useful. If you expand your list of favourite strengths to about five, you are on much more solid ground and will find a number of ways to reinvent your work into new areas.

Overreliance on one or two strengths can lead to:

- Burnout.
- Becoming lopsided or one-dimensional, which may irritate or bore other people.
- Selling yourself short – who knows what you could do if you developed your other strengths as well?
- Difficulty in adapting to changing circumstances, or not having enough flexibility to move between different work tasks.

Do you overuse your favourite strength?

Ignoring relevant weaknesses

You'll get much further in your career by polishing strengths than by compensating for weaknesses, with one exception: weaknesses that are central to your work and that are holding you back.

Maybe you're a gifted verbal negotiator but struggle to convey your thoughts on paper in your final reports. Or you are great at logical analysis but not so good at presenting your results in a meeting.

I have personal experience here because numbers are not my thing. When I was about 15, my school maths teacher told me that if I wanted to go to university (which I did), then I should drop maths immediately (which I did). This proved to be an excellent strategy, as lawyers don't need maths skills beyond the ability to calculate their fees in six-minute increments – and naturally they have staff or technology to do that kind of task for them.

So all was good, until I started my own business. I couldn't afford a bookkeeper in the beginning, so I had to master basic accounting skills. I had to learn to use spreadsheets and enter expenses correctly. I had to read a balance sheet and invoice my clients for the right amounts, work with GST calculations and understand a Business Activity Statment (BAS). As you might imagine, it was a nightmare. However, there was no way I could run a successful business without doing these things, so I slowly developed a minimal competence at them.

I persevered long enough to ensure this weakness of mine was not hampering my business growth, and then, as soon as I had some spare cash, I hired a bookkeeper. In this I was aided by a very nice letter from the Australian Taxation Office, effectively saying that while they didn't think I was being deceptive, there had been at least one error in each of my last three Business Activity Statements, and so perhaps it would be a good idea if I got some help. (Seriously.)

If a weakness is all that stands between you and your next career or opportunity, try these strategies:

- Do a short course, read a book or get some hands-on help to lift your skills.
- Find another strength through which you can create a workaround to bridge the gap.
- Connect with someone who has the strength you lack, and who could benefit from one of your strengths in return.

Remember, it's only necessary to work with weaknesses that are holding you back and only to the extent needed to allow your strengths to shine.

Do you have any relevant weaknesses you need to look at?

What are your skills?

Although strengths are the ultimate building blocks when you're reinventing your career, skills are also very relevant. Many of our top skills are built on strengths or talents, and thus are the most useful pathway to a new career or job. When you're writing a résumé, the focus should be more on skills than strengths or talents, as employers think in terms of skills and interview questions will call on you to look through this lens.

You may also be able to use existing skills, even ones that you don't particularly love, to get a 'journey job'. This is my expression for the kind of job that isn't your ultimate ideal, but which matches your present skill set and pays the bills while you think about other possibilities, or allows you entry into an interesting new world. If you want to break into a new field, taking a journey job in that area may not pay brilliantly but could enable you to develop skills or to get to know the industry or find people who may lead you to your next big step. For example, I had a client who was in PR and wanted to become an event planner, so she took a PR job in an event company while she retrained and built a network in this new line of work.

When I was transitioning from my legal career, I had a number of journey jobs, mostly part-time legal or compliance-management contracts. These took some financial pressure off while I was building up my new business, and it was also reassuring to keep up some old skills, in case I ever needed to supplement my income again.

When you're building your skills inventory, it's good to drill into your experience and think about underlying skills. You might describe yourself as 'a lawyer' but that involves a bunch of skills, some of which all lawyers have (like the ability to digest complex arguments), and some that those in your specialty have (thinking on your feet, in or out of a courtroom), and maybe some that not many lawyers have (like writing clear English).

Exercise: Your skills

In the table starting on page 116 are some categories of skills. As you think about them, don't restrict yourself to formal qualifications – after all, you are trying to move beyond what you are currently doing, into new worlds where the ability to relate to children or fix a dripping tap could be just what's needed.

Read each skill, and without thinking too much about it, rank yourself 'Very Skilled', 'Adequate' or 'Not Skilled'. Don't underestimate yourself – as we mature, we can downplay our experience, assuming everyone can do the things we find easy. It isn't so.

Look at the skills in the 'Adequate' or 'Not Skilled' columns. Put a second tick in the box for those you enjoy. Are there any skills you enjoy that you'd like to develop further? Make a list of those that you'd like to expand over the next year or so.

Now look at the skills in the 'Very Skilled' column. Put a second tick in the box for the ones you enjoy. These will be the easiest to leverage in finding new work.

What else can you list? It may well be that you have skills which don't show up on a general list like this but are the very things that will set you apart from other candidates and convince an employer (or an investor in your new business) to say 'yes'.

Skills categories

Formal or technical skills required for your job

These might be formal qualifications, short courses, skills you have learned on the job or through hobbies. Take some time to make your own list of these.

Generic or transferable skills

These are having a revival at the moment, with both recruiters and employers taking more notice of them than was the case a decade or so ago. It can be helpful to think about these skills in categories, so you don't take any for granted. I have clustered them as 'people', 'organisational', 'communications', 'thinking' and 'personal attributes', but you can rearrange these or add to them to suit your skill profile.

YOUR SKILLS			
People skills	Very skilled	Adequate	Not skilled
Working in teams			
Leading teams			
Coaching or mentoring			
Getting on with people			
Selling your ideas, persuading, influencing			
Negotiating			
Dealing with difficult people			
Customer service			
Inspiring or encouraging others			

YOUR SKILLS			
Organisational skills	**Very skilled**	**Adequate**	**Not skilled**
Goal setting			
Achieving your goals			
Working to deadlines			
Solving technical issues			
Planning projects or tasks			
Budgeting, allocating resources			
Time management, productivity			
Business savvy			
Leadership			
Networking			
Diversity			
Communication skills	**Very skilled**	**Adequate**	**Not skilled**
Making presentations			
Training, facilitating			
Oral communication			
Written communication			
Foreign languages			
Thinking skills	**Very skilled**	**Adequate**	**Not skilled**
Critical thinking			
Creative thinking			
Designing			
Diagnosis			
Idea generation			
Decision-making			
Problem-solving			
Getting the gist of something			

YOUR SKILLS			
Personal attributes	Very skilled	Adequate	Not skilled
Self-improver			
Keeping a cool head under pressure			
Determined, persistent			
Self-directed			
Adaptable			
Assertive			
Helpful, supportive			
Team player			
Trustworthy			
Reliable			
Taking initiative			
Fast learner			
Professional			

Psychometric assessments

You may like to further your understanding of your abilities, talents and strengths by doing one of the many psychometric assessments that are available these days, such as Myers-Briggs Type Indicator (MBTI), DISC (Dominance, Influence, Steadiness, Conscientiousness), Herrmann Brain Dominance Instrument (HBDI) or the Clifton StrengthsFinder.

Psychometric assessments can be most useful, provided you know what you want to find out about yourself and do some research to select the assessment that best matches your needs. Psychometric assessments fall into two main categories:

- Personality tests, which look at your personality or behavioural style. They generally rely on self-reporting, where you answer questions about yourself, and vary greatly in their reliability.
- Aptitude or ability tests, which test your level of competency at verbal, numerical or thinking tasks, for example.

One of the first tests created was the Rorschach inkblot test, an open-ended, relatively simple exercise. These days there are thousands of tests to pick from, ranging from quick, free online tests to very complex instruments that cost a lot of money and require a lengthy debrief by a licensed provider. Here are some well-known ones, most of which I have experienced. They are in no particular order and come with no particular endorsement from me. I will leave you to read about them and think about whether the information they provide is going to be useful to you:

- Myers-Briggs Type Indicator (MBTI)
- Herrmann Brain Dominance Instrument (HBDI)
- Dominance, Influence, Steadiness, Conscientiousness (DISC)
- Minnesota Multiphasic Personality Inventory (MMPI)
- HEXACO Personality Inventory
- Hogan Personality Inventory
- Strengthscope
- Enneagram personality system
- Harrison Career Assessment
- Highlands Ability Battery (HAB).

There are also numerous tests based on the 'big five' personality traits. In the psychometrics world, these are: Openness to experience, Conscientiousness, Extraversion, Agreeableness and Neuroticism, or OCEAN. (You may have noticed by now that people who develop these tests are fond of acronyms.)

The instrument I use with all my reinvention clients is the Highlands Ability Battery. While the name is reminiscent of something nasty connected with Scottish chooks, it is actually a rigorous and extremely in-depth look at your hardwired natural abilities. I spoke to Dori Stiles, PhD, Director of Training & Research at The Highlands Company, about the benefits of assessments. Stiles notes that while many adults have been through a number of assessments during their lifetime as part of work evaluations, very few have actually been through an objective assessment of their abilities. When you're at a career crossroads, you have an opportunity to look at yourself with the sole purpose of finding clarity about your strengths and what you want to do, with nobody else evaluating you for it.

This is especially true for people over 50, says Stiles, because you have less and less to prove to other people and more and more you just want to satisfy yourself. As she says, 'People over 50 just want to cut to the chase, remove all the layers of "what ifs" and possibilities, and do something that really represents themselves authentically. People at this age know a whole lot about what they don't want to do anymore and so an assessment gives a lot of confirmation about, "That's why I don't want to do that" and, "Wow, this is telling me exactly why I want to do this other thing."'

Stiles agrees that almost any assessment gives people a point of reference, rather than just a gut feel that they are good or not so great at something. It gives them confirmation and data to work with. It's easier to hold on to a piece of data than to wonder if your ideas about your abilities are in fact correct.

When I work with clients who use assessments, they often find something that they really haven't paid much attention to that ends up being something really strong for them. Stiles finds the same thing and says that people often overlook their top abilities because they come so naturally to them. 'A classic example is people who are extroverted or who have been in sales positions, they often hear, "Oh, you're such a people person" and think, "Yeah well, so is everybody else out there." And all of a sudden after doing a test, they have that point of reference that allows them to see how different that is from the rest of the world.'

Stiles says that people over 50 are absolutely clear on their performance, because they've received feedback on this, whether it's in terms of pay rises, advancement or career success, but what most people don't really understand is that performance draws on our abilities. I see the same thing. Often people are not clear about the underlying abilities that have driven their success so far – and it is these abilities that allow you to learn skills in new fields and transport yourself into a different career.

Final advice from Dori Stiles: 'It's never too late to be reflective and to look and take care of yourself, it's never too late to get involved in something that is totally your own creation, meaning your own direction, your own career and how you want to shape it and sculpt it. And the 50-plus group is a very energetic group and they have lots of experience and lots of wonderful ideas, and they're really ready to explode with it and they just need side rails to help guide them, like those bumper lanes in a bowling alley, and that's what this is all about. Get the information, use your energy and, gosh, you can really be happy.'

Looking at your strengths or abilities can be very helpful, but they are not an instant solution to your career dilemma. I sometimes have clients who have done a heap of assessments in their search for a Holy Grail that will hand them a career with guaranteed satisfaction and success. However, as with any tool you use to navigate your career (including this book), assessments are only helpful if you are prepared to take them on board, reflect on them and really do the work needed to integrate the results and apply them to your career search.

You will also have to take into account the other things that we look at in this book, such as your interests, your needs from work, your beliefs about yourself and what's possible for you and, of course, your values.

Christie, 50

Christie was a client of mine who understood the importance of looking at all aspects of herself as she planned her next stage. She did the Myers Briggs Type Indicator and the Highlands Ability Battery, but her comments apply equally to any of the many good instruments you can choose from. She also relied on the other strengths exercises I have included in this book when thinking about her best future options.

I've been coordinating a course and lecturing for five years, as well as other teaching, and I just know it's not what I should be doing. I really want to realise my potential in some better way. I want to make sure I plan something that is really valuable for me when I get older.

Although I did various assessments when I was younger, doing one now, at 50, was excellent because it is a confidence thing. It's just one aspect of planning, so you are looking at this in a context of what are your needs, or your wants, and how you want to balance your life. It was such a confidence booster because I could see that I was very good at some things, and then there were other things I was not good at and I could just let them go. It was quite liberating.

Strengths and abilities are really important to me at the moment. I've had many assessments over the years. I've done the MBTI, which gives you a general overview, general capacities, and I've read books that help you work out what your strengths are. But because you're using your own head or you're doing an assessment where you tell someone else what you think your strengths are, it can be limiting. It doesn't necessarily get you out of what you are doing now. It doesn't really help you think differently about your strengths.

Doing the Highlands Ability Battery highlighted areas where I was really surprised that I did well and also some where I didn't do so well. I've never thought about it that way before. I saw that I had very specific strengths, and they make sense for where I am right now. It was really good to have a benchmark, so I wasn't just relying on things I read in a book or thought about myself.

There were also a couple of weaknesses, which was a relief because you could just throw those things away. One I was worried about was the spatial, 3D-thinking area, because I had always worried that I should've been an architect, but now I could see that it wouldn't have come naturally, so I had instinctively avoided the wrong path when I was younger. That was a relief.

Thinking about my strengths I have come to see that all my strengths also come with weaknesses. For example, I'm great at generating ideas, but that means that I can be indecisive, or not see some things through and that was really helpful because it is unfortunately true.

I've found that I have a whole lot of strengths which I've actually used in my career until now, but I discovered that they were real and got better with age. I worried that it would be limiting to find out my abilities, but I don't think it is because you discover that there are certain abilities you might have or not have, but it doesn't mean you can't be something. You can build most careers around your abilities, if you know what they are. You still have lots of options.

CHAPTER 7

Past lives

On these magic shores children at play are for ever beaching
their coracles. We too have been there; we can still hear
the sound of the surf, though we shall land no more.

J.M. Barrie, *Peter Pan*

The title of this chapter doesn't mean you have to tap into your
inner Roman soldier, or the time you were a member of the
Versailles court. This chapter is all about your present life but
looking back to find clues from the things you loved to do when
you were younger and the values you have developed over time.

While I firmly believe that change is possible (or I wouldn't do
what I do), it's also true that many of the things that interested
us as children or teenagers continue to crop up throughout our
lives, and can be an excellent indication of themes that lead us
to truly sustaining and satisfying work. Remember David's story
in Chapter 3? He has returned to his love of music and is now
weaving it through his work in a couple of different ways.

I had a client some years ago, a woman in her 30s, who was
a very unhappy corporate executive. On doing some exercises
about childhood interests, she reconnected with her old love of
creating tea parties for her dolls and teddies. Nothing in that, you
might think, but even aged four or five, she went much further
than you or I probably would have – proper food, invitations,
decorations, entertainment and as many human guests as she
could corral. Every week. This memory proved to be a vital link in

her reinvention, leading to a new direction in events management. She was able to use her existing business skills in a field that fascinated her.

You may be reading this thinking, 'I can't remember my childhood', and it's true, many people struggle to recall their early years in any detail. However, as many of my clients have found, siblings, parents, other close relatives or family friends can be a very useful source of information. In fact, my tea-party client reconnected with her inner hostess via a conversation with a favourite aunt, who had lost none of *her* memories of helping to write the party invitations, having stimulating conversations with the teddy bear or doll she was seated next to – and the look of absolute delight on her young niece's face.

Exercise: Your archaeological dig

This exercise is about going back to the things that fired you up in childhood, the things that made you forget time passing because you were lost in a daydream or totally absorbed in an activity. It's like going on an archaeological dig where you sift through the layers between the present and the past, looking for clues to understand earlier times and find the links between then and now.

1. Think about these questions:
- What were your earliest memories of doing just what you wanted to do, no matter how unproductive or unimportant it seems to you now?
- List five things you enjoyed as a small child, five as a teenager and five as a young adult.
- What gave you pleasure about these activities?
- What was the setting, where were you?
- Were you alone or with others?

- Was there a purpose, a finished product, a task to be done?
- Did you have a secret place as a child? What did you do there? What did you dream or think about?

2. What was your favourite childhood story?

What did you like about it? (Storybook heroes tell us about qualities we admire and situations we enjoy or dislike. Children use fairytales to process issues in their real lives, to understand their world and explore capabilities and challenges.)

3. As a child, what did you want to be when you grew up?

4. Rediscover your childhood by filling in the following:

When I was a child:

- My favourite movie or TV program was …
- I dreamed about …
- I loved to …
- I hated to …
- My favourite game/pastime was …
- I wished I could …
- I wished I had …
- I was frightened of …
- I looked forward to …

These can be big questions, with many layers. You might find things bubble away, with memories surfacing when least expected.

Keep in mind that it's not about becoming the person you were or wanted to be aged five. Childhood has useful clues for us, but just because you dreamed of being a fireman or a doctor when you were little doesn't mean you should become that now. When I was very young, I wanted to be either an alien-space explorer or a kindergarten teacher. Neither of these came to pass, and nor would I want to be either of those now. But both of them were about belonging versus not belonging, as well as collecting new knowledge and ideas to share with others, and these are themes that have informed my work in many different ways over the half-century since, including this book.

As well as reminding you of your longstanding interests, the 'archaeological dig' exercise takes you back to a time when many of your beliefs about the world were laid down. These might include things like 'the world is a happy (or harsh) place', or 'I always (or never) get what I want', among many examples. Some beliefs are useful, but others hold us back if we assume they are still true, so it's good to make a note of these beliefs as you encounter them. Chapter 14 has plenty of practical strategies for working with beliefs and other things that could derail your work-reinvention process.

This process of stepping back from your day-to-day life and taking time to reconnect with things you used to love was helpful for one of my clients, Alistair, who left a long career in artisan food when he was 57. While he reflected on his next move, he focused on working around the house, painting and repairing, gardening, caring for his three kids and engaging with his local community. These activities all tapped into important life themes that he had let slide when in full-on career mode.

From these simple activities, he built some threads, reconnecting with his past self, with things he enjoyed and which made him happy.

He came to see me for some coaching, to get clear and settle on his new direction. He tossed up a number of ideas – growing things to sell at the local organic markets, sourcing produce or making his own (such as a range of chutneys), starting a B&B or running a pub.

During this period, the family decided to move house, so he readied the property for sale. He loved doing that and did it so well it was snapped up on the first weekend of showing. He thought some more, then came up with the idea of setting up a business getting properties ready to sell, not full renovations, but doing all the little (or not so little) things that make the difference, and show the house to its best advantage.

Alistair hasn't made a final decision yet, and it is likely he will end up with a portfolio of activities from his shortlist. For him, it is all about going back to longstanding basic themes in his life and using them as his guides and building blocks.

Sparking joy

Have you read *The Life-changing Magic of Tidying Up*, by the wonderful Japanese decluttering expert Marie Kondo?[1] Her core concept is that you take every piece of clothing you own or every kitchen item or every book and place them on the floor. One by one, you pick up each article and ask, 'Does this spark joy?' If so, keep it. If not, thank it for its service to you and discard it.

I have used the technique to great effect with my clothes, and recommend it to anyone who needs to declutter as it's both effective and fun. And it makes it much easier to discard things – Kondo's advice that you thank the article for its service to you and then pass it on for someone else to love, works a treat. (Until you go shopping to fill the new gaps in your wardrobe, that is. Hopefully Kondo will write a book about that.)

I've applied the technique in my work as well as my home. I started in my office, and found it helpful for getting rid of the miscellany that hangs around me – articles I cut out of the newspaper before I went digital, notes I scribbled to myself years ago, and so on. I did find a limitation to the office-decluttering application when it came to tax records, however. Do they spark joy? Decidedly not. Should I keep them anyway? Decidedly yes.

But the place where 'spark of joy' has really captured my imagination is in thinking about my work activities. I adopted 'spark of joy' as my highest work value for 2015, and I still think about all my existing and potential projects through this filter. It's proving really helpful in deciding where to spend my time, especially in choosing between different possibilities. Should I develop this workshop or that one? Should I complete this writing project or that one? Do I want to take my business down this road or not?

And on days when I am in a rut I ask myself, 'What could I do to add a spark of joy?' In fact, I am in danger of becoming a Spark of Joy Tragic, although I hope my deeply ingrained cynicism will save me from that dreadful fate.

It is a really useful filter when you are thinking about ways to create the next stage of your work and your life. Heather and Brian in Chapter 3 used their adult gap year to find new sparks of joy to use in order to create new paths, and Jan's story, which comes up next, shows how a spark of joy from a hobby can turn into a money-making adventure.

Jan, 68

Jan was a client of mine who has become a friend, so I have enjoyed seeing her several career reinventions. Now in her late 60s, she has returned to a longstanding interest in jewellery and accessories, in order to create a small business making and selling things that she loves.

I went from managing an alternative health centre to doing a diversional therapy course and becoming an activities officer in a cancer centre, where country people came to Sydney to stay for weeks while they had their cancer treatment and I organised all their fun and craft activities. It was just the best job, but the centre closed.

That's when I realised how much I liked making jewellery and doing mosaics, and so since then I have done courses in jewellery, resin jewellery and beading, and mosaics. I'm not a knitter or crocheter or embroiderer. I hate following patterns, so I like things where I can create my own style, and I don't ever do the same thing twice because it's just too much fun to do something different.

It's my one time where I'm really living in the moment. Nothing else going on in my head except what's happening and a whole day can just disappear. It's my form of meditation in a way, it's fabulous. It's when I'm really, really happy.

Now I'm setting up a little business. I make sets of scarves with matching beads, bracelets, earrings, things like that, and I make individual pieces. I'm starting to do resin and putting little mosaic patterns or crystals or whatever in pendants or earrings, put photos inside them, and so on.

I've always loved jewellery and wearing jewellery. Obviously with a busy lifestyle, children, the whole thing, you don't really get into all of this stuff so easily, but once my time became more my time I just realised how good it was. So when the cancer centre closed I started thinking I could make a little business out of this to supplement my income.

I don't think I consciously thought about whether I'd still be working at 68, but I'm really happy that I'm still actively involved in doing things. I can't really imagine not doing something. It would be nice to make a few extra dollars, but yes, I just really like it. If it comes to not being able to sell a piece, I'm happy to give it away to a charity or something.

Word of mouth has been really good for me, and I did do one market stall. I thought about an online shop, but I don't think it's ideal because I'm not really so big on computers. I'd rather be selling face to face or through a shop. My things look a lot better, I feel, when you actually see them as a real thing, rather than a picture on a screen. It doesn't do them justice, I think they look cold.

I did 'angel' earrings at Christmas and everyone went nuts. I made a pair and started wearing them to my volunteering job and to my Zumba class and people were saying, 'I've got to have angel earrings' and I was getting orders all over the place. At other times, when people saw what I was wearing they would say, 'I really, really like that' and so then I'd say,

'Okay, I can make it.' In the beginning I'd just say, 'Okay, thanks' but then my daughter said, 'So you have to say, "I make this jewellery and I could make some for you if you'd like me to, I take orders."' I was like, is that how it works? And it does work.

I am learning new skills in jewellery making but also business skills. There are some difficulties because I'm not very business-conscious. I think it's interesting to try this and see where it goes and yes, it's my intention to keep going with it and give it, I don't know, three to five years and see what happens.

In many areas we're very wise in our 60s because we've learned a lot and reached this age and we've sorted things out, but there's always more to learn and experience.

10,000 hours

As part of thinking back over your life, it's useful to consider areas in which you have achieved expertise or mastery, sometimes described as amounting to '10,000 hours' of practice. The good news for older workers is that we have had plenty of years of experience, and likely built up our 10,000 hours in at least one field, often more. This is a very valuable asset in a work reinvention.

Malcolm Gladwell's well-known book, *Outliers: The Story of Success*,[2] develops a convincing argument that the most successful people are successful not necessarily because they are more talented but because they practised more. He devotes chapters to the lives of the Beatles, Bill Gates and others, demonstrating that none of them had the overnight success we might have thought. Professional chess players, musicians, in fact everyone who excels, devote years to learning and practice before they master their field.

As you reflect on the things that are important to you, think back over your past and factor in the areas in which you have achieved real excellence. What are the things you do really well, where are the arenas in which you shine? You may have

10,000 hours as an electrician, for example, but this will probably also mean you have 10,000 hours as a small business owner, a customer-relations expert, a workplace-hazards master and more. So, really drill down into your experience and make a good list.

Values

Many people orient their careers around their needs or wants (or other people's needs and wants). It's a very useful step in creating a truly satisfying career to go deeper and identify your values and create your work around them.

Values are your principles or standards, the things you think are important or valuable to you. It is your values that make you 'you'. If you can articulate your values, they will serve as a litmus test for career decisions and planning: Does this move fit with my values? What will best reflect my values in this situation? You'll be able to solve dilemmas more easily, and you'll have fewer regrets. Most importantly, you'll live a life that truly reflects the best you can be. Reading stories like that of Ross, my plumber, in Chapter 2, it's easy to see how satisfying a value-driven life can be.

If you ignore your values when making career choices, job satisfaction is almost certain to be elusive. You may just feel incomplete or dissatisfied, or (if the value mismatch is extreme) the work environment will become intolerable. In my early career, when I was trying all kinds of different legal work in an attempt to find my work tribe, I didn't understand how important my values were, particularly those around authenticity, creativity and fairness. Because of this, more than once I was seduced by what I call Bright Shiny Objects and took jobs that were never going to suit me deep down. For me, the BSOs were things like interesting clients, good money, opportunities for travel and feeling appreciated. There is of course nothing wrong with any of these things, but the jobs involved compromising my core values, which rendered all those lovely BSOs essentially meaningless. It took me a while to learn to put my values first, but as soon as I did, my career change was much clearer to me.

I sometimes see a version of this with clients who value family highly. If a parent or other close family member is very attached to Fred or Susie becoming a doctor, lawyer, accountant or IT professional (very common parental choices) and Fred or Susie value family highly, they often comply with the plan that is laid out for them. If this matches their strengths, abilities and interests, it may not matter too much. But of course, frequently it does not, and that can be a huge dilemma, because to change careers also means managing family expectations without losing the relationships.

I had a client a while ago who became a doctor to fulfil his immigrant parents' dearest wish for their only child. He values family very highly and he had the marks to do medicine, so he became a medico. However, his secret dream of being an artist refused to die and over the years, he became more and more unhappy. When he came to see me, he was in a real bind – follow his art dreams and break his parents' hearts, or stay at the hospital and break his own heart? He found the courage to talk to his parents, and discovered that they had noticed how miserable he was and really only cared about him doing whatever would restore his happiness. So it all worked out fine, but not before all concerned had gone through some suffering as they worked through the values issues.

Look at the list of values that follows. Without thinking too much about it, circle the ones that resonate with you. You may already be clear on your values, but keep an open mind as you read through the list, as values can change through your life. There is no right or wrong, and no need to justify your list to anyone.

VALUES			
Creativity	Competence	Participation	Respect ✓
Helping	Risk-taking	Elegance	Excitement
Making	Loyalty ✓	Authenticity ✓	Being amused
Family	Learning ✓	Sensuality ✓	Empowerment
Happiness	Discovering	Service	Thinking
Self-respect ✓	Growth	Excellence	Relationships
Generosity	Touching	Aesthetics	Community
Inspiring	Grace	Health ✓	Connection
Strength ✓	Involvement	Zest	Nurturing
Observing	Co-operation	Tradition	Presence
Recognition	Culture	Productivity	Enthusiasm
Peace ✓	Integrity ✓	Status	Independence
Competitiveness	Responsibility	Vitality ✓	Compassion
Wisdom ✓	Adventure	Faith	Mastery
Planning	Fame	Honesty ✓	Passion
Humour ✓	Harmony ✓	Free spirit	Connectedness
Magnificence	Experimenting	Contribution	Accomplishment
Friendship	Power	Precision	Awareness
Advancement	Daring	Progress	Acceptance
Perceiving	Wealth	Teaching	Being right
Discerning	Security	Orderliness	Success
Encouraging	Pleasure	Expertise	Performance
Spirituality	Impacting	Dominance	Collaboration
Stimulation	Directness	Having fun	Mateship
Good taste	Partnership	Romance	Self-expression
Building	Trust ✓	Leadership	Fairness
Affection	Beauty ✓	Joy ✓	Focus

- What are your top values?
- Are there any others that are not on that list?
- Can you identify the top ten?
- Can you identify the top three?

Values provide the bedrock for a life well-lived, so I explored this topic further with values specialist Karynne Courts, who sees values as our unconscious motivators. Unless you understand what drives you and what motivates you, you are often guessing and you're only playing on the surface. Values are essential if you want to get right to what really connects you and gives you your energy.

I often find when my clients start to examine their values closely, they come to see that many of their most important values have been absorbed from others, rather than developed through their own experiences and reflections. Courts agrees.

'People often discover the values they think are really important to them aren't even theirs. It's often our grandmother's values or beliefs and assumptions we have inherited from our childhood that can stop us from moving forward, like not making a career change because "good mothers don't work". We might hold values like tradition, rights, respect, courtesy, and similar values that sound really nice but are actually constraints that can stop people from looking into their future. They may have got us to here, but they're not always useful to take into the next part of our lives.'

For many years, I believed that values were fixed, that the things that guided your life early on would remain your compass forever and that they would retain the same ranking for you – if 'family' was your number-one value it would always stay number one. It was during one of my early conversations with Karynne Courts that I realised this was not so. She says that you can change your values, or you can choose the ones that you want to live by through self-reflection. 'There are several ways to change your values, including a significant emotional event which changes them in an instant, or naturally over time, or conscious choice. So you can actually choose your values and orient your life around the ones that give you energy and excite you. It's not as easy as it sounds, but it's liberating to realise that you can choose five or seven values around which to create what it is that you really want to do and who you really want to be.'

Courts sums up the essence of her work by quoting Antoine de Saint-Exupéry in *The Wind, Sand and Stars*: 'perhaps love is the process of my leading you gently back to yourself.' She says it's the same with values, that in the end it comes back to 'Who am I and how do I peel away all the other stuff to say, "If this is really who I am, how do I live that into the world?"'

If you ignore your deep values when making a career change, sooner or later your body will tell you, and eventually it will come out. If your heart literally isn't in it, you end up having no energy. In extreme cases, you can't get up in the morning.

I remember a day towards the end of my legal career when I picked up my briefcase and tried to walk to my front door but my feet literally wouldn't move. I just sat on my sofa for hours, until my then partner came home and we talked. Eventually, I did go to the office and I didn't resign that day. But in that moment when I couldn't force myself to leave the house I knew this was it: either surrender to a life of quiet desperation, or take out my old dream, dust it off and find a way to live it. Which I did.

Peter, 80

Peter, at 80, is able to reflect on a long life that has been lived very much through his values.

I was born on the land and I studied Agricultural Science at Sydney University, which I loved. And I've been on the land ever since. Early on, I had the choice of a career in business, but then I got the opportunity to work for myself, on a very small scale and with a very large debt. Preserving the space to be able to make my own decisions, that's what I value most, independence and autonomy.

I think probably the most valuable thing in the world is to be your own boss. The chance to make your own mistakes is what I prize the most. It limits the scope of what you can do, if you're your own boss, but I don't think that's as important as being able to make your own choices.

About 20 years ago we moved out of Poll Hereford beef cattle and into Wagyus. That turned out to be good and just this year we've sold it all to a

Chinese company. We will stay living on the property, and new owners want our son to run their beef business for them.

I've served on boards and in local government. I went back into local government because I was concerned at the advance of coal and coal seam gas in the Hunter Valley. I was also concerned that they were tending to address their financial issues by increasing rates rather than improving economies. So I went back.

I'm still interested in the humanities and the arts. I'm more interested in the arts than anything. I was at a book launch on Saturday in Newcastle, a poetry book launch called *Home is the Hunter* and I had some poems published in that.

Money has been a driver, but it's not *the* driver. You can't ignore money, but it's not the goal. Life satisfaction as far as I'm concerned is the outcome for the family, really. You're not aware of it when you're young, it comes when you have kids.

As well it's about how many challenges you didn't squib and which ones you did, you know. It's always the ones you dodge that you're disappointed at. There's not that many of them.

You never know what's next, do you? I'm going to keep writing. We're really in quite a profound change because we're now officially divorced from the land, which has been the central affair for 60 years. I will still have an interest in the Wagyu industry, but it's much more of a strategic nature now.

I like taking risks, but not just for the sake of taking a risk. I like to find issues that have potentially serious rewards and then try to work out whether it's worth it. Life is a risk. I've no idea what's next. Something interesting might turn up, and I expect I will give the odd strategic nudge to people. You learn to trust your instincts on matters that interest you. It's important that you trust where your interest will lead you.

I'm never bored, never lonely, always seem to have more things to do than I have time for.

If you're born enthusiastic, you're very lucky. I've always got a shelf of things I want to do.

Exercise: Essential you

Step 1

Reflect on everything you've learned about yourself in the last few chapters of this book. Think about your values, interests, the context of your life. Bring in your strengths, skills and talents. Take another look at the mind map from Chapter 3 and the 'your story' exercise in Chapter 4.

As you go, jot down the key things – a good idea is to make a list of the top three in each category and call it 'Essential elements of me' or some other name that appeals to you. Or if you enjoyed the first mind map, do another one that brings together the key aspects of you. The important thing is to capture these essentials on one sheet of paper – A3 size is ideal.

Areas to start with might include:
- Skills, talents and strengths
- Values
- Beliefs
- Interests
- Temperament.

Step 2

Now you will apply the things you've captured in Step 1 to each of the five types of work we looked at in Chapter 2. Even if you are not considering some of these types of work, it's useful to go through all five as it may highlight the reasons why you favour one over another.

- First, think about you in relation to the area of encore careers. Bearing in mind what you know about yourself now, what would be the pros and cons of an encore career for you?
- Write down at least five reasons why an encore career would suit you, or would otherwise be a good choice.

Then write at least five reasons why an encore career might be a bad choice for you.

- Next, repeat this process in relation to each of the areas of same–same-but-different careers, starting a business, giving back and finally, landing a job.

This is the start of your process of filtering possibilities, which will continue and deepen in Section 3 of this book.

CHAPTER 8

Money and more

Be steady and well-ordered in your life so that
you can be fierce and original in your work.

Gustave Flaubert

This book is about your working life, but 'work' and 'life' are overlapping parts of one whole (as we saw in Chapter 3), so in this chapter we look at the functions of work and at life arenas that strongly impact work.

Five functions of work

Much has been written about the functions of work, the economic, psychological and other benefits we derive from employment. It is often in pretty technical language, and most actual workers would find it hard to recognise themselves in the jargon. The most useful categorisation of the benefits of work that I've seen is by Richard P. Johnson, a former president of the American Association for Adult Development and Aging. He founded the Retirement Options consultancy for mature life planning and I came across his work while I was training through Retirement Options to become a certified retirement coach.

Johnson says that there are five benefits (perhaps even needs) that bring us satisfaction through work.[1]

Financial remuneration

Money is (of course) a key work driver. An income is essential to almost all of us in order to remain independent, create a lifestyle and save for future needs. The fact that it is paid in regular increments also makes money management easier. The need for money drives many people in their 50s and 60s to keep working, and although it's not always the main reason people delay retirement, the loss of a reliable and regular income can be a major challenge.

Time management/structuring

Being an employee or a business owner gives structure to your days: you are handed (or you create) a schedule that takes you from Monday morning through Friday evening and sometimes into the weekends. I've had several clients who are terrified by the thought of the empty, unstructured time that will loom if they stop working. Whether currently employed or not, we need to become more proactive about time management as we age, and find ways to create a schedule that allows us to do the things that are most important to our wellbeing.

Socialisation

This is about having mates to swap weekend stories with, colleagues with whom to work and share ideas and even the development of lifelong friendships. It's an important reason people keep working, and can be a huge challenge once your working life ends, or if you trade being an employee for a solo business start-up.

Status/identity

Work provides us with a role, a place in the world. It can be critical in developing a sense of identity and a way to explain ourselves to others: when we meet a new person at a party, the 'What do you do?' question is often our first attempt to get to know them.

The use of 'status' here doesn't mean high status, it's more about knowing who we are and where we belong in the world. The loss of this can be very stressful and much has also been written about people who retire and find themselves suffering from 'relevance deprivation syndrome'.[2] The expression was coined by former Australian Foreign Affairs Minister Gareth Evans after his retirement, but affects all sorts of people who give up a busy and useful working identity only to feel suddenly irrelevant in their new life.

Usefulness

The final benefit of work is to provide a sense of usefulness, a purpose to our days. Work is not the only way to derive meaning – my years as a mother have been at least as significant to me as my work – but it is often the simplest way to feel useful, and is certainly the most common. Work becomes our 'cause', our contribution to something larger than our immediate world.

Work keeps you in touch with the world, helps you build strengths, develop competencies and use your talents. It grounds your sense of who you are and what you offer. We frequently take the benefits of work for granted until they disappear, leaving us puzzled, sometimes shocked by the void. When we take on a new venture, we generally consider the impact on our financial position, but often that's all. As you consider the work options in this book, take the time to also reflect through the lens of the five functions of work and think about which of them may be either satisfied or challenged by different choices.

Because of their central importance to work reinvention, we are going to take a closer look now at two of the five – finances and identity.

Finances

I am sure I'm not the only person who spent large chunks of their early life deliberately *not* examining their financial position closely, and avoiding any consideration of the future implications of their current lifestyle. Eventually, I realised that even if you don't value the accumulation of vast wealth, you must know where you stand, and develop a plan to ensure you can remain independent for as long as possible and can live a life that makes you happy.

Some people find it natural to consider and plan far ahead, to delay gratification now so as to create a better future in years to come. Others are more likely to go for immediate pleasure and like Scarlett O'Hara in *Gone with the Wind* postpone future planning on the grounds that tomorrow is another day.

However you feel about it, you must take stock of your finances, get some advice and know where you stand.

It's never too late to seek help, but after 50, your time horizon for earning income becomes compressed. Even if you're happy to work until 70, or your early 70s, you have about 20 years and so good decisions and not-so-good ones will both be magnified.

I spoke to financial planner Kate McCallum about the most important things to think about at this stage. She talks about organising your finances through the concept of buckets of money. One key bucket is the money saved to support you when you stop working permanently – when you hang up your boots is there sufficient money to provide the income to live the life you'd like to live? 'It's very personal and I recommend people build a bottom-up budget for retirement so they say, "This is the life I want to lead, I want to be able to travel and visit friends in Australia or overseas once or twice a year, I want to play golf or go out to dinner with friends." You cost it and build it up as a budget.'

It can be helpful to think in decades, because say from 65 to 75 you may have a certain type of life you'd like to lead (in my case I am planning for plenty of travel, for example), but in the next decade to 85 you may have a different set of expenses. As McCallum says, 'You need to put it in a spreadsheet, with all the other things like gifts or health care. Housing and accommodation are important and these days we're seeing clients who will have a mortgage as they near 50 or 60. Is that something you want to repay or are you comfortable with a certain level of debt? There's no right answer, it's very personal.'

McCallum had a client who went through a really nasty divorce. 'She's in her early 60s and was able to afford a property in a place where she enjoys living, and we've worked out what she needs in terms of the retirement bucket. Her three children are her world and they all live overseas. So she travels to see them every year because you don't get this time back. The trade-off is she's quite happy that she'll work until she's 70. She budgets really tightly, and she doesn't get to buy everything she wants, but it's about asking, "What do you value most and how do we make sure that's where you spend the money, not on things that you don't truly value?"'

If you are reinventing your work at 50 plus, you need to be very clear about which buckets or areas of life are important to you and how much money you need to have saved or coming in as income while you make your transition. Having this clarity lifts the weight off your shoulders and frees you up to make decisions.

Even if the news is challenging, and sometimes it will be, the fact that you know and can make conscious decisions about it is itself liberating.

McCallum has a good suggestion for people who have had regular predictable income every fortnight or month and face a big challenge around managing cash flow when they no longer have this regular income stream. She suggests that you will feel a lot more in control if you actually draw an income stream as though it was a salary. You would do a bottom-up budget, work out what you need to cover expenses so you're not worrying, and that's the amount that you pay yourself to replicate that sense of an income stream.

McCallum also sees many people who are planning a career shift and don't have regular income because they are looking for a new employment role or building a business. She says this can cause emotional stress because you're relying on savings, or a redundancy or an existing buffer, and that means you're drawing on your capital, which can feel uncomfortable. Her advice is to be very clear about what you need to spend, and to know your overall position so you understand the implications of your decisions.

On the other side, she also sees people being more frugal than they need to be and not giving themselves permission to do something that's exciting. As she says, 'I look at people who have made really good decisions for everybody else in their life, particularly their children. They're not thinking about what they really want and often your 50s and 60s is a fabulous time to do that. So if you've got sufficient assets and income, why hold back?'

Kate McCallum's tips

1. Prepare for left field

You can have the best plans and then something comes from left field like a health issue. You have to consciously think about those 'what if' scenarios so that they don't completely blindside you. Make sure you have assets you can access easily if you can't continue working or somebody needs lump-sum funds to help with medical treatment, or you suddenly need to go to a child overseas.

2. Insurance

People working in larger firms may have insurance such as income protection, life insurance, total and permanent disability, and trauma or critical illness. I strongly recommend in any career change that you reassess insurances, and think about what you need.

3. Superannuation

We often see people paying total fees of 2 per cent on their superannuation, when you should be paying around about 0.8 per cent, at most 1 per cent. That's just money out of your returns. Above 1 per cent? There will be a fund out there that will give you a better deal.

We also see people overexposed to risky assets, when in your 50s you may not want to be. Make a conscious decision about this – and don't just look at the name of the fund because a balanced fund could have 70 per cent in equity-like assets and 30 per cent in defensive assets, or it could have 50:50, which is what I consider balanced. Shares or equities and listed property make up growth assets; defensive, non-risky assets are fixed interest or bonds and cash. People are often surprised at how far a 70:30 balanced portfolio can fall in a downturn like the financial crisis. It can be a 30 per cent drop in your portfolio and if you're 50 that makes a very big difference in the quality of lifestyle you're going to have.

4. Get clear on your priorities

The first question we ask is, 'What's most important to you when it comes to money?' and then we ask about your goals. They can be professional goals, whatever you want to do with your career shift; they're personal goals; they can be goals about key people who are important to you – children, parents, close friends; and then for many of us there's a contribution we want to make to community. The only job of financial planning is to enable you to achieve all of those things.

5. Have a plan

Analyse your current situation, work out where you want to be, understand the gaps, and develop a logical step-by-step approach to give you the best chance of getting from where you are to where you want to be.

6. Couples

Have the conversation. There's the rational side, which is about money decisions, and there's the emotional side, which is about values and what's most important to you. Once you understand each person's core values you'll make better financial decisions. I'm not saying that there's no compromise, but once you've had the discussion you can see why it's so valuable to the other person to have that experience or that outcome, and you somehow find a place where it works for both of you.

7. Think about risk

In your 20s or 30s there's less to lose so you may make riskier decisions, whereas in your 50s I think you're always very careful not to undermine what you've already established and built up. It's really about thinking about how comfortable you are to take risks and then evaluating all your decisions in the context of your goals and your comfort zone because, at the end of the day, we're all different.

8. Be prepared to challenge the norms

There's a lot of 'should dos' out there and I think you must ask yourself, 'What's right for me in my situation'? There'll always be naysayers saying, 'Oh no, it's too risky, don't start a new business, don't make a career change, it's too risky, you can't' or 'You have to repay the debt on the home, you have to do this and you have to do that.' Get rid of 'have to' and 'should' and build a very, very personal plan.

The next two stories are both about working with your finances at a time of change in your life, but from the perspective of people with quite different life stories and circumstances.

Andy, 56

Andy spent time in advance to create a solid strategy for his 50s and beyond, getting advice but also researching for himself and tailoring a very personal and satisfying plan.

Age 52 was my target, which was when the youngest was due to leave high school, and I thought it would be good to stop work, take some time off completely and then look to perhaps work part-time and do bits and pieces through to age 75-ish.

The idea was to buy something smaller in the Southern Highlands, work on the house to allow us to holiday let it to bring in a bit of money and then I would continue to do basic consulting. I liked that idea. That meant I actually had to do something with my finances that will enable it. Essentially, it meant not consuming and spending as much money at this end of the scale because you want to spend it at the other end of the scale.

We talked about it for a while and then we got our financial planner to validate that I wasn't making some stupid assumptions, and he said, 'You can do it.' So we decided to go ahead. The kids had both finished school, so we told them we were moving and they both decided to follow us, which damn …

The proceeds from the sale of the house mean that I don't have to work and earn as much money as I have had to in the past, so that has helped. I see myself as an apprentice retiree.

Our plan is not well-supported by the financial system because the financial system is still based on the model where you can't access your super until later. And I have a reluctance to put all of my retirement savings in the hands of the government so they can change the rules whenever they feel like it, so I've had some going in to super and some as a separate fund that I can use when I feel like it.

I have a fear that it's more difficult, and it may become even more difficult the older I am, to actually earn an income if I need to. If I'd done this at 35, then getting back into the workforce and being able to command a decent salary would be easy. I see that it's more difficult now at 56 and it will be more difficult later on.

The pot becomes sort of finite and it's harder to top it up. I have a sum of money that has got to last me from here to here and if I've got a leak in it somewhere I may not be able to plug the leak and then top it up.

I remember the first financial planner I had asked me, 'What are your ambitions and goals?' and I said, 'To die poor. On the final day I intend to spend my final dollar.' So we look at the house as being part of our retirement fund to pay for aged care and that sort of stuff.

I was at an international company in England in the 1990s when they started making very attractive redundancies. There was a guy who'd been there for 24 years and was not enjoying his work at all, and I said, 'You haven't taken the payout, what are you doing?' He had a picture on his pinboard of a fourteenth-century coach house in the hills and he said, 'I can't afford to because we've got this property and we need the income.'

What I then saw was I wanted the financial flexibility to do whatever I wanted to do at that time. And it could have been carry on working or it could be change, but I wanted that degree of flexibility. That's part of the, 'Why do I want a huge house with a massive mortgage? Why do I want a luxury car?'

Pauline, 62

Pauline's story is an inspiring example of someone who has had a tough life in many ways and avoided thinking about her financial future until recently. She has still been able to make decisions that will allow her to manage in her 60s and beyond, negotiating flexible work arrangements, finding a place she can afford outside Sydney and creating a solid plan for earning an income during the years ahead.

I've never been dedicated to a career. I always wanted to have a large family, and work was always incidental to that. After I had my first child, work was just not really a thing. I had a few little forays into work, but they didn't really work out and I'd stay home and have more babies.

When I started full-time work as an editor with a publishing firm I had four children. Then I had another baby, later my marriage broke up and I had three of the children with me. One of the banks lent me $5000, which was enough to buy some stuff and rent a unit.

I worked at home three days a week for years in that job and then I took on a bigger role and I worked in the office three days a week, at home two.

When my ex-husband left Australia, I ended up having all five children so working from home made a big difference.

I was pretty hard up; my ex-husband paid maintenance, but that wasn't a great deal. I got family payments so we managed; we lived very frugally. Then my mother gave me $50,000 so I could have a deposit and I bought a modest two-bedroom unit, where I live now. I still had two children at home, so my daughter had a bedroom and my son had to sleep in the dining room.

I put my head in the sand about the future. I used to laugh and say, 'Oh, John Howard says we have to work till we're 70, I suppose I will.' And then when I turned 60 I got a letter from my superannuation fund saying, 'Now you've turned 60, we've got to start thinking about retirement' and I was so upset.

After that, I started thinking about the future, I started evaluating everything. I didn't think I could afford to live in Sydney when I retire, so I decided I will move to the south coast.

I think working is important, but after I had this wakeup call I was thinking, 'I can't work in the office five days a week till I am 66 when I get the pension.' I found some information about applying to work flexibly under the *Fair Work Act*, which says that for various categories of workers, the employer should accommodate them unless there is a business reason for refusal. I applied to my employer to work flexibly and although it was a bit of a process, I was given two days working from home. It was terrific.

Even when I retire, I want to still continue doing freelance proofreading and editing. I'm also thinking of doing some advising to authors, just offering advice and explaining what things mean. I think if you can still contribute and earn money and do things you like when you get to a certain age, why not?

Identity

Identity is another of the five functions of work, and as we live for longer, it becomes more important than ever to be able to play with our sense of identity, our sense of who we are in our private and public worlds. There are threads of identity that stay with us forever, no matter how life changes. These give us our sense of 'I' and allow us to find connection between all the parts of our lives day to day, as well as over time. However, we also need to be able to reshape parts of our identity, explore new sides of ourselves and become more flexible if we're going to navigate this changing world. We need to take charge of ourselves, develop a sense of being in charge, so as to make the most of new and different opportunities.

In *The 100-Year Life*,[3] Lynda Gratton and Andrew Scott stress that as our lives become longer, we need to be able to experiment with ourselves, to create a multi-stage life that works for us. As traditional age and stage-of-life models break down, we need to be able to make our own choices in a world with many more possible futures – and possible future identities. It can have remarkable benefits and it doesn't have to be an enormous challenge: a simple change of perspective can alter everything, as I discovered on a research trip to the United States in 2014.

I met with a New York clergyman, who ran a soup kitchen for homeless people. It was a pretty standard set-up – they came in every day, stood in line and had their meal served to them by volunteers who also did the cooking and cleaning up. And the people would eat their meal and they would go.

This clergyman became interested in 'asset-based community development', an approach where you look at what a person can offer, irrespective of their past work history or circumstances, so he sat down with each visitor and asked, 'What are the gifts that you have?' And in doing that he found some people who could cook, even if not professionally. And he found others who played a musical instrument, so he said to them, 'Okay, you're now the band. So we'll get you instruments, you're gonna play music during lunch when everybody else is coming in', which they did.

Then there were people who used to be on the receiving end of the line who were now cooking or serving the visitors. After a while he found they didn't need the volunteers to do that alone, they had these people who had taken over their own process. As he said to me, 'And so you could give people names like, you know, not "John the homeless guy who came to the soup kitchen every day" but he was "John the cook" now or "Joe the musician" or whatever. In this way, you can help remove people from "I was an office worker and now I am unemployed". It gives people an identity and a sense of purpose.'

So, whatever your circumstances, you can reshape and reclaim your identity.

I spoke to counsellor and psychotherapist Alex Roberts on how to work with identity in times of change. She says that most people are identified by their work, at least to some degree, so if that changes suddenly you can 'flail about and land in your dressing gown for a few days'. If you are the type who likes to have a routine, then it is important to create a new schedule for yourself by finding things you like to do and making diary appointments with yourself to do them. Even if it's a gym class or a coffee with a friend, this creates a structure to your day which is enormously reassuring.

Roberts also makes the important point that we can absolutely create a new sense of identity, 'but if you're changing a career, first there is very much a grief process. Even if it was your idea to give up that career, you're still going to grieve. But if we can work through the anger and perhaps depression about what's gone, we can rise like the phoenix from that, with a new identity.' As a serial reinventor, I particularly like this idea of the phoenix.

A new identity takes work, though. Roberts believes we have a choice; that we can choose to have a positive reaction or a negative one: if life throws you lemons, make lemonade. She says that 'so many people live a fantasy world where they believe that they should still be able to do this and still be able to do that, but the reality is that you can't anymore. It's about acceptance. We all have a tendency to not want to acknowledge reality if it's not a positive reality. But if you're looking for a job and you're 60, you have to be realistic that it may be harder to get a position and not to let that deter you.'

It can be a real problem if you don't accept the reality and instead chase unreachable dreams. Both Roberts and I believe that dreams are critical, but they must be tempered by reality and approached with flexibility. Perhaps you can't be the CEO in your next job, but that may be a good thing – if you want to work and you are enjoying what you're doing, does it matter if you're not earning as much? Perhaps it'll be a more interesting experience. You may want to do something entirely different to what you did before and you need to reflect on what it is really that you're looking for.

'If someone's made redundant, for instance, they have a choice: to stay in that hole or to decide to do something different,' says Roberts. 'You either go down a spiral where you go lower and lower or you say, "Okay, this is an opportunity. What can I do? What do I like doing? I've got opportunities now that I couldn't have done 20 years ago because I was paying off my home", or "I had my family then, I had to consider them." Now I've got a choice that I can do things a bit differently. I might have been a CEO, but I could become a dance instructor if that's what I want to do now.'

Roberts tells the story of a client who was a high-flyer in IT, very good at what they did, but when it came to dealing with people they didn't have a clue. The client came to Roberts when they were made redundant and needed to get another job. 'Their confidence had gone down, so they came to see me as a psychotherapist to unravel what was happening. Once they'd done that, they realised that they didn't actually want to be in that kind of job anymore, they wanted to do something totally different, and it changed their life. And I don't mean just the job, it changed their identity, who they were and how they thought and how they performed and how they related to people.'

This 'unravelling' process can be painful, but it is critical if you want to learn from the experience and then move forward with a fresh identity and sense of possibility. You have to realise, as Roberts says, 'that anything that's gone in the past is actually gone. You cannot change it. As much as you would like to, you really can't, so put your past on the shelf. Use it for experience, but don't let it define who you are now.'

Elaine, 62

Elaine thought she had an identity that would carry her through her working life, but realised at 49 that she needed to take time to reflect and rediscover who she wanted to be in her 50s and beyond. It has not always been easy or straightforward, but she has re-crafted her story to take her in new and exciting directions.

I'd been working as a banker when I finished a job at age 49, with nothing to go to. I was in Singapore giving a keynote address and it was the last thing I did in that job, so when I went to the airport to come home to Australia, I was officially unemployed. It was the first time since I was 17 that I didn't have a job.

I was sitting in business class, in a suit, and the executive next to me told me everything about what he did. Then he said, 'What do you do?' and I looked at him and I said, 'I don't know.' I watched him flinch, actually pull back from me and I suddenly thought, 'My God, there's no room to even ask me questions if I don't have an identity or a title or a card.' He didn't know where to put me. And then I realised that *I* didn't know where to put me. I felt really ashamed because it was like, you should know what you do. That was implicit in his reaction, if you don't know then you must be mad.

Back home, I went to a transition consultant at an outplacement service, and that was the most demoralising and demeaning experience of my life because she handed me a book and said, 'Work through this' as though I was a child. And I remember sitting in this soulless room with all these men walking around looking dazed and lost and confused, thinking, 'I have got no idea who I am or what I'm doing.'

Because I've always been so rational and analytical, I didn't expect that emotion would come and get me and I didn't know what to do, I didn't have any way of dealing with it. I lost my visible cloak in a way, I just didn't know who I was anymore. I wasn't able to come up with a strategy. Given I was an internationally known strategist it was kind of ironic, but when it came to me I was completely frozen.

Finally, I decided to set up my own business because I didn't see any other option. At first it was tough because I had no idea where to start and I missed having people around. I would do three or four months with a client and then move to the next one. Then somebody asked me to help them set up a new business as CEO so I did that for two years and absolutely loved it. Then I went back to consulting, but of course I had to build it all up again.

I think I didn't have resilience, which surprises me. I had lost the way in my own story. I had always been the youngest at whatever I did in my career and suddenly I felt I was the oldest, in a culture where being an older woman was not at all valued.

Over time, with a lot of reflection and finding good people to talk it over with, I found my place and re-crafted the story around what I was doing. It's an ongoing process. Jane Fonda talks about her third age from 60 on and that you need to understand and learn from the first two. That's been very powerful because I've come to realise that everything I've done has purpose and now it's just a matter of pulling it together and using it in a constructive way. So it's a big shift.

I've read every book on finding your purpose, looking for somebody to come and tell me. Now I've actually realised that you have to find it yourself. If you have purpose, you don't have time for shame because you get excited and passionate and you have an identity in that. But I still find myself at meetings and things slipping back into the known and comfortable. And yet I know that therein lies danger, that's not the way.

The conversation has definitely changed in Australia. We see older women in positions of power now more and more, and it is seen as having gravitas. There are role models, there's discussion, the whole landscape's changed. I want to be one of those role models. I plan to be working into my 90s if I'm compos mentis.

I'm peeking out from that corporate wall, I'm jumping out from time to time, but when I can walk out and stand in front of it then I'll know I'm home.

Exercise: Money and more

How much do you understand about your financial position now? And what it might be in 5, 10, 20 years? Who do you need to talk to about this – your partner, a financial planner, your children?

How much does your work define who you are? What else makes up your identity now? If someone asked you, 'Who are you?' what would you say? How might this change in your next stage?

What else do you need to think about now, so that your work reinvention is as successful as it can be? Think about these elements of your life:

- Health
- Leisure
- Relationships – family and friends
- Self-development
- Community or spiritual life
- Legacy.

Think about the five benefits of work:

- Financial remuneration
- Time management
- Socialisation
- Status/identity
- Utility/usefulness.

Which of these are most important to you now? What about in the future? How do you currently get what you need from work, and how will you shape this in years to come?

SECTION 3

RESEARCH

CHAPTER 9

New directions

No one saves us but ourselves. No one can and no
one may. We ourselves must walk the path.

Buddha

As you start this research phase, you may already have definite ideas about work avenues, or it still could be a bit unclear. Either way, if you can do the exercises in this chapter it will set you up for the rest of the steps in the book – and help you come up with promising ideas that may never otherwise occur to you.

From now on you will generate ideas and drill down into them, finding out as much as you can about your various possibilities. So far we have spent time looking at *you*, but now your focus will turn outwards, to find the best intersection between your talents and the needs of the world. Some readers will be heaving sighs of relief at this point, at last able to stop navel gazing and get into action. If that's you, jump in now.

If that's not you, jump in now anyway, because after a certain amount of imagining, there is no way forward except via action.

Here we go ...

Exercise: Lots of questions

In your search for the ideal work pathway, some of your questions need to be answered in the external world, like, 'What training would I need for this new field of work?' and some will demand that you dive into your inner world, like, 'Does your job define you, or do you define your job?'

The best way to encourage lots of good questions, and therefore lots of good answers, is to keep a notebook or journal where you can record questions, reflections and results of your research.

Some questions need to simmer on the back burner for a while – often you will keep a question in mind for days or weeks before the answer 'pops into your head'. (Of course it doesn't actually pop into your head from nowhere; it is the result of all that reflection, of moving your attention into the right space.)

Here are some questions to get you started – but the best questions will always be the ones that you come up with yourself, the ones that are personal to your own career search. So, as you work your way through this list, pay attention to any new thoughts or ideas that occur to you, things you are curious about – write them down and set aside time to think about them.

Take the time to write out each question and compose an answer. It is very powerful to put pen to paper (or fingers to keyboard) and see the words taking shape in front of you. Some questions may be reminiscent of earlier exercises in the book, but it's worth taking a fresh look at this stage – you may find your thinking is changing.

There are many questions here, so it's important not to get overwhelmed. You could start by deleting the questions that aren't relevant and those you are already clear about. Then perhaps pick 10 of the most interesting to you, and set aside some time to work with them. If writing isn't for you, why not use them as discussion starters with your partner or a friend?

Questions about work and purpose
In this context, 'work' may mean paid work, or activities that give purpose and structure to your life, such as giving back, starting

a social enterprise, writing a book and the like. But not hobbies, unless you are turning them into a business-like project.

- How do you feel about work right now?
- Do you want to keep working? Do you need to?
- How do you see your working life in the next five to ten years? What would you still like to achieve at work?
- What's your fantasy work situation in the next five to ten years? Hours, conditions, work environment, role, flexibility, opportunities and so on?
- What are your options in your current job or field of work?
- How confident are you about your ability to find (and keep) ongoing meaningful work?
- What are you an expert at?
- What are you passionate about? What's your greatest enthusiasm?
- What existing strengths and skills and experience could you leverage? Or transport to a new job or a new career?
- What additional skills could you develop – either because you think you will need them, or because you're interested in the area?
- How flexible or adaptable are you about career change? How do you feel about it?
- How much of your sense of identity and purpose (who you are, what you do, what you value) is related to your working life?
- Do you have any beliefs about work that could help or hinder you in the future?
- What have you left on the back burner all these years? Is it time to bring it to the front? What parts of yourself do you want to reclaim?
- Does your job define you, or do you define your job?
- Does your age define you, or do you define your age?

- Does your current identity define you, or do you define your current identity?
- What if you saw your work as a portfolio of projects and activities?

Questions beyond work

- What does 'retirement' mean to you?
- Have you thought about transitioning beyond a full-time career? Do you have a plan?
- Have you thought about completely retiring? Do you have a plan?
- What aspects of working less are you looking forward to?
- What aspects of working less are you not looking forward to, or even dread?

Questions about your life

- Thinking about your life right now, has it unfolded as you expected?
- How do you see your life generally in the next five to ten years?
- What would you still like to do, in order to feel you have a happy/successful/meaningful/satisfying/good life?
- What non-work activities are important to you?
- Have you got an unfulfilled dream or passion that you'd love to activate in some way?
- Do you understand your financial position now, and as it will be in the future – income, debts, investments, superannuation, available benefits? Do you need to seek help or find out more in order to plan your financial future?
- Do you understand your state of health now? How do you hope it will be in the future? Do you need to seek

help or find out more in order to become healthier or maintain your health over the years to come? This includes food, exercise, managing any health risks or conditions, sleep, stress and peace of mind.

- What's the status of your key relationships? Do you need to think about changes in your immediate relationships (partner, family, close friends)? What about your wider social network?
- What are your likely responsibilities over the next five to ten years – caring for children, parents, grandchildren or partner? Will this involve time, focus, support, money?
- Are there any conversations you need to have about the future? These could be with loved ones, professional advisers or people with whom you have any unfinished business.
- Who else needs to be involved in your planning? Who is part of your day-to-day life and focus?
- How would you describe your philosophy of life, or the meaning of life, or the purpose of your life?
- Do you have any beliefs about life that could help or hinder you in the future?
- What will be your legacy? What will you be remembered for?
- What are the other questions you need to answer?

Claire, 50

Claire's story is a great example of someone who is starting to ask herself lots of questions about future directions, and to research and explore some new possibilities. She doesn't have any final answers yet, but she is doing all the right things in exploring new ideas.

I didn't really know what I wanted to do or be when I left school in England, but I had a holiday job in a firm of accountants. And it was just so much fun, the people were really nice and I could understand the work and I could put it into context. And I thought, 'Yeah I can do this.' So then I did an accounting degree and joined an international firm as a graduate. I became an accountant through nothing more than having a good holiday-job experience.

I worked for various employers, ending up moving to Sydney for work. And here I am, 14 years later, still here. Similar industry, similar role and responsibilities, similar reporting lines.

I have always been a reader, I've always been interested in books. When I moved to where I live now, I didn't know anybody, so I joined the local book group. It's run by the owner of a local bookshop, but it's quite a literary book group, not the kind where you just sit around and drink wine. As well as book clubs, the owner of the bookshop also runs writing workshops for adults, so I gave that a go.

I really enjoyed the workshop, I really enjoyed being able to capture what was in my mind and to put it down on paper. Sharing it with other people was a bit confronting, but I quite enjoyed that as well. I haven't done any more workshops since, but it's in the back of my mind, and I've looked at formal courses, online courses and a whole bunch of stuff. It's something to think about over time.

I have taken advantage of opportunities like contributing to our local garden-club newsletter. I've done it over the last three months, and it's something I would never have thought of doing before, because I'm at the learning end of gardening, whereas there are others there who have been gardening for 50 years. The editor said they could do with some contributions and I just find that no one really steps up to help, and it's easy for me to put a couple of hundred words together and a photo about something garden-related.

I don't think I've got as far as thinking of writing as a replacement for accounting yet. But the editor of this garden newsletter said, 'I love receiving your articles because I don't need to change them at all', so that is a good start. I've also submitted an article to our local paper about a garden-club activity, so I hope that that will get picked up as well. But none of that is paid.

At the moment, all I'm doing is seeing opportunities and leveraging them. I'd really like to take some kind of evening class or something I can fit in with work. I don't see how I could make this something I could pay the mortgage with, but I love being in this curious phase, and it's amazing now I think about it more, how many opportunities there seem to be to write.

It's more than just play for me. I would like to learn the formalities around all these things, rather than just keep writing for my own benefit. I've always enjoyed writing, and I did well at it.

I've got a mortgage to pay so earning money's pretty important. As far as corporate roles go, I'm interested in doing a good job, but I'm not on a career ladder now. I've got too many things that I want to do. Learning about things outside of work, and taking the opportunity to get exposed to other things is important. I've been with my current employer for a few years now, and I know that role, and the rhythms of the organisation and the cycles, so that takes the pressure off and allows me to do other things.

I feel frustrated that time is my limiting factor. If I could work even four days a week that would give me an opportunity to do something else like writing on the other three days, even if it isn't paid.

I imagine I'm going to be working forever. I've always wondered about this retiring at 50 thing, because that would leave you with about 30 years of unpaid existence.

You need to work, because you don't want to stay in your pyjamas all day, you've got to get out of bed.

Exercise: Lots of jobs

This next exercise is about looking at lots of jobs, but it's not just about using your logical, analytical brain to select a good role for you. This exercise will help you find the patterns and the deeper satisfaction in different ways of working. Have some paper or a journal handy to jot down your reflections and ideas.

Step 1

Have a look at the list of jobs on page 166. Reading through the list, circle the jobs that you are drawn to, the ones that you think you would find exciting, satisfying and interesting. Don't worry about skills, qualifications or experience, or availability, salary or anything practical at this stage. This is just about the careers that grab your interest. If jobs come to mind that aren't on the list, add them at the end.

Now, pick out the top 10 or so from that list and rank them roughly in order of excitement or interest.

Step 2

Have a look at your top 10. Are there any patterns, clusters of skills or themes – things like 'working outdoors', 'being creative', 'having people contact (or not)', 'running the show', 'thinking/doing/helping/making', or 'solo vs. teamwork', for example. What themes or patterns can you see?

You might also pick up contradictions, such as a bunch of thinking jobs and another bunch of practical doing ones – that's fine, it's all part of the mix, so make a note of those, too.

Step 3

What else do you notice? Do you find memories popping up as you do the exercise? Do you remember a long-abandoned work dream? Or a job experience that you would love (or hate) to repeat? What's going on as you look at your list and think about these things?

Take time to reflect on this exercise, as it can bring up some very useful clues, both obvious and subtler.

JOBS LIST

School teacher – primary or high school

Academic – university teacher and/or researcher

Presenter, public speaker, trainer, facilitator

Coach – career, business, executive, life, etcetera

Carer – for children, adults, people with special needs

Social worker

Psychotherapist or psychologist

Librarian in a public library

Engineer

Architect

Lawyer – private practice, in-house, government, barrister, legal aid, mediator, judge

Hospitality – restaurant owner, manager, waiter, barperson

Minister of religion

Journalist – online, for a paper, magazine, TV, radio, documentary

Blogger

Writer – fiction, non-fiction, plays, copywriter

Linguist, translator, interpreter

Editor or publisher – magazine, newspaper, books

Animal worker – vet, vet nurse, zoo worker

Accountant, bookkeeper, actuary – at an accounting firm, insurance company, business

Visual artist, sculptor

Chef, cook

Medical professional – GP, specialist, surgeon, diagnostician, nurse

Alternative health practitioner

Pharmacist

Business owner – small, large, in between

Entrepreneur

Business consultant

Property developer

Venture capitalist

CEO of a big company

Project manager

Executive in a big company, middle manager

HR manager

Marketing manager in a company

IT expert

Software programmer

Administrative support person

Athlete

Personal trainer, sporting coach

Town planner

Manufacturer – factory owner, manager, worker

Inventor – private, government, corporate

Product developer

Scientist

Driver – bus, train, taxi, truck

Director – stage, film, TV, opera, documentary

Actor – theatre, TV, film, advertisements

TV anchor, newsreader

Tradesperson – electrician, plumber, handyman, mechanic, etcetera

Construction worker, builder

Airline pilot

Hospital administrator

Retail worker, shop manager or assistant

Police officer

Farmer, fisherman

Armed services

Banker – retail, investment

Shop owner

Archaeologist, historian

Member of parliament, local councillor

Recruiter

Explorer

PR agent

Environmental scientist

Social activist

Financial services professional

Interior designer, decorator

Public spokesperson for an organisation

Event organiser, event manager

Diplomat

Real estate agent

Musician, composer

Economist

Non-profit or charity area – caseworker, officer

Other?

Work and life role models

It can be interesting to look for people whose careers or lives you admire. They might be friends, colleagues, people you've read about or seen on TV. They might even be fictional characters from books or movies.

The key question is: whose job (or life) would I most like to have in the whole world?

Then do some research to find out as much as you can about what it would take to get a job or life like that, or what skills or experience you'd need to acquire first. And bear in mind that it may be some aspect of that person's work or life that you admire, such as the ability to travel for work, or the opportunity to help people during a difficult time in their lives. If so, extract that aspect and ask yourself what other roles or pathways you could explore that might give you that same element.

Exercise: Job-card shuffle

For this exercise, you will need a bunch of index cards, or post-it notes, or some other small blank cards.

Write down every single possible job or field or course of study or business or project or significant hobby you have ever wanted to do, no matter how impractical. Put one item per card, and just keep going until all avenues are exhausted.

Your list might include big-picture items such as 'engineer' or 'author', as well as activities like 'do a design certificate' and specific things like 'learn to make my own clothes'. All are equally welcome in your list.

When you have at least 20 cards (and hopefully double or triple that), lay them out on a table in front of you. Look at the cards and see if you've missed any possibilities – if so, include them.

Now, do the following exercises:

Step 1

Pick up two cards at random. What would happen if you connected these two somehow as a job? Say on one card you had 'work in a chocolate shop' and on the other 'teach primary school', how could you connect them? Maybe teach chocolate-making, work in a school canteen or teach children to cook? Put any new ideas onto new cards.

Now pick up two more and try to connect them, then pick up two after that for several more rounds.

Step 2

Eliminate any cards that are of zero interest to you – but not the ones you like but which seem impractical. Looking at the stayers one by one, what draws you towards that idea? You might write the pros and cons on the back of each card. See if they form natural clusters around themes, say 'creative jobs' or 'hands-on' or 'corporate' or whatever.

Step 3

Collect all the remaining cards, and number them '1', '2', '3', etcetera. Each card should have a different number written on it.

Now, look at the matrix diagrams on page 169. A matrix allows you to rank different ideas on the basis of both their practicality and how much you desire them. In the example shown, number 7 is desirable but impractical, 4 is neither practical nor desirable and numbers 3 and 9 are practical but not desirable. The clear initial winners are likely to be 1 and 6. (Another option, of course, would be to go with 7, but work on making it more practical.)

For this exercise, take your card numbered 1, rank it on the basis of its practicality and how much you desire it and put the number '1' in the relevant box on your matrix. Now continue with all the other cards in the same way.

Then, look at the matrix:

Example Matrix

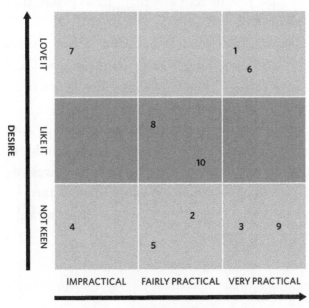

Your Matrix

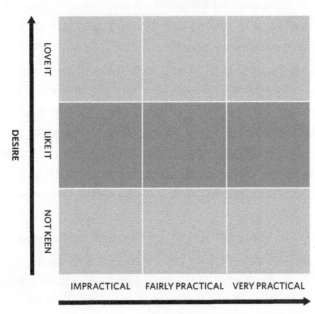

- Which are the jobs or activities that rate as practical as well as desirable?
- What about the ones you love but which are impractical – could you do something to make them more practical?
- What about the less likeable but immediately practical jobs – could you turn one into a 'journey job'? (Remember, a journey job is a job that you can do with your present skill set and pay the bills while you think further about other possibilities, or a job that gives you an entry into a new world from which you can then leverage work that is closer to your new career ideas.)
- Which are your winners?

John, 47

John came to me because he was unhappy and couldn't see a way out. As we worked through his process, it became clear that he wanted to stay in his current job for a while, while he managed his breadwinner responsibilities. But having a strategy and an exciting new venture to plan for and get excited about has changed everything for him.

I've been told we all probably need to keep working until we're 70, but it would be better to do it and actually have fun. I think anybody who has been doing the same thing and is in their 40s and upwards must be thinking what I was thinking: I'm in a rut and I'm not enjoying my job, but I'm in a comfort zone. I wanted to do something else, but I had doubts as to whether I could. Wouldn't it be fantastic to get up every morning and do something you really enjoy?

I have been in the real estate industry for 20-odd years. I've been married for 20 years, too, and we have two children. I'd been grumpy in my job, so my wife sent me along to see Joanna. I went along with a blank canvas and said simply, 'These are the things I enjoy' and we went from there.

We started with lots of questions and I did homework basically trying to find out what I like, what I enjoy and, more importantly, what I didn't like doing. And then breaking that up and heading in that direction of what I'd like to do. Joanna looked at what I was thinking and then helped me put the pieces of the puzzle together: I like motorcycles, I like touring with motorcycles and I like looking after people, so we targeted that I might create a motorcycle-touring-group business.

First of all, I'm not jumping out of what I do now because unfortunately I've still got to pay the bills. So it was more along the lines of the age factor. There seems to be a line at 50 where you become very unmarketable. We discussed that it's probably a good time to do something now, prior to getting into your 50s. But for me I won't immediately take the jump 100 per cent because it mightn't work out and then I'll be struggling to pay the mortgage, pay the bills, feed the kids, that sort of thing. It was more arming me with the things I needed to do to make a decision.

I still have a leg in my old world, but I have a plan now. I have the confidence to pursue my plan and to see if I can do it. You know, I'm a lot more relaxed about my existing job because I know that at any time – when the timing is right – I can do what I really want to do. Worst-case scenario is that you give it a go and it doesn't work; however, even if you just break even it's been an experience. And also having the ability to fall back to what I do at the moment would still be there.

So the main thing was finding out that you are still marketable in your late 40s, you're not dead and buried yet.

Now I'm on a fact-finding mission. Joanna suggested I investigate businesses, what's available and prices. I'm preparing myself to make the jump. I've joined a motorcycle group and we ride together. I'm looking at insurances, weighing up business viability, looking at what competitors are doing and checking out websites. In my current job, I run a group of people and look after budgets, so that's the easy part. It would be great to have someone assisting me, and I'm looking at the amount of riding and the type of motorcycles.

I have never experienced getting up and being happy to go to work before. That's going to be great. Well, it won't be work then, will it?

Showstoppers

For many people, this part of the process is where it starts to get real, and all the ideas that you have been tossing around begin to come alive. You start to 'get' that this process might actually result in change. And that can have some interesting consequences.

You may start to feel excitement building because at last you are doing something to take charge of your future, to create a map that will take you to your next stage of life. There is something very powerful about taking steps in new directions and it often leads to positive feelings and a sense of trust in yourself.

However, you may also (or instead) feel a sense of impossibility, or apprehension, or even dread. This is quite normal and comes from those parts of you that don't like change, or risk, or dealing with the unknown. Because of this, it's important to develop a strategy, so you don't stop the show before you've even had the dress rehearsal.

Chapter 14 contains a full discussion of these 'showstoppers' and plenty of practical strategies for working with them. So if you find anxiety creeping in, or you have a little voice in your head telling you that it's all a waste of time, or you are procrastinating the day away, please jump ahead to read that chapter so you don't lose your momentum.

Context

It's very useful at this stage to get clear about the context of your work. Things like the right work environment and doing work in a way that suits your personality are important but often overlooked.

I've mentioned already that when I was a lawyer, I was drawn towards a number of jobs that were like Bright Shiny Objects, luring me away from my core values. Because of this BSO seduction, I also ended up in workplaces that were never going to let me do my best work – large, competitive, impersonal offices, crisis-driven environments where production was measured in six-minute increments, all recorded in a daily timesheet. Years later I had a conversation with a friend who had stayed in that world, rising to the very top. She mentioned that her firm's sole aim in training young lawyers was to make them 'meaner, leaner, harder and faster'. No wonder it wasn't the world for me.

Exercise: Context questions

Here are some questions about the context of work. Have a look, think about them, and record the things that will be important to remember as you move towards deciding your next pathway.

Questions about the work environment
How do you feel about:
- Working in an office? Working outdoors? At home?
- Large or small company?
- New business or well-established?
- Working for yourself?
- Travelling for work?
- Opportunities for transfer to another division, another city, or overseas?
- Working in the CBD, the suburbs, or the country?
- Are you interested in not-for-profit businesses?
  Or the chance for a corner office? Or a competitive environment? Stable and secure, or risky but exhilarating?

What about:
- Open-plan offices?
- Having lots of people around you?

- Quiet or loud workplace?
- Frequent meetings?
- Working alone or in a team?
- Do you need to have fun at work?

Questions about the work itself

- Do you like being supervised, or self-directed?
- Do you need a clear job description?
- What about opportunities to learn or to develop skills?
- Promotion possibilities?
- Do you prefer a fast-paced job or slow and steady?
- How do you feel about decision-making?
- Do you need a lot of variety, or a steady uniformity?
- How many hours a week are you prepared to work?
- What about availability after hours? Weekend work?
- Is job security important?
- How much retraining or obtaining new qualifications are you prepared to do?
- Do you enjoy creative thinking, problem-solving, generating new ideas?
- Do you like dealing with crises?
- Do you like working on commission?
- Do you want a portable career, one you can do in another city or country?

CHAPTER 10

Experiments

To dare is to lose one's footing momentarily.
Not to dare is to lose oneself.
Soren Kierkegaard

This chapter will help you create some experiments to explore your ideas, and test them as far as possible in the real world before you make any decisions.

For some people (I am one) the opportunity to try new things, to experiment with possible pathways is the most fun of all. However, if you're thinking that you'd rather just keep reading about change instead of actually trying it out, then please pay close attention to the next few paragraphs.

Brain stuff

We often hear that old expression, 'You can't teach an old dog new tricks', usually as an excuse by the speaker for refusing to try something new or take a risk. Now in the case of actual dogs, it may be true that they don't learn new things as they age. Certainly, my much-loved labrador was seemingly incapable of learning tricks at any age, although I suspect he was just special in that way.

But in the case of humans (absent a brain injury or the like), it is rubbish to say that you can't learn or grow or change. Rubbish. Many studies show older people are both interested and quite capable of learning new things.[1] So if you are thinking that all this creating new paths to exciting and different futures is an impossible dream for an older person, read on.

Thanks to huge and ongoing developments in the field of neuroscience, we now know that the brain makes new connections throughout life, and is able to wire and rewire itself in extraordinary ways. Norman Doidge says in *The Brain That Changes Itself* that the concept that the brain can change its own structure is the most significant-ever advance in our ideas about the brain.[2] His book contains numerous examples of people who have rewired their brains after accidents, strokes or illnesses had left them with a loss of brain function. The stories are fascinating and the implications for all of us are extraordinary. If the brain can recover from extreme situations, imagine what is possible in more ordinary circumstances?

And on the subject of ageing brains, Doidge says that old age is not just about decline and decay – older people often develop fresh skills and become wiser and more socially capable than when young. Not only does the brain continue to create connections, it also moves functions from one brain area to another, a form of 'plastic reorganisation' that compensates for some of the inevitable decline of overall function in old age.

There is a trick, though. You have to offer the brain a stimulus to encourage it to change – novelty, challenges, problems to tackle, activities that require sustained concentration. *Rethink Your Career* offers you all of that and more.

Another piece of the puzzle comes from Carol Dweck's research on the difference between having a 'fixed' or a 'growth' mindset, discussed in her book, *Mindset: How You Can Fulfil Your Potential*[3] and her TED talk,[4] 'The Power of Believing You Can Improve'. Dweck researched the significant differences in results from students tackling a tricky problem, one that is in fact just too hard for them to solve. The students who saw the problem as insoluble did much worse on the test than those who decided it was challenging and interesting and they just hadn't solved it yet. She has much evidence to demonstrate that it is possible to change your own mindset from 'fixed' to the much more useful 'growth' mindset. This applies to people of any age, and is a most encouraging thing to remember as you set out to change your life.

There are an increasing number of books about neuroscience and the brain's capacity to change and grow at any age. I'm not an expert in neuroscience, and the field is changing at a very fast pace, so I will leave you to explore further. Whether you read more on this subject or not, if you tackle the experiment-creation process in this chapter from a mindset that at least holds the possibility of growth and change, you'll do well.

You may wish to have cellist Pablo Casals as your role model here. When he was 91 he was approached by a student who asked, 'Master, why do you continue to practise?' Casals replied, 'Because I am making progress.'[5]

And so can you.

Now let's turn to the practical work of this chapter, crafting experiments and research projects to enable you to explore your reinvention ideas further.

Work experiments and investigations

Now that you have some new work ideas (or at least things you are curious about), it's time to find out more about each possibility. The diagram on page 178 has some options, and the closer you can get to the centre, the better. Let's look at each option in turn.

1. Imagine

Do you ever imagine possible futures for yourself? It's certainly been one of my favourite hobbies throughout my life, and continues to be a source of great entertainment. Ever since I hoped that I was an alien as a young child, I've daydreamed about futures as an astronaut, a missionary in Africa, a novelist, a children's barrister, a TED talker, a mother of six living in the country, a perpetual traveller and many more.

This daydreaming is not an essential part of changing your future, but for many people it's the best place to start. Often, your first experiment needs to be the setting up of a vision of where you're going, so you can anchor your actions and relate them to a goal. If this sounds like you, try the 'three futures' exercise on pages 189–90. I use it with all my career clients, and it can be quite profound.

Imagination is an excellent start to this phase, but it won't give you a deep and objective understanding of the work involved in your imagined future life, or many facts about the realities of doing your fantasy job day after day, year after year. That's the job of research.

ZEROING IN

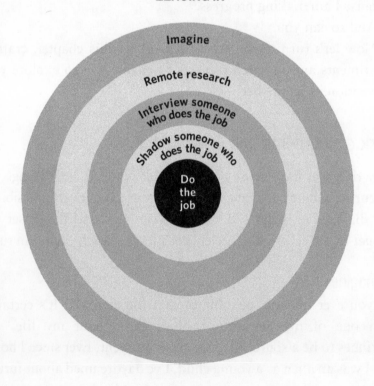

2. Research

This includes internet searches, reading books, even watching TV shows that feature your ideal job. You can find out a lot this way, especially if you drill down and don't just skim the surface of the internet. It also includes talking to people you know to see if they have a colleague or friend who could help you find out more.

You may be able to attend open days or short courses in your field to check out a course that interests you or compare two options. I have had numerous clients who have used this stage to research different training courses, compare their features and outcomes, talk to professors and get clear on the best option for them. Naomi's story below is an excellent example of this approach.

One of the markers of older learners is that we want 'just-in-time' learning that provides exactly what we need when we need it. We are less concerned about prestigious universities or broad educational approaches than perhaps was the case when we were younger. So, it becomes very important to research the options carefully to ensure any retraining you undertake meets your actual current needs. But don't hold yourself back either – I had a client approaching 50 who enrolled in medicine, another who flirted with enrolling at a Parisian university in her 60s (she does speak fluent French) and many others who have embarked on vocational certificates in order to re-enter the workforce after their first retirement. In other words, plan well but dream big.

Naomi, 43

Naomi was a client of mine, looking for a more creative career. I loved her approach to finding a new direction because she took the time to develop some well-considered experiments that would really show her whether her new ideas would bring long-term satisfaction. As she did the experiments, she reflected deeply on what she wanted from her next career. And it paid off, as you will see.

I have worked for many years helping marketing clients make better decisions through a client-service role in a consultancy. I am people-focused in my current job, but at the end of the day financial performance and financial growth count more than anything else, and that's the limiting factor for me. While I am lucky enough to have lots of positive interactions and room for some creativity, in the end it's all about the bottom line. If I rise a lot higher in my current field, the financial pressure will become my sole focus.

So I came to see Joanna to tease out some new options for me, possibilities where I could use my creativity in work where I felt I was helping people and connecting with them. One of the big elements for me was the job cards [see Chapter 9], really writing down all the silly or not-so-silly options, and starting to match them and map them.

And that came together quite nicely with the exercise where I drew a big jungle picture with my values, priorities, skills [see 'Essential you' in Chapter 7 and 'Drawing the threads together' in Chapter 11]. That gave me the framework to map jobs and to get clear on what I'd really like for my future career. I discovered that it's all about accompanying people in times of change and helping them to achieve positive transformations.

Then I did a bit of reading, looking for careers that ticked all the boxes I had identified. Thanks to the internet, I very quickly came across three courses in art therapy. Two of them didn't click, but one of them resonated with me because of the website style and their approach, which was much less university-like and more creative. It was founded by people who were ex-university but wanted to do something different in their field.

In terms of further researching, what really helped were their weekend workshops – they offer Saturday art-therapy workshops so I could try them for myself, and explore how they fitted with my creative side. I also got to see how their style and the therapeutic context sat with me.

I did a couple of these. And I felt very different between the first and the second workshop. I wasn't too sure after the first one, but the second was much more comfortable and familiar, giving me confidence that if I embarked on something like that, while for the first few weeks it might feel very foreign, very different from what I am used to doing, it could grow on me and I would get more comfortable with the interactive learning style. I think if I had only done one workshop it would have still felt a bit wobbly, so doing two was very encouraging.

The final thing was their information session, which is part of the application process and in itself was another therapy workshop, so I had to experience certain techniques and ways of interacting for a third time, and I could really see how that sat with me. And the audience coming to the information workshop was quite different to the other workshops, and it was reassuring to see that a lot of people at the information session were more similar to my personality – showing the spectrum of people who might go into that field and reassuring me that I would fit in well.

Immersion [by doing the workshops] was a real-life test and gave me a glimpse into what working life could look like in that field, and whether it would give me the things I wanted in my career change. I could feel what it was like to do art therapy myself, but also watch the teachers and think what it might feel like if I was practising or teaching.

What was important when I interacted with the various teachers was to see their empathy – that's an element I really miss in the corporate world. In business, it's a lot more about personal agendas and what you want to achieve, and so while in a way people care for each other, there is a line drawn quite quickly about how far they will take it. Whereas the individuals I interacted with in these workshops had the room to be who they were, rather than having to fit into a certain mould and being much more hard-nosed. And that's something I had already identified that I didn't like about corporate, so I think I was consciously looking for a more empathy-based career. So I got to see how would I feel if I was that facilitator, and it was very inspirational and a really good fit with what I was searching for.

It would have been much harder if I had just read a book about it or even had a coffee with one of the teachers. You need to see them in action in their environment. I did read a few books, and they were really interesting, but books on their own wouldn't have given me that 'Yes, I think I want to do this' feeling.

[Naomi enrolled in her course and is thriving.]

3. Interview someone

If you've done your research and identified a few fields that interest you, you might wish you could buy a coffee for someone who does your dream job, sit them down and pick their brain for tips and inspiration. Or maybe you've read about someone who has your ideal lifestyle mix of work and other activities, and wonder how they managed to create that. Why don't you try to set up two or three 'informational interviews' with people who you've come across in your research, or with companies that look interesting?

Good questions to ask might include:
- What's a typical day or week like for you?
- What do you love about your job or your life?
- What are some of the things you'd change if you could?
- What are the three most important qualities needed to excel in this field or to enjoy this lifestyle?
- Are you a member of any networks or professional associations? How do they add value?
- What are the possible career paths, opportunities to learn and advance, options for specialising?
- What is the main reason that people leave this industry?
- Is there anyone else you recommend I talk to?

In my long experience with this tool, I've found that people are generally willing to help, if you:
- Make it clear you're just seeking information, not angling for paid work.
- Ask for 20 minutes only, and arrive and leave on time.
- Offer to meet at their office or the café of their choice (and if the latter, I don't need to tell you to pay for the coffee!).
- Send a hand-written note or polite email thanking them.

If you want to take this to the next level, you could set yourself a structured plan along the lines of a blog I came across a few years ago. A woman who wished to change her life but wasn't sure of her direction decided to have a coffee each week for 50 weeks (a year minus holidays) with people she thought were interesting, or knew something she thought would be useful, or were recommended as role models for an interesting lifestyle. On checking back while researching this book, I noticed there are now numerous '50-coffee' projects out there, so clearly I wasn't the only person who thought it was a good idea.

You can adapt this to 10 or 20 coffees, or to focus on people who have skills you'd like to develop, people with cool hobbies, or people who are wise or brave.

4. Shadow someone

This involves following the person around for an hour or a day, with their permission of course – it's not about stalking or lurking. You follow the person around as they go through their usual work day, noticing everything, asking questions and imagining how it would feel if this was your working life.

Some of the larger corporations have formal job-shadowing programs, though often restricted to current staff or school students doing work experience. It never hurts to ask, though. You might also end an informational interview with a question about shadowing.

You can learn a lot this way about the work itself as well as the workplace. It is a very efficient way to bust daydreams about what a job actually entails. Because of this, it may be the crucial piece of the 'Do I really want to do this as a career' puzzle.

I've had a number of clients who have made their work-reinvention decision based largely on job shadowing. One thought she wanted to be a designer, until she shadowed a real one and saw how much sitting at a desk doing things on a computer was involved. Another was drawn to marine biology, but couldn't build a picture of herself doing it until she managed to get connected with researchers at her local university in Western Australia and go on a short field trip with them, which was when it all fell into place for her.

5. Do the job

This is the ideal scenario – the chance to actually work in the environment, to do some of the tasks that would be part of your career role. It might happen by taking a journey job using current skills but in a relevant workplace and keeping your eye out for opportunities, or by volunteering or interning for a period of time. It might also be possible to isolate a particular core ingredient of that job and find a way to do that, even if it is in a different environment. You may want to try school teaching but find it hard to get an opportunity – so you could experiment by teaching adults in a community setting, which may be easier to set up. It's a bit like adult work experience, though as a mature person you're more likely than a school student to be able to get your hands dirty doing the job, and to better understand the environment around you as well.

Some years ago, I had a client in her 50s who'd worked in an admin role for most of her career. On the side, she made and sold jewellery at her local weekend markets. She loved this, but it wasn't yet enough to pay her mortgage. We brainstormed some plans for setting a date when she could move into doing more of the creative work she loved. Along the way, she confessed that she'd always had a secret dream to make large bronze sculptures, of the kind you see in plazas and other urban spaces. I asked her if she had ever tried doing this, but she'd only daydreamed about it. So we co-created an experiment, and located a foundry where they agreed to let my client try welding.

She went off for two days of adult work experience. She lasted the first day plus an hour of day two before cutting her experiment short. At her next session, she told me it had been the worst – and best – experiment she could imagine. The worst because of the noise, the heat, the heavy equipment (she was a petite woman) and even the smells. Not for her. And that was why it was also the best experiment as she realised that her sculpture fantasy was exactly that, a fantasy. In just over a day, the dream dissolved, freeing her to re-engage with her jewellery work with renewed enthusiasm and creativity.

Are you a design thinker?

Design thinking is a big trend in corporate circles these days. As a trainer in creative thinking, I draw on a number of design-thinking principles in my workshops. And it's interesting to think of your work-reinvention research and experiments this way, too.

Design thinkers look at opportunities or problems through a designer's lens, seeing ways to develop their ideas through questions and experiments in the real world, adapting on the run, discarding things that don't work and pushing further with things that show promise. Tim Brown, CEO of IDEO and a world leader in this area,[6] believes innovations don't come from small tweaks and little improvements, but demand creative questioning and entirely new directions. You can see how this relates to the investigations in this chapter, because you're doing experiments and research to help you design your new future, so you need to be open to new directions. You are both the designer and the subject of the design.

The central methodology in design thinking revolves around 'rapid prototypes', where you put together a working model of your idea, whether it's a product or a service or a lived experience of your potential future. Prototypes should only be given as much time and effort as is required to get useful feedback and shape your idea. In fact, the rougher the better, because if you polish your idea too much at the early stage, and invest huge effort into testing it, you're likely to be very invested in the outcome and become quite attached to this possibility before you know objectively if it's a goer.

It's the same with your experiments – do what you need to do so that you can learn from them, but don't spend weeks crafting one line of investigation. Don't go too far into the planning, or you may commit to something before you're ready and cut off other avenues of research that might have proved more fruitful in the end.

And don't just test out one idea, do multiple experiments so you can compare one with the other and perhaps even fuse together the best bits of several work environments. Stay open, curious and flexible. That way you will design a future that's ideally suited to you.

Kylie, 40

Kylie's story showcases a successful prototyping process as she went through a number of ideas, taking each just far enough to see if it was really for her. In the end, she found the ideal career, though it wasn't at all where she expected.

I came to see Joanna while I was working in marketing and communications for a multinational recruitment company in the city. I knew I was unhappy, and that I wanted to do something that was more meaningful, that I felt had inspiration, something that I felt was important to get up and do every day. Through our conversations, we were thinking about my working at key points in people's lives, helping people at times of life transitions.

I actually worked at [Sydney's] BridgeClimb many years ago, and did a bit of research about going back there, but it didn't feel interesting enough. Another idea was to be a funeral director, which was top of mind at that time because I had helped with my granddad who died. We've had a lot of deaths in our family, I think we had 13 in 18 months, it was just a ridiculous run, and I've had three offers from funeral directors to join their companies, which I think is quite odd, so I obviously have a knack for that. I did think that it would be something I'd be good at, in terms of the organisation and the creativity around the ideas of how to remember people and relating with people who are going through that. It would certainly be meaningful, a job that matters. But it didn't feel right as a career for me.

I had a passion for kids, so we worked out three other areas that I was interested in – primary school teaching, child psychology and then I briefly flirted with the idea of midwifery.

In the thinking phase, we went through the whole spectrum, from birth to death. We zeroed in on the areas involving children and started with midwifery. We set up an experiment for me to talk to people who had children. I also decided to watch a childbirth video because I don't have children and had never seen a birth. The idea of being a midwife died pretty quickly with the video. Then my sister-in-law gave birth and I went in there when the baby was maybe 45 minutes old and there was blood all over her legs and she hadn't had a shower yet, and I thought, 'Yep, that's definitely not for me.'

It helped me realise that I wanted to work with children, and midwifery isn't really about the children, it's more about the medical side of the woman giving birth and her body and the safety of the baby and not so much about the bonding with the child, which is what I was interested in doing.

I was still exploring different ways that I could work with children. Next, I flirted with the idea of child psychology and read a couple of books about what it's like being a psychologist. Even though I've got a huge interest in psychology and I've read a lot of books about it, this was different because it was actually a book about what it's like to be a psychologist.

The writer had many pros and cons, but he talked about how really draining it was and I was reminded of my own experience doing amateur counselling of other people. And my sister has severe depression and alcohol issues, and I didn't think that I'd have the capacity to take on more people's problems than I have already in my own family.

That left primary school teaching. I signed up for a teaching course at university and the first subject I picked up, deliberately, was 'prac' teaching, so I could arrange to work for two weeks legitimately in a school.

One thing that stood out really clearly to me after the two weeks was that I loved working with the kids and I got good feedback. But, as an introvert it took a lot of energy to be in front of people all day, even if they are six years old, because in my old job I could be in my own little world doing my own thing.

Also, I realised that the youngest primary kids would be five or six, in kindy, and up to 12 years old, and the kids that I really loved were the ones who were two, three, four years old. I thought about being a preschool teacher and talked to a woman who was, and she said there's not a lot of money in it; that it's really long day care, it's not really teaching.

I kept thinking and decided to mix my old career and my love of kids in a different way. Now I do freelance work for a group which has 70 childcare centres around Australia and that's where I get my childcare fix, I get to write about kids. I love it.

I also do work for a small company writing about Aboriginal health, immunisation, cancer, all the kinds of things that I feel are important and giving people awareness. I get to meet patients and talk to them about their experiences and I love that.

I was looking for more meaningful work and I sure found it. Just not where I thought it would be.

The main thing I valued from the experiments was getting clarity and not having any regrets. The idea to work with kids had always been in the back of my head and I thought if I don't at least explore it I will always regret it. The immersion experience [teaching kids] was good because you do see what it would be like day to day, and because when you just think about it, you can either glorify it or you can put up barriers that may not actually be there. But when you go and do it, you find out how it actually is in real life and then you can make a more informed decision about whether it's for you or not. So it was definitely valuable to do those two weeks, otherwise I'd still be sitting here thinking, 'Should I be doing primary school teaching?'

Exercise: Three futures

In this exercise, you look at three possible different futures and really play out how your life might look after, say, five years of living each of them.

Step 1

Start by thinking of all the things that might get in the way of change for you – is it money, financial commitments, investment in a particular work identity, status, family stuff, or ...?

Now, for the moment, just sweep them aside. We aren't ignoring them, just moving them off centre stage for a minute. Then, imagine a world where there are NO obstacles to whatever future you might consider, none. And ask yourself this question: what future would bring me the most satisfaction or success or happiness?

Try to come up with at least three futures. Often, our first thought is a future that looks very much like a continuation of our present working life. Our second future may be a twist on that, for example a future where you stay in your current career but upscale or move to a different work context – or sometimes our second future is the fantasy opposite of our first. By the time you come to a third future, you are likely to be thinking more broadly and tapping into deeper desires and interests.

If there is only one winner, go to Step 2A. If you have more than one clear answer, move on to Step 2B.

Step 2A (if you selected one future)

Imagine your life in say five years' time, living your future. Think about a typical day:

- Where are you?
- Who are you with?
- What is happening?

- What are you doing?
- How do you feel?
- What do you see?
- What do you hear?
- What about smells, tastes, touch?
- What about spiritual elements, physical elements, mental elements?

Capture this in whatever way you like – a journal, collage, mind map, list, story, recording.

Step 2B (if you selected multiple futures)

Zero in on the top three possibilities for a future direction, picking the three that seem the most attractive or compelling or interesting, NOT the three that are most practical or easiest to achieve. Remember that for the moment there are no obstacles in the way of achieving these dreams.

Now, pick one of the three and put it through the Step 2A process. Repeat for the other two in turn.

Thinking about the three, which one seems more compelling or inviting?

Step 3

Taking your top pick, bring all those obstacles – money, time, status, identity, fear – back into view. Make a list of them, thinking of them as logistics challenges rather than reasons not to move forward.

Looking at them one by one, brainstorm ways you could overcome the obstacles. Assume that there *is* a way around each challenge without losing your dream. (We will be doing more on this in Section 4 so don't worry if you get a bit stuck doing this step now.)

Exercise: Your experiments

Thinking about each of your work ideas in turn, how could you learn more about the idea through:

- Imagining yourself doing that work, using the 'three futures' exercise.
- Researching the idea, or training options for it, or workplaces where you might apply for a job.
- Interviewing people.
- Shadowing someone who does that work.
- Doing the work yourself.

What questions do you have at each of these five stages? The list that follows is only a starter, your own curiosity should inform most of your questions:

- What is involved in this work?
- Where could I do it?
- Who do I need to talk to?
- Why do I want to do this experiment/research?
- When will I do the experiment/research?
- How could I find out more?

Now for each of your work ideas, make a list of the experiments you will be doing. Make them clear and detailed enough that you will know how to achieve them, but don't get bogged down in planning – remember the design-thinking tips on rapid prototyping and do only as much as you need to answer your questions.

Next, make a table that looks like the example on page 192.

As you do each experiment, reflect on it in terms of what worked and what didn't, what elements were interesting, what you learned, what the next steps might be, and anything else that strikes you. This is valuable data to take into the next phase of your process.

EXPERIMENT TABLE				
Experiment	Details	Logistics (where, when, who, etc.)	Results and learning

CHAPTER 11

Decisions

There is a tide in the affairs of men, Which taken at the
flood, leads on to fortune. Omitted, all the voyage of
their life is bound in shallows and in miseries. On such
a full sea are we now afloat. And we must take the
current when it serves, or lose our ventures.

William Shakespeare, *Julius Caesar*

You have reached the moment of truth. It's time to decide.

For some people, this moment cannot come too soon, as they love to move into action and are often quite uncomfortable sitting in uncertainty, mulling over options and thinking about alternatives. If you are that person, and you have jumped straight to this section without going through the earlier processes thoroughly, then I am sorry, but as the road sign says, 'GO BACK, YOU ARE GOING THE WRONG WAY.' Investigations, thinking about options and looking at different angles all contribute to informed, better decision-making. Please don't skip over those earlier steps.

However, for others, the temptation is to stay in the research phase for far too long, in order to postpone that evil moment where you have to actually choose one option and forget about the rest. If you're that person, then congratulations for getting to here. You are in the right place.

And of course, if you're the one following the middle way, chapter by chapter, you too have done well and are absolutely on track.

The process you've been following so far in this book is carefully designed to give you the best possible chance of making a good decision about your future. It has brought you to here.

Now it's crunch time.

So far in this book you have looked at the essence of 'you' from various angles, and you've done some research and experiments to test your ideas. Now we put it all together and see how the whole picture is developing. This will make it much easier to draw connections between things, see the big-picture patterns and identify any areas that still need more thought. It will summarise your work so far and lead to clearer decision-making.

It's time to prepare your summary sheet or map of the key things about you and your career-change process. In a sense this is an update of the 'essential you' map you did in Chapter 7 and you might like to revisit that map now. But your thinking may have shifted since then, plus of course you have been experimenting and drilling down into possibilities, so you need to be open to new ideas and conclusions.

Exercise: Drawing the threads together

First, gather together your work on the exercises from the previous chapters (and any other things you have done so far). You may also have done previous research on specific careers, or thought about different life possibilities; if so, include that as well.

Read through the instructions below before you start – and feel free to design and adapt things in the way that will be most meaningful for you. For example, if there is particular information from other research or exercises that you want to include, by all means add another section for that.

Copy the sample diagram on page 195 onto a piece of paper or cardboard (ideally at least A3 size), modifying it to include the sections that are important to you. If you prefer to design your own diagram from scratch, please do so. You could draw a mind map or a treasure map (or branches of a tree, or rooms in a house, or ...), with the same headings, or whatever headings seem useful to you. Some clients have created works of art, such as Naomi from Chapter 10, who did a beautiful jungle picture. Others have done complex spreadsheets or collages. The more personalised it is, the better it will work for you, but the main thing is to capture the key information on one page.

Fill in each area, circle, branch or room with the distilled results of your pondering and research (and of course any new inspirations that strike along the way). A good guide is to list your top three in each area, so you will have your top three skills, top three interests, top three strengths and so on.

Then, spend some time looking at it all together on the page. Think about links between elements, ways that different sections might come together. Start to think about possible futures that could bring all this together, even if you are not able to see how to get there just yet.

DRAWING THE THREADS TOGETHER

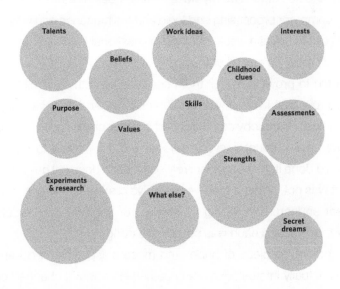

Talents, Work ideas, Interests, Beliefs, Childhood clues, Purpose, Skills, Assessments, Values, Strengths, Experiments & research, What else?, Secret dreams

If you are short on ideas, show your work to a trusted friend or colleague, or search online for some of the keywords and see what comes up. Talk to anyone you can think of who might know something useful or who can point you in the direction of someone else who might help.

Meditate on it, pin it up on the wall, let it bubble away in the back of your mind.

Robert, 70

Robert's story emphasises the importance of valuing your life and work experience. He says that nothing is wasted, but there comes a time when you need to reflect on your life and find out what you really want in your next stage. Along the way, you may discover your sense of achievement becomes more internal (and that's a good thing ...).

In 1964 I was in computers, working on mainframes that filled up basements in Barrack Street in Sydney. I had a passion for that because it was new and here was I, 19 years old with an opportunity to work on these fantastic machines and so I dedicated my life to it, really got stuck into it. I became an expert in computer processing and logic and maintenance and was working up to 100 or 110 hours a week, but then my relationship fell to pieces, I didn't see my kids grow up and all of that story.

I wanted to prove to myself that I could do something significant in the world, to prove that I was powerful in some form. And one day I realised in a blinding flash of the obvious that I had built an organisation, 180 people, it was across the country, even overseas, so if I wanted to prove I was powerful, I'd done it. In the instant I realised that I'd done it, I never had to do it again. It was not, 'What a fool I've been, I've climbed the wrong mountain', but in fact an incredible feeling of freedom of knowing that I could keep doing this, or not, and each was equally satisfying.

So I took out a piece of paper and made a list of half a dozen things that I was actually interested in doing something about. I changed careers,

I worked nights and finally got employed in personal development for about a third of the salary that I'd been on, but I had sufficient funds.

So, if you are thinking, 'It's all I know how to do, I've done this for 30 years, you know, I'm not good at anything else', that's only true in the very simplest sense. If you're highly logical like me, strong and independent and you've done that for 30 or 40 years, that's always going to be a talent you've got, you can use it whenever appropriate. But you can also explore some entirely other part of you, explore the possibilities, take an art class.

Then you'll start to wonder, what do I want my life to be about? What do I want to do in the world? When we start off, it's all about what we are good at and how hard we work at it. Our achievements are stuck up on the wall, or in trophies or in the vehicle I drive or what I have achieved. Wisdom comes when you realise that no matter what you achieve out there, there will always be somebody who will do it faster, smarter, better than you. So if your self-esteem is hung up on what you've achieved in the world, it's going to be short-lived.

You need to step back from your working life and reflect. We're so busy that we don't do much real reflection: Is my life how I really want it to be or has it just happened to me? Is this all I can expect? And to recognise when you get to the top of the mountain, it may well be the wrong mountain. That doesn't matter, because you are now a person who can climb a mountain and so you could climb any mountain, or perhaps now you want to swim in the ocean. So nothing is a waste of time in this world. Nothing.

Collage

As your ideas about your new direction become clearer, you might do a collage as a storyboard or blueprint of those ideas, also sometimes called a vision board. In collage, you collect images that speak to you and arrange them on paper. You could use personal photos or drawings, magazine illustrations or other images. You might add words or create texture with leaves or scraps of fabric or feathers. The aim is to represent something differently and interrupt your usual thought patterns. Collage taps into the power of the verbal, linear, logical parts of the brain and also the holistic, visual, big-picture, intuition parts.

Making a collage of your work-reinvention ideas can be very powerful. If you're still at a crossroads, you might want to free associate about your current life, or what is important to you. Or you may wish to collage about 'success' or 'meaning' or 'values' and build on the mind map in Chapter 3.

A few years ago, a client was struggling to get clear on a new life direction. We'd done a number of exercises, discussed options and played with possibilities, but she was still stuck, so I suggested collage. Two weeks later she returned with her finished work. She had divided it into four quadrants – three were each about a part of her present life, with the fourth headlined by the words 'north star' and 'leap of faith'. As a result of the process, she had a realisation that she couldn't make change by talking about it, but only by taking actions, maybe small at first, maybe experiments or trial experiences, but actions nonetheless.

The process helped her bypass the logical (and in her case, cautious) part of her brain in order to tap into her imagination and create a compelling image of two possible futures – one if she kept on doing what she was doing, and the other if she took her leap of faith and headed in the direction of her north star. This spurred her on to take action and start her new life.

Some of the best results come from people who aren't 'naturals' at this process. My favourite example was a builder in his 60s in a group program many years ago. When I introduced collage as our next group exercise, he looked at me as if I had suggested he leap up and dance *Swan Lake* for us, but eventually and very reluctantly he agreed to give it a try. By the end of the night, he cornered me to ask quietly if he could take home some of the magazines and the glue to keep working on his creation – and the end result changed his life.

Here are some collage tips:

- Take time collecting and arranging before you grab the glue.
- Find your own style. Everyone will be different – some collages have lots of elements, some a few, some have more words, some more pictures.
- Don't worry about interpreting your choices at this stage.
- When it's finished, sit with it for a while and then ask:
  - Does it need anything more?
  - What do you see? How do you feel about it?
  - Are there people? Animals or nature? Objects, man-made structures?
  - What do the patterns tell you?
  - Are you drawn to some elements more than others?
  - Are some things there because you felt they 'should' be part of it?
  - What did you leave out?

The power of three

In Chapter 10, I introduced the 'three futures' exercise, which allowed you to imagine your life in different ways. It's one of my most popular and effective client exercises because you can get a sense of possibilities without having to spend time and money exploring them in the real world. And when you're ready to make decisions, you might like to revisit the 'three futures' exercise and use it to test your final ideas again.

There are a couple of other 'power-of-three' techniques that work really well.

Three solutions are better than one

This is a great technique: whenever you have a problem to solve, or need to come up with a fresh idea, challenge yourself to come up with at least three ideas, not just one. I use this technique in my corporate creative-thinking sessions, in all sorts of contexts. For our purposes, you can use it to challenge yourself to come up with three possible work-reinvention pathways, which may be subtly or wildly different from each other. Or three ways to overcome an obstacle, or three ways to find the answer to part of your career puzzle.

I once had a client who'd been landed with the job of liaising with his company's European offices by phone, which from Sydney meant late-night phone calls, often for two or three hours or more. He had limited time off in lieu, but the main problem was that he had a young family who missed out on his company at night, and he was left feeling both tired and resentful. When I quizzed him, I discovered this had gone on for over four years, up to four nights each week, so I challenged him to find a way of stopping it, and soon.

His first idea was to write an email suggesting they find someone in Europe to give this support (though he already knew there was no budget for it). His second solution was simply to refuse to do it anymore, effectively threatening to resign. A high-risk strategy, that one. When I explained that I always encourage clients to find three solutions, he thought for a few minutes and said, with a look of dawning possibility on his face, 'I could tell them I'm not available after next week for phone discussions outside Sydney business hours, but if they summarise the top challenges or concerns at the end of their phone meeting and email it to me, I will respond by email within 24 hours.' He left my office soon afterwards, already drafting his memo in his head – and it worked a treat.

The thinking behind this is that we often settle for the first halfway-decent idea, either because of time pressure, laziness, or lack of belief in our ability to come up with a really innovative winner. By 'forcing' yourself to have at least three ideas, you have a fighting chance of digging deeper to something really fresh.

The trick is not to edit yourself at this early phase, to be as wild as you can. It's not as if every idea has to be practical, a proven winner, or even cheap or legal – those considerations kick in later. For now, the wildest idea is likely to be the one that contains the seed of the really brilliant solution.

What are your three work ideas?

P.S. If you are up for a real challenge, what about coming up with five or even ten options? It's more demanding, but I have seen in workshops and with clients that sometimes the fun doesn't really start until the first five or more 'easy' ideas are out of the way, clearing the air for more radical stuff, and forcing you to dig below the surface.

Top three choices

Once you've narrowed down your new work choices to a top three (or two, or four, or even five), it can be useful to answer the following questions for each choice. It's a great filter, and a way to summarise the results of all your experiments and research.

- Name the career or work activity. Add a short description of what the work involves.
- What are the entry-level qualifications and other requirements? What would you have to do to get these (years of study, job experience etcetera)?
- List five advantages, benefits or good aspects of this career or activity.
- List five disadvantages, drawbacks or bad aspects of this career or activity.
- How hard is it to work in this field? Are prospects getting better or worse, is it a growing field or a shrinking one?
- What career paths are available? Where could you go with this career or activity? Is there a promotion path, or different directions or specialities you could take?

- On a scale of one to ten, where one is 'not at all' and ten is 'a great deal', how would you rate this career or activity for:
  - Practicality (how logical or sensible it is)?
  - Desire (how much you would love it)?

The last question in the above list will remind you of the decision matrix that was part of the 'job-card shuffle' exercise in Chapter 9. If you found that exercise useful, you could revisit the technique now, using it as framework to filter your short list of possibilities.

Sara, 52

If you are interested in trialling something new alongside your existing work for a while, check out Sara's story. She has had a few careers and is now happily juggling two ventures, trading and travel.

I graduated from ANU and went into the corporate world. Around 2003, I started dabbling in trading – I'd done a Masters in Finance, so it seemed a natural fit. Since then I did my own thing for over 10 years. By 2015, I was feeling a little bit isolated. It can be lonely working from home, and it's amazing the amount of energy you get from just dressing up and going out of the house sometimes.

I looked at corporate opportunities, but I didn't really have a sense that I would get anywhere because I was too disconnected – and because of my age. Also, whatever I did needed an element of office work or some intellectual component to it, otherwise I'd feel a little embarrassed around my peer group. Although I know any work is better than nothing, I had a sense of identity at work to preserve, but also in my social milieu. If I stack shelves at a supermarket down the road or work in one of the cafés – I'm quite well-known in the community – I would feel embarrassed.

Anyway, there was an opportunity in travel with some friends. It wasn't really earning money; it was more like an intern and so I thought, 'What have I got to lose?' I did some free courses with them, basically they couldn't shake me off, and I just kept learning. They weren't quite sure about a position but they weren't quite sure how to get rid of me either, so I became a contractor doing my own thing. It's one day a week in the office, but it's doing your own business whenever the opportunity comes up.

I always did the travel planning for the family, for friends, so I was just fascinated with the subject and I thought, 'This I can do.' It's a slog, and the margins are tiny, remuneration is minuscule, but it fitted in with my identity. I could carry it off.

I still do trading. The two of them fit in pretty neatly and I've got three screens, so I can have the markets on one and a bit of travel on the other. My office is 150 metres from home, so it's neat like that. I think the trading has got better because now I leave it alone more – the saying in trading is you make the most money when you sit, when you don't 'do' all the time. The travel is all about building my networks, building up critical mass, but in the meantime, it just comes in in dribs and I've got lots of time to really work it through, not take shortcuts.

When I was younger I didn't take work seriously and I didn't make the best of opportunities. I always thought it would be so straightforward and easy. Maybe if I'd had to work harder for things I would have gone much further. I started living on my own from the age of 16 and there weren't people to advise me on those choices, particularly in my 20s. I didn't have the life experience, the information, and that's why I took certain paths.

At the moment, if there was an opportunity in travel to work six or seven days a week and really long hours I would just jump on it because I've got the energy level. I think in a sense I've landed on my feet, I've been fortunate. Even though I've said I regret not having taken things seriously at a younger age and being a little bit more driven, now it's like I've got another chance, so maybe I'm blessed.

Decision-making tips

Only you can make your decision, but here are some tips that may be helpful.

1. Look at the broader context

You have done this in chapters 1, 2 and 3, but if you feel that your thinking has become very focused on you in isolation from a social context, perhaps it would be good to start by reviewing these sections of the book.

2. Multiple possibilities

This is about going beyond just considering the pros and cons of a decision, the 'should I do this or that?' focus. We love the deceptive simplicity of this binary kind of decision-making, but it often cuts us off from wider possibilities or solutions. My 'power of three' exercises earlier in this chapter are a good example of widening your choices, as are most creative-thinking strategies such as mind mapping or brainstorming. They help us to see beyond the obvious, and to consider more lateral possibilities. I often recommend Chip and Dan Heath's book *Decisive*,[1] in particular for its discussion of the importance of moving away from binary decisions, from 'stay' or 'go', or 'yes' or 'no' choices. In the context of your work reinvention, instead of asking, 'Should I set up my own business or not?' it's much better to ask, 'What is the best way to remain productive, earn money and remain engaged over the next 10 years?'

3. Confirmation bias

One of the devilish psychological challenges in making good decisions is known as confirmation bias. We develop a tendency or view about something, then pay attention only to evidence that supports that belief, discrediting or ignoring anything to the contrary. This is insidious, and affects much of our lives – think of the last time you set your heart on a particular car or dress or house or holiday spot, and then magically found all the information that supported your choice. (Or the last time you discussed politics with a friend ...)

We may think we have done a great job of making a balanced

decision, or that our views are entirely logical, but often of course that's not the case. My science-loving son introduced me to this confirmation-bias concept a few years ago, and since then, I see it everywhere, including frequently and sadly in my own decision-making. My personal favourite version of this is to set up alternatives that I can consider, but (often unconsciously) making sure the alternatives are quite unrealistic or unpalatable, so that my preferred choice is the only sensible one left. Hmmm. The good news is that once you are aware of it, you can make sure you seek out evidence more widely, and consider it more carefully.

4. Find a fresh angle

A number of the exercises you have done in this book are aimed at helping you see your position from different angles, which is a key part of creative thinking, and helps us find fresh, often better perspectives. Think of the mind-mapping, career-story, collage, prototyping and experiment processes as examples. The aim is to shine a light on all the options, and to break us out of thinking ruts. You know, those loops when your mind goes round and round, time and time again, same old same old, which is both exhausting and unproductive.

Other tricks for seeing things differently that I use in my workshops include asking questions like:

- What would Kim Kardashian or His Holiness the Dalai Lama or a fish do now?
- Who could I talk to about this, someone who sees the world very differently from the way I do?
- What experts can I tap into?
- Who do I know that has done this before?
- What am I missing, what else can I consider?
- What if I couldn't choose that, what else might I do?
- What questions am I avoiding?
- How can I test this belief or decision or idea?

- If I was really brave, what would I do now?
- How does this decision fit with my values?
- What's the worst-case scenario? What's the best case? How will I handle either?
- What is niggling in the back of my mind? Do I have a hunch about what needs to happen?
- What am I prepared to do to make this happen? What am I prepared to give up?
- What assumptions am I making?
- What sacred cows or old beliefs am I preserving?

5. Cover all the angles

It's easy to fall into the habit of considering decisions from only a few favourite vantage points. For example, if you're naturally a rational thinker, you might make all decisions as if you were a Vulcan science officer on *Star Trek*. If you see the world optimistically, you might be a decision-making Pollyanna. And if you live mainly through your feelings, your role model might be *Pride and Prejudice*'s Mrs Bennet.

What you need is a way to ensure you tease out all the aspects of a decision, not just look at it through your habitual lenses. Techniques such as Edward de Bono's *Six Thinking Hats*,[2] where a group takes it in turns to think about a problem through a particular lens (wearing a particular 'hat') such as 'factual', or 'creative' or 'positive', can work really well. You can try this on your own, or with a partner or friend.

You might list a number of ways of thinking about an issue, and consider them in turn. My list includes the following lenses:

- What are the true facts – all of them?
- How do I feel about them?
- What could go right?
- What could go wrong?
- What am I assuming?
- How does each assumption sit with my values?

- How will each assumption fit with the rest of my life?
- What will each assumption look like in 10 years?

You can use this list, or create your own, ensuring you include your particular blind spot or least-favourite lenses. If you know you really struggle with one aspect, such as hard cold facts, find someone for whom this comes naturally, ask them what they think or how they would approach the issue.

6. Understand that things will change

I would hate you to think that once you make a decision, that's it. This is a creative process, and so your decision will develop, pivot one way and perhaps back again, and may even morph into some whole new thing. Provided you are responding to the nuances of your project and not bouncing around following whims, this evolving, organic process is exactly how it should happen.

7. Don't give in to obstacles

I've had plenty of clients who reach the brink of a decision, and then say, 'That would be ideal, but I don't have the money or time or skills or courage or ability to go back to university or whatever.' If you really want to do something, frame these obstacles as logistical steps, or practical problems to be solved. Don't let them stop you choosing what you want to do. You may have to modify your dream in the end, but don't give up.

The danger of no decision

Some people reading this book will have no choice but to make a decision, often in a pretty short timeframe – losing your job and having no cash to pay the mortgage concentrates the mind powerfully. Others will find that by the time they reach this chapter, they have pretty well decided already.

However, if you know that you could muddle on indefinitely while you ponder the perfect next step, you might think about the fact that after a certain time, no decision becomes a decision to stick with the status quo or to be tossed around by the actions of other people. If that's your end result, you have likely sold yourself short – and wasted a heap of time. It also leaves you at the mercy of a changing world, rather than having a sense of where you want to go and some tools and strategies to weather the storms.

One technique that I have used successfully is to give myself a deadline. Yes, it is an artifice, but it often works well. If the decision is a serious one, and your stuck-ness is severe, you might do this in two phases – tell yourself you will forget the problem, not think of it at all for a period of time (say a week to a month or more, depending on the circumstances) and then you will use the time from that first deadline to a preset future date to make a decision.

I understand the difficulty inherent in decision-making. Many years ago when I taught journalism at community college, I had a student who was talking about how hard it was to take an idea out of her head and actually commit it to a finite written form and send it off into the world. She had tears in her eyes as she told the class that it all felt so beautiful and perfect in her mind, but as soon as it was translated onto paper, something was lost and it would never again be as wonderful and full of potential. This resonated with many in the class, and with me also. However, the result of allowing this mindset to rule you is that you actually create nothing at all.

So, if all else fails, any decision may be better than no decision. I remember reading Luke Rhinehart's *The Dice Man* as a teenager in the early 1970s, equally intrigued by its graphic (by my then unworldly standards) content and its compelling central premise – a man who lives by making all his decisions on the roll of a dice. Now, I am not recommending this as a strategy, but I am strangely attracted to it as a possible exit mechanism when desperation strikes.

SECTION 4

REDESIGN

CHAPTER 12

Some practicalities

Put your shoulder to the wheel.
Aesop

In Chapter 2 we looked at five types of work – encore careers, business start-up, same–same but different, volunteering and landing a job. Since then you have had a chance to think about which direction might appeal to you, and then to do some research and experiments to test your first ideas.

Now it's time to delve a bit deeper into the practicalities of each of these work types. Of course, what follows will be general guidelines rather than the tailored pathways I develop with my individual clients. But there will be plenty of tips and tricks here that you can adapt to your own work reinvention.

Tips for everyone

No matter where you are headed with your reinvention, here are some relevant practicalities.

1. Take your time
You will have realised by now that reinventing your working life takes time and reflection. The more you can sit with uncertainty and possibilities in the beginning, the better your final decisions will be. And now you have your new direction, don't skip over the building blocks in this section – whether it is ensuring your

LinkedIn profile is up to date, brushing up on the new world of job hunting or creating stories to bridge your experience into a new world.

2. Be flexible and (a bit) adventurous

A man in his late 50s was referred to me last year by a friend, after being made redundant from an IT communications job he had held for 14 years. We had a coffee and a chat, and it was clear that he was very angry. That's quite understandable, and I think being able to rant is a very useful part of the process. However, this bloke was nowhere near ready to think about updating his résumé, or applying his (considerable) skills in a new field. He just wanted to spit the dummy until 'they' fixed his world so that he didn't have to change. I genuinely wished him well, suggested he take some time to have his feelings and call me if he wanted to try a new approach. So far, no word.

It would be lovely if we were in charge of change, but the truth is that we are never in full control of our career path. We certainly don't have to be tossed about like victims, but we do have to be both creative and strategic. As surfers do, we must look at the ocean, see where the waves of opportunity are, and where the sea is flat. We must pick the right board for the conditions, learn new skills if necessary and be very determined about the whole thing, paddling out time and time again until we find the right wave to ride. Like surfers, we work with reality and create the best opportunities we can within it.

This means you may need to consider a sideways move into a new industry, or take a pay cut while you navigate the next steps. You may have to report to a younger boss, or lose that important-sounding title on your business card. It may feel uncomfortable, but you never know, it could be liberating and even fun.

3. Hang out with like-minded people

It's often helpful to talk to people of a similar age. Some areas have online or real-world groups that will be relevant to you, or you could create your own. Participants in my workshops frequently tell me how much they value the opportunity to talk to others, to share ideas and to see that they are not alone.

Support and trained guidance make a measurable difference to success. A 2014 MIT Sloan School of Management study[1] on older long-term unemployed workers found that those who had support from a career coach or a support group were significantly more likely to have found work during the study period, and also found the unemployment experience less damaging to their sense of self.

On my research trip to the United States in 2014, I came across a number of sponsored programs offering training and support to older unemployed people. I was very impressed by the success rates of these programs, which generally ran for several months, offering job-hunting tips, retraining and ongoing support in finding a job. Here in Australia, similar programs are offered at different times through government or not-for-profit bodies, so keep an eye out for these in your local area. Your local community centre or council may have leads, or you can always search online for upcoming courses.

If hanging about in groups is not for you, find a trusted friend or coach so you can talk through your ideas, get feedback on your résumé or even run a mock interview. You could find one or two others on a similar path and arrange to meet say once a week, talk over issues and set goals together. You could use this time to plan, brainstorm, work through obstacles, prop each other up and celebrate victories.

4. Keep perspective

I've long thought that 'Don't worry, be happy' is one of the silliest-ever sayings. I mean, who would pick anxiety over happiness if they felt they had a choice?

So now I risk ridicule by telling you that you should 'be confident', 'persevere', 'be resilient' and 'keep an open, flexible mind'. In my defence, I'm not thinking that you will read this and say, 'I get it now, if only I'd known earlier that confidence was important ...' But however you work with these concepts, it's undeniable that your reinvention will be more successful if you can cultivate qualities like confidence, perseverance, resilience and creative, flexible thinking. (Not worrying and being happy are also pretty good.)

There are suggestions for developing some of these qualities in Chapter 14. There are some excellent books around and friends can be wonderfully supportive. And many people swear by having motivational quotes stuck up all over their house – I find these a bit irritating, as I inevitably encounter them on really bad days and just want to scribble rude words all over them, but they may work for you.

If you know you struggle with one or more blocks like these, and you're not able to overcome them, please do yourself a big favour and seek professional help. There is no need to let these issues hold you back from creating your excellent new life. Seriously.

5. Do you need to upskill or re-skill?

As you focus on planning and practicalities for your new working life, make sure you revisit your strengths and skills inventory from Chapter 6. Skills are always important, especially in changing times, and there is evidence that the need to upskill or re-skill is a particularly big issue for those over 45. Some older workers resent having to do training or feel they can't get their head around new things, while others sense they are being denied access to learning.

It's clear that those who can access training (formal or informal) and keep their skills current have a decided advantage in the workplace. It's not just about keeping up with technology, though that is important. There are whole new areas of career focus that experienced workers can leverage if they have the required skills. And adult-learning research clearly shows older adults are just as capable of upskilling as younger people, though they may require re-entry support if it is a long time since they were in the formal education system.[2]

I'm always interested when clients tell me they want to change careers, go for a big promotion, or start their own business – and expect to make this shift without a learning curve. I remember one of my clients was planning a total career overhaul. She had a plan of action and plenty of motivation (so far so good). But when I suggested that she might need to take an entry-level position in her new field while she learned on the job and did a couple of short courses, she was clearly taken aback. 'I can't afford a pay cut, and I've invested so much time getting where I am. I know I'll show my talent in my new field, isn't that enough?'

Er, no.

You'd be horrified if your doctor or lawyer was given a licence just because she was motivated or talented or had 20 years' experience as an accountant, or if the CEO of your bank was unskilled. But when it comes to starting a business or that fabulous new career path that we suddenly realised is our true calling now that we are 55, sometimes we assume that because we have life experience and one solid career behind us, the rest will be easy. These will always help, but for task-specific skills, there are no shortcuts to excellence.

6. Portfolio options

We have already touched on portfolio careers, where you might do a number of different things to make up your working week. It could be a couple of part-time jobs, or a job plus a microbusiness, or a number of projects. I am a great fan of this kind of working, and I love my portfolios of teaching, writing, coaching, corporate gigs and community work. (Though I am not sure I like being described by the new term 'slasher', as in teacher/writer/coach/corporate trainer/community worker.)

Charles Handy is known as the 'father of the portfolio career'. Author of fascinating books about future trends such as *The Age of Unreason*[3] and *The Second Curve*,[4] he sees great advantages in having a number of irons in the fire in a changing world, because if you have a range of clients or several kinds of work, if one fails you still have others. He says that people with 'proper' full-time jobs are in the minority, a trend that will only increase over time.

Portfolio advantages include variety, having a number of strings to your bow, flexibility and the ability to tap into more of your strengths. Disadvantages include challenges with cash flow and time management, feeling like a dilettante and the difficulty with questions like, 'What do you do?' It's not for everyone, but it's certainly worth a thought.

Tips for business start-ups

If you've decided that a small business is the way to go, then there are myriad things you need to do. You'd be well-advised to read a recently published Australian book about business start-up such as *Managing a Small Business in Australia: The Complete Handbook*,[5] or do a short course. I've taught small business start-up for over a decade now, so here's a list of things to think about, based on the curriculum of the Sydney Community College program I facilitate:

- why a business?
- building and testing your business concept
- identifying your target market
- understanding the competition
- identifying skills and skill gaps
- your online presence

- websites and SEO (search engine optimisation)
- social networking and blogs
- creating your brand and your unique selling proposition
- pitching your business
- marketing
- the right business structure
- legal aspects of business start-up
- insurance
- compliance and WHS (work, health and safety)
- managing risk
- customer acquisition
- customer retention
- business operations
- business planning
- accounting systems
- staffing
- pricing, margins and profit
- tax
- record keeping
- cash flow
- organisation and time management.

This is not a complete list, nor is it meant to scare you. Much of this you will already know something about, and none of it is rocket science. There is plenty of good-quality information on the internet and advisers like accountants and lawyers can be useful if your business is complex. The main thing at this stage is to list the things you need to find out and include them in an action plan, so you can tick them off one by one.

I'm involved in a national network called Seniorpreneurs, which delivers learning, development and support to people over 50 who are interested in exploring business. I asked co-founder Bambi Price for some tips.

Bambi Price's tips

1. Think before you spend

Don't spend a lot of money on courses (like how to market your business, how to get your business up and running, how to do social media) until you think about your needs and understand what you're trying to find out.

2. Is there a market?

We've had people come in who have been working on an idea for 10 years and still don't know if there's a market for it. Don't go and ask family and friends, they love you, they want you to succeed, of course they'll say it's a great idea. Go out, talk to people you don't know and ask them if they'll pay for it. You need a prototype or some mechanism to explain it to people and then get out there and talk to your potential target market.

3. Know your strengths

A lot of people think they want to start a business, but they're not comfortable talking to people about their product or services. That's an issue. We work with people about understanding their capabilities and then what are they missing? You might have all the technology skills, but you couldn't make a cold call, talk to a client or negotiate a deal.

It's nonsensical to think you can do everything. There's only so much a) that you can actually devote the time to, and b) that you're good at or that you want to do. I know when I try to force myself to do things I really don't want to do, it's only at the last death knell when I've got to have it done for tomorrow that I'll sit down and do it, and then I do an appalling job.

4. Be wary of tapping into your super

I'm concerned that many people are drawing on their superannuation. Superannuation wasn't compulsory until 1992, none of us have enough to retire for 30, 35 years on the money we would like to have. We don't recommend people draw down on super to start a business unless they've really gone through a validated program to know what they're trying to achieve, something that will actually make them sit down and look at their product, look at the market, talk to their customers and find out whether they can deliver it, whether they want to deliver what the market's looking for.

5. Understand tech

If you don't understand technology, it seems to be this black hole that people are terrified of. Also, everyone's got the fear of God in them at the moment about cybersecurity. Technology appears to be an enigma to many people and they're not really sure how to utilise it to enhance their business, but you need to come to grips with this.

6. Value your time

A lot of people assume their time's worth nothing, they never factor that in when they're looking at what they're doing and how they're doing it. If you set the bar low in the beginning the bar will always stay low. If you're starting your own business and you don't value your time properly, no one else will either.

7. Know what you want

Know what you're trying to achieve, like what are your exit strategies. Are you looking for a lifestyle business, a home-hobby business, a part-time business, something that's going to actually go global? What do you want? If you know what you're trying to get to, it gives you a different mindset. Then your expectations are certain and when people ask, 'Can you do this or that?' you respond with, 'Well, is this beneficial to my business?' Elon Musk said, 'When you are starting out every single thing you do, meeting, email, you have to say to yourself, "Is this going to benefit my business?"' If it's not, then don't do it.

Giving back

Volunteering is a practical option for work reinvention because it could lead to a paid position, and at the very least will expand your network and give you new skills and achievements for your résumé. Volunteering Australia data[6] shows that 92 per cent of volunteers (of all ages) are either 'very satisfied' or 'satisfied' with their volunteering experience. They also say volunteers are happier, healthier, live longer, have a greater sense of life meaning and even sleep better (and who wouldn't want that?).

If you're interested in volunteering, you can contact an organisation directly or go through an umbrella agency such as Volunteering Australia or its state branches. Chairperson of The Centre for Volunteering in New South Wales, Valerie Hoogstad, has three tips for new volunteers:

- Try to fit in, get a feeling for the culture and fit in and not be Mr or Mrs Know-All. That's not acceptable, and it doesn't go down very well.
- Treat it like a job in the sense of turning up on time and regularly, and behaving in a professional way. However, if you need to take a break, as long as you tell your organisation that you're going away and are respectful of that, they know that you're a volunteer and it needs to be flexible. Just don't suddenly not turn up.
- Either use your skills or do something you're interested in, so you make sure you find something that's meaningful for you, something that will give you job satisfaction.

Job hunting

We've looked at some of the practicalities of business start-ups and volunteering, so now it's time for the other three of our 'big five', which are encore careers, same–same but different and landing a job. These all involve being an employee, so we're going to look at the core elements of job hunting – résumés, interview skills, telling career stories and more.

Before we do, I want to briefly revisit age discrimination, the elephant in the job-hunting room. There is no doubt that ageism is a reality, and if you are looking for a job, you will likely encounter ageist attitudes.

People often don't realise they're being ageist – they think their comments or behaviour reflect reality, that the stereotype is a simple truth. Research shows that younger people may believe that older workers:

- lack mental capacity
- need flexibility
- have declining health
- can't learn new things (especially technology)
- are unwilling to learn
- are unskilled
- don't like change
- don't like working for someone younger
- are not committed
- are unproductive or slow.[7]

These stereotypes persist even though studies consistently demonstrate that in fact age is generally not related to job performance. We've looked at some of these studies in the early part of this book, and my special report (downloadable from my website) contains many more references.

I'm not suggesting that we can remove stereotyping just by talking about it here, but there are two practical things you can do.

The first is to counter it where possible. Whether you are looking for work, or in a job already, when you suspect you are being judged based on stereotypes, do whatever you can to disprove them by your actions. I heard a great story recently from someone who commented on one of my social media posts, in relation to challenging the myth that older workers can't handle technology. He said that whenever he went to a job interview, he would make sure his latest-model smartphone was on display, perhaps even using it to reference something or make a note of a particular point. Nothing was said, nothing needed to be.

If ageist comments are made in your presence, you can rationally point out the fallacy, using the data in this book or from elsewhere to establish the facts. If it is something said as a joke, you don't have to laugh along.

The other thing you can do is make sure you don't start believing the stereotypes yourself. Remember that research from 2012 I mentioned earlier, suggesting many older workers retire around the age of 65 because social norms say that's the right age to retire? And statistics show that Australians aged 50 plus may be discouraged from entering the workforce due to anticipation of discrimination. You don't have to be one of them.

You can also use some creativity to maximise your chances. We looked at Leanne's story in the 'Land that job' section of Chapter 2, and now I want to share one of her job-hunting strategies that I thought was particularly clever and creative.

Leanne's strategy

Initially in my job search, I probably took rejection a little bit personally: 'What am I doing wrong?' I was telling a close girlfriend that I'm really concerned I'm doing something wrong or I'm projecting something incorrectly about my persona and she said, 'Why don't you go and have a mock interview with my husband?' I know her husband extremely well – he's general manager in a company. It was a very clever idea and very generous. So I went in to the city, to his business and he interviewed me like he would a potential employee for his company. We did it exceptionally professionally, as though I didn't know him.

As soon as it was over, he said to me, 'Leanne, you were fantastic, the way you conducted yourself, the way you spoke.' He talked about the first two minutes of an interview, you know when you make a bit of conversation, you might talk about the weather or would you like a coffee, whatever. And he said, 'You almost froze. I could see a little bit of panic on your face. But once you got through those first few minutes, you just launched into being so great and professional and at ease.'

I adored him for taking the time out to do it. I know him well enough that if I'd done something wrong or was portraying something that he saw as a negative he would have told me. It made me feel so much better.

You might try Leanne's strategy, or use her approach as a springboard for developing your own ideas. Whatever you do, being creative with your job hunt can make all the difference.

You need to find ways to bypass ageist gatekeepers, to turn your years in the workforce into an 'experience advantage', and to find an imaginative way to stand out from the competition.

You might find the employers who do appreciate experienced workers by scanning the media for articles about age-friendly workplaces, do a brainstorm for networking connections that could help you, or list ways you can bridge a skills gap or become tech savvy. Older-worker job boards are starting to appear, which specialise in matching experienced workers with employers who value that experience. I haven't listed any particular ones as they are new and it's not yet clear who the stayers will be, so check out local ones for yourself.

It may not be fun or even fair to have to find ways of countering ageism in your work search, but that extra effort will pay off.

I have a friend who was keen on a job that was advertised in a large company. She was perfectly qualified but couldn't get past the gatekeeper, a young HR woman who clearly thought that at 45 (yes, 45) she was past it. So my friend explored lateral avenues, talking to friends, contacts, anyone who could connect her with someone senior in the company. She managed to meet with one of the directors, who hired her on the spot.

When you reach Paul's story in the next chapter, you'll see he was both thorough and creative in his job search, too. It's always worth thinking about different job-hunting strategies, using networking, or being proactive in contacting organisations that interest you, or volunteering in a place you'd like to work, or doing something else that can help you get noticed.

Résumés

There is no join-the-dots formula for writing a résumé. You need to take into account the industry, the type and seniority of the position, and any application form or job criteria for each job. Experts debate how many pages, whether to include names of referees and even if it's 'CV' or 'résumé' or even 'resume'. Here are a few overall comments that might be helpful.

- Tailor your résumé to each job application. Write a first-page summary drawing out the achievements, experiences and skills that most closely match that job description. Include a brief profile of who you are and a very brief career history.
- Give some thought to how you present your work experience. Lying is never appropriate or clever, but if you don't present yourself with your best foot forward, you won't even make it to an interview. Focus on achievements, strengths and successes, not a chronological list of job descriptions and duties. You have maybe 30 seconds to grab the reader's attention, so make sure you emphasise recent successes – unless that job you did 15 years ago has a compelling relevance, the barest information about it is enough.
- Look over the skills exercises in this book. The language used can be useful for describing your skills in a résumé, if you make them specific and business-like – for

example, say 'mentored seven staff members over two years' not 'helped people'. Use active verbs such as 'solving', 'managing', 'facilitating' and the like, and language that is as specific as possible: How many staff? What kind of project? What exactly did you do? Say 'managed over 1000 accounts receivable and payable accounts, liaising directly with the Chief Financial Officer' not 'maintained accounts receivable and accounts payable system'.

- Use a clean modern font such as Arial, Calibri or Helvetica. Unless you are a talented designer *and* going for a job in that industry, don't be cute – no fancy covers, multiple fonts or colours. If you don't have a good template, there are plenty of free ones available online.
- If there are job criteria or a duties statement in the advertisement, address these in your application, item by item. Don't just paraphrase their descriptions, give a real example of how you have used each skill.
- Don't put anything under 'interests' unless it is relevant to the job or you can wax lyrical about it on demand. But volunteering experience is always good, as it demonstrates skills and a willingness to work.

I spoke to job-seeking expert Anne-Marie Kane at Resumes for Results about her insights and tips for résumés of older workers, to help you navigate the modern minefield of job hunting. Here's our combined list:

1. Let go of old ways of thinking

It may be 20 years since you last put together a résumé or sat down with the local classified job ads and a cup of tea. Times have changed, and you need to change your techniques to match. Everything is done online now. Your résumé may be read first by an applicant-tracking system, scanning for keywords that relate to the role you're applying for. If you don't use the relevant keywords on the first page of your résumé, it may be binned without being seen by human eyes.

2. No dates, no photos

Anti-discrimination laws mean you don't need to put age, date of birth or photo on your résumé or job application. Don't share when you finished high school. You may be justifiably proud of your 40 years' experience, but avoid being so specific in your résumé – describe it as 'deep expertise' or 'being a seasoned executive'.

3. Be succinct

Your résumé should be no more than three pages, focusing on what is most relevant to the specific job requirements – you don't need to detail every job you've ever done, just the last two or three and any qualifications or earlier experience that may be useful for this role. Ideally, you'll submit it in PDF format as this keeps the layout stable. However, except with very small companies, it's likely your résumé will go to applicant-tracking software, which doesn't always scan PDFs, so check if you can – and if in doubt use a Word document instead of a PDF.

4. Flip your résumé to focus on achievements (not duties)

Think of your résumé as a way to explain the skills you can quickly transfer into a new role. To do that, you need to show them what you have achieved in the past for previous employers. Be specific – if you wrote a manual, ran a training program, doubled sales or won an award, make sure you mention it up front. List all your key achievements and skills on the front page, as that's where they'll be scanned to see if they match the position. If you're struggling to work out what your achievements are, think about what might happen in your workplace if you left your job tomorrow.

5. Show you invest time in your own development

It's important to keep your skills up to date, and you can do many reputable courses online for free or very little cost. Proving you have IT skills by completing an online course (whether in IT or not) may help overcome an assumption that older workers are less tech savvy.

Interview tips

Interviews can be scary, especially if you haven't done one for a while. But it might help to think that most are a conversation with someone about your skills and their job, with a focus on three areas:

- Do you have the skills and experience required to do the job?
- Do you fit into the company culture, do your values match those of the company and will you 'get' the work environment?
- Do they like you personally and could they work with you every day?

Here are my top tips:

1. Do your homework

Check your target employer's website, search online for their name (and the interviewer's if you know it), read their last annual report and interviews with the CEO or whatever else you can find. Think about their situation and be prepared to ask intelligent questions that show you're aware of their challenges and opportunities.

2. Look smart

I'm not going to give you fashion or styling tips, but there's no doubt that it's worth spending some time and money updating your look. An interviewer will judge you before you even open your mouth, and you can minimise negative or age-related assumptions by looking smart and contemporary. There's no need for a 'mutton-dressed-as-lamb' look, and in fact, trying to appear younger than your age can backfire. But if you're not sure how you come across, seek advice from a stylish friend or an expert. When I started to do more speaking and video work, I invested in a few hours with a stylist and it was worth every cent.

Check your body language so that you stand up straight, put your hands in a natural-looking place (not in your pockets or on your hips), make eye contact and smile. If you have a nervous fiddling habit, drill yourself out of it. If you learn to breathe slowly and steadily it will help you control all sorts of other mannerisms, such as a shaky voice or sweaty palms. If you're not sure how you come across, do a role play with a friend and have them give you feedback, or video yourself.

3. Answering questions

It is often suggested you should aim to talk for half the time in an interview and listen for the other half. Keep your replies informative but not rambling – about one to two minutes is a good guide. You have a lifetime of communication skills, common sense, wisdom, maturity and experience, so weave examples through your answers. Tell succinct stories that show a willingness to keep learning and a curiosity about new ways of doing things.

A word of caution: I know you have all this valuable experience, but it's also important not to be a know-it-all and disrespect your (probably) younger interviewer. Don't ram your experience down their throat, or use expressions like 'in my day'. Act as if age is irrelevant (because it should be). Show by how you talk and behave that you have no issue with younger people, that you're interested in trading your abilities, not your chronological age, and that you will easily fit into a team of others, irrespective of age.

4. Asking questions

You're trying to suss out whether this is the right work situation for you, so do ask questions about the things that matter to you, such as community involvement, training, friendliness of the workplace, opportunities to develop new skills or whatever. (Don't ask if you can have an overseas transfer in the first year, though ...)

5. What not to discuss

Don't discuss money or conditions at the first interview, unless they push you to give an estimate. In particular, if you need special arrangements (such as holiday leave in the first few months), wait until the stage when details are being finalised or you will risk looking difficult or half-hearted.

6. Ditch the anger

Don't whinge or get angry about your situation. Whatever your age, it's never a good look to approach the job hunt with this mindset, so do yourself a favour and deal with the feelings first. Find a counsellor to help you with this, or talk it through with a partner or friend. You need to be relaxed and 100 per cent enthusiastic when you begin looking for a new job.

7. Dealing with your age

You don't have to give your age at any stage of the interview process, even if asked directly. If you have to provide ID, try to find something that doesn't include your date of birth. If you're asked in an interview, deflect the question with something like, 'I'm energetic and committed, and intend to keep working for many years.'

Sometimes language may come across as outdated, so avoid saying things like 'back in the day', 'we used to use telex machines' or 'the young girls in the office'.

8. Act positive

Acting positive will improve your chances of landing a good job. Candidates who are proactive, upbeat, engaged and have an energetic 'can-do' attitude are more likely to get hired, whatever their age or experience.

9. Do your prep

Think about the questions you're likely to be asked and prepare answers. Find ways to weave in your successes and strengths, and to present your failures, weaknesses or gaps in experience in a positive light. Never bag a past employer, or betray confidential information (you knew that already, of course).

10. Tricky questions

There are two questions that often crop up with older candidates. The first is, 'Aren't you over-experienced?' Here it's useful to emphasise that you are interested, love working, keen to be involved but not looking to take over the joint (unless you are …). Stress the benefits you will bring to the team, and how much you enjoy being part of a multi-generational workplace.

The other big question is, 'Can you do digital?' and the answer must be 'Yes'. Make sure you're familiar with all things online, are across social media and then drop references to your use of online platforms during your interview. Emphasise that you love learning about new technology and using it, to deflect any assumptions about old dogs and new tricks.

Telling tales

In Chapter 4 you worked with your career story, and now you can apply that to telling stories in interviews or to creating your bio on LinkedIn, or to find the founding story for your business.

In the interview context, the most well-known story format is Situation, Action, Result, Benefit, or SARB. As it suggests, you tell a story about a work experience or demonstrate a skill by describing the situation, then the action you took, the result and finally, the benefit to your employer. It's good to develop a number of these vignettes, and practise them until they come easily. If each story takes about 60 seconds, that's perfect.

Claire Scobie, founder of the Wordstruck consultancy and author, gave me her tips for telling a great work story.

Claire Scobie's tips

1. Stories are very useful in a job interview

Stories show that you are still current, relevant and in-the-know. They position you and take away that little assumption that old people can't keep up. If you went into a job interview and said, 'I'm a really good leader' that won't wash, people will think you're talking yourself up or wonder, 'Where's the evidence?' Whereas if you had a story about being a marketing person in a big company when your boss was taken off sick suddenly and you had to roll out this huge marketing program, that would show leadership skills indirectly, also that you're someone who can step up, be creative and make this all happen in half the time. It's a way for people to 'get' you and feel like they know you quite quickly.

2. It's not something that you come up with overnight

Start in your childhood, your teen years, your 20s, looking for stories that show something that became a life theme. One client in his 50s ran leadership workshops in his teen years, and he uses that story to say, 'Since then that's been a theme throughout my life and I now really enjoy working with younger people to encourage their leadership skills.'

3. Choose what to foreground in your life

You can't change the events of your life, but you can choose what to highlight and what to leave in the background. Maybe you spent 10 years working in an office, but now that's not relevant because you're 58, about to set yourself up in business and you need money from the bank. Rather than emphasise the office work, you talk about other parts of your life which show you're very entrepreneurial. Particularly if you're going for lots of job interviews, think about having a bank of stories. Often the same story can have three or four different purposes.

4. Good stories normally have:

- A time marker, such as 'in 2010'.
- Characters (yourself or others) if possible, with names, because we connect more to a named individual than a faceless person.
- Some colour, a bit of description about how you were feeling at that time, so you're bringing in the senses. If you say, 'My stomach was churning as I went for the interview. I was 55 and terrified, I didn't know if I'd ever get another job again', that 'stomach churning' means we feel it, too.
- Something unanticipated. When you tell a story other people often lean towards you, and that's because they're being drawn into your story. So if you can have something unanticipated then they get the payoff, the result.

Exercise: Practicalities

This chapter has been all about the practicalities, so go back through the chapter and write down everything that seems relevant to you. Then turn each item into an action statement – so 'be more flexible' might become a list of three practical things you can do to investigate other industries you could explore for job opportunities.

This list of actions will feed straight into the action plan you will create in the next chapter.

CHAPTER 13

Time for action

The beginning is the most important part of the work.

Plato

Once you have come to a decision, and looked at the practicalities, it's time for an action plan. Most of you will already have a way of planning things that works for you, so I'm not going to cover the many methods of project planning. If you do want to improve your planning skills, just do an online search for 'project planning' and you will find a plethora of ideas to experiment with.

My major planning tools are mind maps combined with an app called Trello, which takes to-do lists to the extreme. I came to these by trying a heap of other ideas that didn't stick, mainly because they didn't mesh with how my mind works. That's the most important thing – to find a system that works with the way you think.

Overall, the way I look at creating new things in my life is resonant with the ideas of Robert Fritz, whose work I have loved and used for over 20 years. In 2011, I had the privilege of doing one of his week-long workshops in Vermont and it was a great treat. I highly recommend his books, such as *Path of Least Resistance*,[1] for a detailed examination of creating new things in your life.

What follows is my core model, which I have developed over 20 years. It started with an adaptation of some of Fritz's ideas on creation, coupled with some material from the well-known coaching GROW model (Goal, Reality, Obstacles/Options, Way forward), and is now thoroughly infused with years of experience with clients and creating my own projects, including this book.

My model has four stages:

- What do I want?
- Where am I now?
- How will I get there?
- How will I keep momentum?

Step 1: What do I want?

If you want to create something new in your life, the most important step is to first create a vision of it. Whether it's a work reinvention, a creative project or a whole life overhaul, success is far more likely if you first get really clear about what it is that you want. If the word 'vision' sounds airy-fairy, you can use 'goal', but only if you don't let it limit your thinking. This is the time to dream big, not to restrict your sense of what's possible.

Useful questions include:

- What is it I really want? What end result am I looking for? If you are not sure if your first answer is a final result, ask yourself, 'Why do I want it?' as that may lead you deeper.
- How will I know when I have it? What will my life look like? Make this as clear as you can – what will it look like, feel like, sound and smell like, what are all the elements of the end picture? The more detail, the better.

If you jump over this step and start from process ('How will I get there?'), you limit yourself to what you already know and cut off wider possibilities. So, if you want a new job, don't start by looking at job advertisements. First, imagine your working life when you have a great job, think about what would make you feel satisfied and happy, like the 'three futures' exercise in Chapter 10.

This is not wishful thinking or playing with pixie dust – it's very hard to reach what you don't aim for. Of course, some things aren't possible, but they are a lot fewer than you might think, and you can't know which ones are impossible and which are not at this stage of the process. Go for it all now, and let practicalities take care of themselves for a while. Even if your end result is a variation on the original vision, you'll end up with a much more satisfying future than if you had compromised at the start.

As much as possible, have a blank canvas – pretend you have no idea already of what you think is possible, or what you have done before. Try to cultivate what the Buddhists call 'beginner's mind', because if your mind is full of what you already know, there's no room for anything new.

This book starts with the section called 'Reimagine' for this reason, so that you can get your imagination firing, envisaging lots of possible new futures before looking at the practical nitty-gritty. I know from working with hundreds of clients that it's vital to allow big dreams. I promise all my clients that we will end up with a practical plan at the end, but it's critical that they don't limit themselves at the start. The same is true for you – if you haven't let yourself imagine the best possible life, do so now.

Step 2: Where am I now?

After your vision is as clear as you can make it and truly tantalising so you really want it to happen, you might think the next step is to make an action plan, but actually it's important to first get clear about the reality of your current situation.

Often we try to ignore reality, such as the fact that you don't yet have the skills or the money to do a particular project. However, unless you can accept how things are right now, you can't successfully move on to create something different in the future. For each vision you create, or each major goal, ask yourself the following:

- What is my reality in relation to this goal or vision currently *really* like?
- What's working for me in these areas right now?
- What's not working for me in these areas right now?
- What needs to change?
- What useful tools, skills and qualities do I already have?
- What tools, skills and qualities do I need to develop or outsource?

Section 2 of this book (Review) is all about your present reality – looking at your life situation, your strengths and skills, interests, identity, purpose and much more. We spend quite a bit of time on this so that you end up with a clear map of your assets and your limitations.

This process of Step 1 (What do I want?) and Step 2 (Where am I now?) worked very well for my client Ahmad, who had been a cook on a big mining site for some years, but wanted to change careers. He had quit his job and was very unsure what might be next. As we went through Step 1 together, I encouraged him to dream big, and he did. He told me he'd always wanted to build space stations (as in actual stations, in actual space). He was keen, but looking at Step 2, it became clear that Ahmad had neither the desire nor the aptitude to undertake the long formal studies that would be necessary to join a space program.

We talked more about his dream, and over a couple of long, structured conversations, we looked in detail at why he wanted to build space stations, and when we drilled down we realised that what Ahmad really loved to do was to create something from scratch, starting with an empty canvas and ending with a new creation that would make people happy. (Interestingly, this description also fitted his work as a cook, and it is often true that when you drill down into a life theme, it covers several activities that otherwise look quite disparate.)

We then went back to his strengths and interests, to see how he could apply this theme to a practical field of work. One of Ahmad's top interests was plants and nature, whether it was herbs and vegetables for cooking, walking in a national park, or digging in his garden. We explored the area of landscape gardening, as it was a perfect fit for creating something from scratch that would make people happy. Ahmad did some research and experiments to see what training he would need, what the work would be like day to day and the likely job prospects. He became very excited about this idea, and the last I knew of him he was working as a gardener while studying landscape gardening at TAFE.

Step 3: How will I get there?

Now you have a vision and a clear idea of your present situation in relation to that vision, you can start to list the actions that will bridge the gap and get you to where you want to go. This listing process is the simplest form of project planning and one that we all have used, if only to create a shopping list or a to-do list of chores.

Your project plan may be fairly complete, especially if you have done some research and experimenting along the way. However, if there are gaps, steps that are hazy, don't worry. It isn't necessary to see every step right now, and in fact, it's likely that actions will change as you move towards your goals, so it can be a trap to over-plan. You need to have a direction and some steps in place, but not to be too constricted by your sense of how it will happen.

Once you've created your action steps, you can ask yourself: if I did all these steps, would I get to my vision? If the answer is 'No', see if it is your vision or the action steps that need to change. If you don't know which just yet, stay curious as to how you can find the answers as you proceed.

Section 3 of this book (Research) supports Step 3 by helping you get clear about what's actually involved in your new work idea, and what actions you need to take. Then this chapter and the previous one help you create your action plan.

Step 4: How will I keep momentum?

Now that you have your plan, you start moving from here to there. You do this by working the tension between your picture of where you are right now and your picture of where you want to be. We're all familiar with this tension, as it arises whenever we have a gap between what we want and what we currently have.

The simplest example is that feeling when we realise we are hungry but for whatever reason don't want to or can't eat immediately. A more complex example is the tension when we need a job but don't have one, or are unhappy in our current work but haven't found a new plan. The act of creating this tension (through Steps 1–3) starts to move you towards your vision.

Exercise: Your plan

If you haven't already, it's time to create a written plan for your next stage. The easiest way to do this is to write detailed answers to each of the four questions in my model, using the tips suggested in the matching section for each question earlier in this chapter:

- What do I want?
- Where am I now?
- How will I get there?
- How will I keep momentum?

Be as clear as possible, but don't worry if there are gaps. Don't leave out the bits you don't like doing or find difficult, and do check your actions are specific and achievable, even if they are challenging. If you can, add some due dates as this is extremely motivating and helps ensure your plans are realistic. It's also useful to have a trusted friend or adviser 'sanity check' your plan and help you spot gaps or places where you are either playing small or being over-optimistic about what's possible.

If you like, you can create a spreadsheet or to-do list for each phase or time period. Twenty years ago now, my very first coaching client created a plan for her life change that involved several sheets of cardboard taped together, on which she stuck the most comprehensive spreadsheet I have ever seen. It had multiple rows for every month, which she then broke into weeks and categorised into areas like 'work', 'family', 'decisions' and many more. She used a complex system of colour coding and symbols to identify various themes and updated it daily using tiny sticky notes.

Every session, she would unroll her chart on the floor and we would track her progress together. It was complex, intricate and far more detailed than I could have created (or would have found useful). But it was exactly what she needed to successfully reinvent herself. So, as you develop your plan, adapt it to suit your way of thinking and make it so that you look forward to using it as you reinvent your work.

Paul, 57

Paul was made redundant in his 50s and developed a job-search plan that played to his strengths and personality. He went beyond passively responding to job ads – and it paid off.

I was at a media company for 17 years, for the last 12 as head of internal audit. I was made redundant at 55. I had already noticed that I had a number of friends who were finding it difficult to find a new job and, although no one ever said it, there seemed to be some type of ageism in the recruitment process.

I had never been out of a job before, so I looked forward to the opportunity of having some time where I didn't have to work, but I knew I wanted to get back to work so I made a plan that in the afternoons I was going to concentrate on getting a job.

I went to an outplacement firm a few times. They were quite helpful, especially in getting me prepared for job interviews – which I hadn't actually done since 1996. I got my LinkedIn profile updated, they showed me how to include words in my title that would come up in searches.

Every day I'd check what jobs were on offer. I'd ring up the employment agencies and say, 'Hi, Paul here, just checking to see if there's anything that's come up, anything in the pipeline?' to keep the contacts rolling over. Even coming into town and meeting with old colleagues and having a cup of coffee and saying, 'I'm here looking, just in case you find anything' just to keep my name front of mind.

I had a couple of interviews but they never seemed to go anywhere. Again, did I think it was ageist? I think it was. So to expand my horizons, because I'd been in the corporate world all my life, I opened myself up to public service opportunities because I knew ageism isn't as much of a problem there.

It's very easy to get disheartened and just rely on a daily online prompt that tells you what jobs are available and decide nothing is suitable. You need to get out and talk to people and meet with people, to actually cold call. I read the *Financial Review* to find companies that had problems. As an auditor, I look after governance and compliance and controls, and for example, there was one business that was having problems – they were having profit downgrades – so I found a connection who knew someone there and I got them to introduce me to the CFO. I went to him and said, 'Okay, here I am, I've got this skill set, I notice you're having problems. If you need me I'm here, willing to come up and contract with you for a set fee to set up your function, etcetera.'

So they're the types of things I did, being proactive. Having a plan was really important to me.

I did try to look more modern when I went to an interview or meeting. I wore my most modern suit rather than just a black suit with a white shirt.

Having not been through an interview process for a long time, you need to prepare, you need to know what your achievements are, and what you can achieve for them. It's no good saying that I've had 25 years' experience doing internal audits; you've got to sell yourself, 'Well, I can build an internal audit function from scratch, set up all the procedures, the methodologies, all the structures and the systems, and I can do that within the first hundred days and have the function running smoothly within six months' or whatever.

Just before Christmas I saw an ad for a job in the New South Wales public service for a head of internal audit and I submitted an application. I followed my strategy and nearly two-and-a-half months later I was offered the job. That's where I am now.

Personal environments

If you need to make big changes in your life, you may want to take your planning to another level and develop personal structures or environments that help to make it easier to succeed than to fail. It's about orienting your whole life around your vision or goals.

You might think change is about willpower, but in fact willpower is just about the worst-ever way to try to change your life. Resolutions based on willpower just set up an internal war between the part of you that wants to change, and the part that wants to stay doing things the old way – and inertia being the powerful force it is, the odds are heavily stacked in favour of the status quo. Willpower can be a powerful kick-starting force but has great limitations as your main tool for change.

There is an easier way. Rather than trying to modify your behaviour, go deeper and take a look at the underlying structures and environments in your life, such as your home environment, the people you hang out with, the way you start your day and many other things. We've built these structures over many years (or fallen into existing structures and made them ours) and often we're not even aware they're there. These environments, habits and belief systems come to run our lives, and any effort at change is largely doomed if we don't take them into account.

The best place to make lasting and profound change in our lives is at this level. If you change the structures, you create a new underlying channel that will make it easier to succeed than to fail, and you won't need nearly as much effort or willpower to introduce and maintain changes. You'll no longer be fighting yourself.

Many people believe that by changing your behaviour, you automatically change the underlying environments and structures of your life. In fact, the reverse is true – first change the structures and then your behaviour will change with much less effort. If you have a big goal like changing careers or setting up a new business, start with the frameworks and structures through which you live. This way you can create systems around you that make it easier to achieve your dream than not to achieve your dream.

The trick is to set things up so that the environment pulls you towards your goal. Great athletes, writers and successful people of all kinds set up their lives so they live their dream 24/7 and make favourable outcomes much more likely. When I decided to make the writing of this book a priority project, I structured my life around that goal. I changed my workspace, only saw clients on certain days, scheduled in long walks, cut down on many activities, booked a couple of writing weeks away, made sure I had the right software (Scrivener, it's brilliant) and found ways to spend less time cooking and cleaning.

We can't all be single-minded about our project (I still had family, friends and clients who were important to me), but we can systematically go through every area of our life and make it work for us as much as possible. Once you start to focus on this, it is amazing how many elements of your life you can control, how much you can change or modify to pull yourself towards your vision. It's a combination of bringing in all the things that support your goals (for example, blocking off diary time each day to work on your plans) and removing all the things that don't (clearing out all the junk from the spare room so it can be your office). It doesn't have to cost big money – you can be creative with it and still achieve great results.

I heard about a woman who started piano lessons at 63. She plays music all the time, goes to concerts, puts up posters of composers and performers, rents a piano for her living room, has oriented her time, focus and life as much as is practical around her dream, so that in two years she has become very skilled in what was a lifelong dream. You can do it, too.

It's not about being the most talented person or having 24 hours a day and a million dollars to devote to your dreams. It's about choosing to live differently, one bit, one day, at a time. We create our lives in every minute, so why not choose to create the work and life you really want?

Exercise: Changing your environments

Have a look at these – what are five ways you could enhance each of these parts of your life to help you reach your goals?
- Physical: home, office, possessions, clothes, lighting, sounds, air, visual elements.
- Self: body, food and drink, exercise, values, energy, feelings, wellbeing.
- Relationships: friends, family, supporters, time wasters.
- Ideas: new ideas, reflection, concepts, mental stimulation.
- Networks: social, clients, online, colleagues, support.
- Money: assets, debt, income, savings, financial planning.
- Creativity: space, outlets, activities.
- What other environments are important to you?

Exercise: Your personal vision

Some people are keen on vision statements and some think they are beyond tacky. As I sit somewhere in between these extremes,

I offer an optional exercise here to take your work in this chapter into another form and create a vision statement for yourself. This is more than your vision for your work, as it encompasses all of life and goes beyond the pragmatic and into the philosophical.

Ideally it will be pretty concise, say up to 100 words, 150 maximum. It will be simple and easy to memorise and it will serve as a guiding principle for your future actions. If you search online you'll find plenty of tips and examples.

You could write a free-form vision that starts with words such as, 'My vision for my life is ...'

Or you could give it more structure by using a template like this:

- I am a [describe yourself through your values, e.g., kind, creative, logical] person who cares about [e.g., family, helping others, the environment].
- I want to [insert your vision or major goals here].
- I am living a life [e.g., in the country or with my family or around my values or ...].
- My life is meaningful or satisfying because ...

Personal brand

Part of your action plan should include how you present yourself to others, as it's an essential part of changing careers or finding a new job. However, I need to start this discussion with a confession: until recently, I was not a fan of the whole personal-brand thing. You know, where you think of yourself as if you were a brand, like Telstra or Qantas, and you see your job hunt as a marketing exercise. It seemed just a bit contrived to me, like an endless selfie.

I still believe caution is required, but I have come around to the concept. One of the main triggers for my change of heart was working with Scarlett Vespa, who is an expert at this personal-brand stuff.

Vespa says everyone has a personal brand, whether they like it or not. 'You know, you wear it, you express it, you talk it; it's there all the time. The question I always ask people is, "What are you selling in your personal brand?" and making sure they take ownership of that. Personal branding is literally your image, how you relate. Ultimately, it's how you emotionally connect and how people emotionally connect with you.'

So, are you a Fiat or a Ferrari? A Mac or a PC?

Vespa has a model for working with personal branding, in four sections.

Scarlett Vespa's model

1. Values and beliefs

This is about acknowledging your values and beliefs, which we looked at in Section 2.

2. Practical skills

What can you do that people will pay money for? Again, we have looked at this, in Chapter 6. Vespa emphasises that you should think outside the box here, and really dig down to find those transportable skills. You need to work with what's true, so for example, if you have no tertiary education, stress that you are a hard worker and a fast learner.

3. Physical appearance

Relax, we are not talking about plastic surgery, weight loss or even 6 a.m. gym classes. This area involves authenticity and self-acceptance first, then making the most of yourself with a great haircut, stylish clothes, accessories and a big smile. I tend to tell my clients that your skills matter more than the colour of your tie, but there's no doubt that first impressions are critical, too. As Vespa says, 'In an environment where people wear very casual clothes, someone may say, "Look, clothing's not important to me, it's all about my talent." But what that can communicate to others is, "I don't care about myself and how I look, therefore I'm not going to care about my clients and how they look."'

Of course, different working environments have different dress codes – you wouldn't show up to an interview for a job as a children's soccer coach dressed like a corporate banker. But your image does communicate, so you have to be very literal and ask yourself, 'What am I saying with my nail polish or the style of my shoes? What am I communicating? Is that the best I can be, and is it appropriate for the environment I will be in?'

At the end of the day, you'll be selected for a job based on deeper qualities than nail-polish choice (unless you're going for a job selling cosmetics). But if you don't pay attention to first impressions, you may never get to the final short list.

4. Emotional disposition

In this area you look at your emotional self and identify what is true for you. Are you fearful or confident? A risk-taker or more cautious? Are you a 'yes' person or more opinionated? If there are aspects of you that don't fit with your brand and are hindering your attempts to get the job you want, think about how you can work with them to become more positive. For example, if you think of yourself as a 'yes' person, could you start to reframe that towards being positive and flexible? If you're fearful, could that be recast as being aware of challenges and ready to meet them? And if you don't trust easily, it's likely you're also very responsible, which is a much more attractive way to think about this aspect of you. This can be a difficult area to work on by yourself, so you may wish to seek help from a coach or trusted friend.

Exercise: Brand audit

This exercise may feel premature if you're not sure of your new career direction, but it's useful to do it now and fine-tune it as your new career starts to come into focus.

- Mark up a large sheet of paper into four quarters, one for each of Vespa's four dimensions of personal brand. Under each heading, write down words that convey your brand identity in that area. Aspirational is good, fantasy is not. As an example, for physical appearance I could never write 'model thin' or 'young' and so it would be a waste of time and energy for me to yearn in those directions. But what I can focus on and work towards are things like 'stylish', 'wise' and 'confident'. That gives me a great guide for ways I can polish myself.
- Make sure the content of each quadrant is consistent – it's quite damaging to your brand if your physical appearance screams 'utterly self-assured' and your emotional demeanour says 'scared rabbit'.
- Make an action list for the things that need work. This might include items as diverse as 'get a haircut', 'read a book on confidence' or 'do a course in project management to bridge a skills gap'.
- Do the things on your action list.

Getting your personal brand right can make a huge difference to how consistent and memorable you are when you meet new people.

A final warning: authenticity is vital in creating your personal brand, and most people can smell a fake a mile off. Even if you could fool an interviewer, remember that you would then have to act out that persona every day on the job.

Networking

Once you have your personal brand sorted, it's time to take it on the road. This means networking.

People sometimes turn up their noses at networking or find the idea more terrifying than being locked in a room with 20 spiders. Possibly this used to be me. But if you want to take charge of your working life, the reality is that networking is not optional. Some estimate that 60 per cent of jobs are never advertised, maybe more, so pull out those business cards, brush up on your small talk, and off we go.

It doesn't have to be horrific, I promise ...

One warning, however. Networking is not an instant fix to be activated only when you're looking for a job. Networks take time to build and are based on relationships and reciprocity – getting to know people and focusing first on what you can do for them. Manipulative or inauthentic networking is a real turn-off and quite counter-productive.

Networking is not just about getting jobs; it's also excellent for finding information about companies that appreciate older workers, having a sounding board for a current dilemma, seeking out training opportunities or just hanging out with people who actually understand your working world.

Social media should be part of your networking plan. Most people know someone who got a job or a piece of work or a good contact through an online network, and recruitment firms and employers looking to hire use it frequently. Check out the sites that fit your needs, industry and available time, but at the very least, you must be on LinkedIn. Making contributions to blogs in your area of interest is a very good strategy, and depending where you're headed, you could even start your own blog. I've also read a number of articles recently that talk about building an online portfolio or résumé through creating a simple website. Depending on your field, it might be a place to collect your résumé, testimonials and other information, or to show samples of your work, or even be really creative.

LinkedIn tips

1. Create your professional profile

Write a succinct summary of your most recent job history, including achievements and key skills for which your connections can endorse you. Include a recent professional photo that reflects how you look in the workplace, not on holiday.

2. Include job-related keywords

It's important to include job-related keywords and summary sections that will help potential contacts or employers find you.

3. Connect with everyone you know

This includes friends, ex-colleagues, old employers, people from school or university.

4. Ask for recommendations

Don't be shy, it only takes your connections a few minutes and it adds a lot of credibility.

5. Join groups

Join industry groups or those in an interest area, make comments and share knowledge, be part of the conversation.

6. Research organisations you'd like to work for

Do this by following their company pages. You can get information on their employee policies, who is coming and going, and any 'connections of connections' you could be introduced to.

Our world is a series of relationships. 'Six degrees of separation' is a cliché now, but it was based on scientific research showing that we can reach anyone on the planet in only six connections, often less. Even if your first contact can't help you, they may well know someone who can and be willing to connect you with them. We saw earlier in this chapter how Paul activated existing connections and created new ones to maximise his chances of job-hunting success.

Formal networking groups abound, and are often tailored to age groups, industries or locations. If you feel uncomfortable going alone, take a friend, but don't spend all night in a corner talking only to him or her. Informal networking (through family, sporting clubs, gyms, friends and so on) may be the best way of all to forge links, as it's based on common interests and connections, and may feel less stressful and more authentic.

Suzy Jacobs, She Business founder, is one of the best networkers I know so I asked her for some tips. Jacobs makes the excellent point that networks occur in different parts of your life – such as professional, social, family, sporting clubs or hobby groups – and it's worth exploring all of them.

Younger people have grown up with the online space, so it's absolutely natural for them to use it for networking, whether social or for business. We older people may see networking much more as face to face, but the first thing people do when you meet them is check you out on LinkedIn. As Jacobs says, 'If somebody rings me, I'm already online searching them and generally straight into LinkedIn while we're talking. So, you must have an up-to-date LinkedIn profile at the very least and then you might have a personal website.'

If networking is not something you've incorporated consistently throughout your life you may be apprehensive about where to go to create networks, and how to know which one to choose. When I started my business, I visited numerous networking groups before I found two that offered me the sense of having a tribe and the contacts that I was looking for. Although you will need to shop around, Jacobs rightly points out, 'the biggest trap for new networkers is being random, being social and not valuing your time. Networking can be brilliant, but not if you're going out every night and spending money on a ticket, and spending your time without thinking about a return on your investment. Handing out business cards in a haphazard way can lead to a lot of nothingness and be quite disappointing, so we need to be strategic'.

Suzy Jacobs' tips

1. Have a buddy

You'll need a partner who's supporting you on your journey. Who can be a support team for you going out and achieving this goal?

2. Don't make a vast plan

One activity, one result you're looking for, that is a really valuable use of your time. Sit down with somebody who knows you well in a professional sense and work out one thing you're looking to achieve, and then together work out who might be useful.

3. Be persistent

Don't be put off if the first few don't go well. Acknowledge yourself, congratulate yourself that you actually got on the bus, got to the networking event. Go back home and regroup, get your support team around you and go back out again.

4. Focus on others

Being interested in what the other person does is important. Listen for the opportunity to be able to give back. It may be something unrelated to what you're talking about, but really listen for that opportunity. It's about building a relationship.

5. Be prepared

Take the time to do some background work before you walk into that networking event.

6. Make your meetings very specific

Ask them for 15 minutes of their time, particularly if they're busy, and really keep it structured.

7. Say thanks

Always deliver an email of thanks or a phone call. And if something comes from that meeting or you make headway, let them know. You're developing a network where ongoing conversation is important.

8. Focus your efforts

Aim for networks in three key areas: personal growth, professional development, support and accountability.

Exercise: Your networks

Try this exercise to see what networks you already belong to and how you might deepen those relationships:

Step 1

- Draw two circles, one inside the other. In the inside circle take some time to write down all the clubs, groups, organisations, communities and circles of friends of which you are part.
- Then, in the outside circle, write down all the people who are leaders or influential in those groups.
- In the space outside the bigger circle, write down all the clubs, groups, organisations, communities and circles of friends that these people are (or you think might be) connected to.

Step 2

- Repeat the process with new circles for your business networks.

Step 3

- Now, have a look at the two maps. What do you notice? Are there any connections you would like to deepen? How could you do that?
- What are three steps you could take to find out more about these connections and/or deepen some of them?

CHAPTER 14

Showstoppers

*The first rule is to keep an untroubled spirit. The second is
to look things in the face and know them for what they are.*
Marcus Aurelius

It's tempting to think that all you need is a plan and a goal, and
everything will be fine. But in fact, the challenge often lies in
keeping momentum, overcoming the things that sneak up and
derail your best efforts, like the inner critic, procrastination,
anxiety and beliefs about yourself and your ability to change.
We're going to meet these potential showstoppers in this chapter
and look at very practical strategies to handle them before they
have a chance to stop *your* show.

The inner critic

Do you have a little voice that pops up in your mind with criticisms
or dire warnings such as 'If you try that, you will fail', 'Everyone
will laugh', 'You're not clever', or 'Don't be ridiculous'? You could
call this voice the inner critic, or the voice of doubt. We are all
particularly open to inner-critic attacks when starting something
new. Anything that is risky or outside your current comfort zone is
likely to arouse the curiosity of your critic. By definition, if you're
thinking about crafting a new approach to your work and life, the
inner critic will want to offer an opinion.

If you don't learn how to put the critic in its place, it can rule your life, keeping you very safe but also keeping you from learning and growing and trying something new, such as starting your own business or asking for more flexible work arrangements. You may never be able to silence the critic permanently, but you can most definitely stop it conducting your orchestra, you can send it to the back row and relegate it to an occasional crash of cymbals.

It's helpful to distinguish between the inner critic and the inner editor. There comes a stage when you need some discernment about your ideas, but then you need your inner editor, that part of you who makes objective and specific comments about what will actually work and what won't. The editor is pertinent and helpful. The critic makes generalised ('You will *never* do this right', '*Everyone* will laugh') and negative comments, often showing up in our most vulnerable moments, such as at 3 a.m., just before you quit your job or as you're about to pitch your business idea to an investor.

Tips for dealing with the inner critic
Some of these ideas may sound a little strange, but as we have just agreed that you have inner voices trying to control you, please go with me this one step further and try some of these tips, as they may change your life. I've tried all of them and they've certainly changed mine.

1. Study your critic's habits
Start to notice patterns – are you most open to your critic when tired, hungry or stressed, or when you're alone or lonely? When does it pop up, what does it say? Does it comment more in a particular area of your life such as work, social activities or when you are trying something new? What does it want? How does it contribute to your life? How does it limit you?

Think of it like studying the habits of a wild creature. If you were to make a David Attenborough–style documentary called *The Habits of My Inner Critic*, what would it feature?

2. Deal firmly with the voice

When you are aware of a voice of doubt, deal with it as you would a stranger offering advice. Thank it for giving you its opinion and politely ask it to leave. Point out that it is not in charge of you. Imagine it moving away, like a voice coming from a far-off room.

3. Give your critic a hearing

You can try journal writing – maybe writing down your thoughts, or writing a dialogue with the critic. You can write a statement like, 'I am able to change my life' and notice if an objection comes up, 'No you aren't' or whatever. Write it out, all the comments, voices and feelings, however silly they sound. You can do this once a day for as long as you like – eventually the critic starts to get bored, its objections are exhausted and you are freer.

4. Turn your mind off, and your body on

Physical work (cleaning out cupboards, washing windows, gardening) or movement (walking, gym, swimming, dance) can be very effective. Just watch out if you find you are spending all day at these tasks – you may have swapped your inner critic for your inner procrastinator.

5. Put it in its place

You can dispute the correctness of its conclusions by pointing out an occasion when you did display creativity or when your project did succeed, but please avoid getting sucked into a long point-by-point argument with it, as this will only reinvest it with power over you.

6. Bribe it with some quality time

If the voice comes at an inconvenient time like the middle of the night or during an important meeting, you can make an appointment with yourself to hear it out at a later (specific) time such as 10 a.m. In the meantime, visualise yourself putting the voice in a bucket and closing the lid. This technique sounds a bit mad, but it's extremely effective.

7. Develop your own strategies

After all, you know your critic better than anyone else – what would best put it in its place? Experiment and develop a personal toolkit.

However you handle it, make it clear that the inner critic no longer dominates your decision-making process. It's time to take charge and deal with it, so you can move forward into a more satisfying life.

Procrastination

Procrastination is a devilish problem for many people. Often we start a project full of optimism and drive, then after a while, sometimes only a very little while, momentum slows down and we find almost anything else is more important. What is going on here, and how do we keep things moving?

Procrastination falls into two broad categories: skill-based and feeling-based. Skill-based or task-based procrastination is easier to deal with. It usually comes down to one of these:

- poor time management, an inaccurate sense of time available or needed
- not knowing how to prioritise
- too much to do
- not having the necessary skills or knowledge
- the task being irrelevant or not meaningful
- lack of problem-solving skills
- not understanding what is required.

Once you identify the issue, there are plenty of resources, such as books, internet sources or more experienced colleagues, to help you handle this.

Feeling-based procrastination is a decidedly sneakier beast. Types include:

- anxiety about the task, so you spend time worrying rather than doing
- difficulty concentrating
- feeling overwhelmed
- fearing the unknown, not knowing how you'll manage
- fearing failing or not meeting your own standards
- worrying about not meeting external standards (family, peers)
- fearing success
- setting unrealistic standards, perfectionism
- avoiding things you dislike or find boring or hard.

The underlying psychological reasons can be many and varied but generally come down to some kind of fear – be it fear of failure, fear of moving outside one's comfort zone, fear of ridicule, fear of risk-taking or even fear of success.

Tips for dealing with procrastination

1. Put it away

If you are blocked with a specific project, and time allows, put the project away for a week. Don't let yourself do anything connected with it at all.

2. Try something new

Try something new, like listening to different music or taking a walk somewhere you've never been. Follow your impulses and see where you end up.

3. Do something else

Do some simple and mechanical tasks like housework, cleaning out a cupboard, organising your office or gardening. This gets you moving, lets you start and finish something, gives a sense of achievement, tires you out and takes your mind off things.

4. Move your body

Get moving – dance, walk, swim, jiggle, shake. Feelings exist in the body and they can be shifted by moving the body and letting the feelings find a way out.

5. Explore the feelings

Stop for a moment, relax, and explore what you're feeling. Is it feeling overwhelmed, pressured, frustrated, indecisive, anxious, panicked? Whatever it is, accept the feeling. You can journal, walk with it, breathe through it, meditate – there are many ways through this, but naming the feeling and accepting it are crucial.

6. Do it anyway

This one seems like the opposite of the first suggestion, but is equally useful. Notice that you have feelings about the project, be gentle with them, but do the work anyway. Whatever it takes. Separating feelings from work has been a huge breakthrough for many people, myself included.

7. Follow that whim

If impulses arise, follow them. What looks at first like a detour may be exactly where you need to go next, or may give you information or ideas that will help you when you resume your project.

8. Baby steps

When you feel ready to get back to your project, or if you have a deadline and can't wait for inspiration to strike, then try taking baby steps. When trekking in the Himalayas, I was told that the way over a seemingly endless mountain crossing was 'baby steps, baby steps' and it is a very powerful way to get from here to there.

Just do a very little bit of your project – open a book, find that phone number, sharpen the pencil – then leave it for an hour or a day, then do the next step and so on. It's simple but it really does work. Try doing five minutes at the same time each morning, and five minutes at the same time each night, which sounds like nothing but can add up to real progress over a relatively short time. And quite often you end up so engrossed in your project that you just keep going with it anyway.

9. Bribery
Bribe yourself: do 30 minutes on the dreaded project and then have the reward.

10. Move your attention away
Whatever else you do, don't talk endlessly about the procrastination or focus on it as an issue – it just gives it energy and importance. Find something more compelling to do for a while, then slowly, slowly start again.

Anxiety

When you're anxious, it's very difficult to think clearly. You can't make sensible decisions about small things, let alone real dilemmas, and your perspective can become quite distorted. The ability to be creative or innovative is badly compromised when you are frightened, and if fear or even low-level anxiety persists over time your whole being can suffer.

Tips for dealing with anxiety

Here are some effective strategies for dealing with anxiety and worry.

1. A cuppa with a friend

It's very useful to talk through your worries with a friend, to get a caring but objective view on your problem. Maybe it's all just in your head, or maybe not, but either way sharing your concerns is a very good thing.

2. Worst case

Ask yourself: what is the worst that could happen here? Often it is not nearly as bad as you are thinking. Most worries are based on our fears of the unknown, so once we bring things into a real-world scenario, we can develop strategies to combat likely events. It is much easier to deal with the devil you know.

3. Make an appointment with yourself

Set aside a time for worrying then put it out of your mind until that time arrives. For chronic anxieties, you may need to give yourself 10 minutes every day at the same time.

4. Do what you can

Decide whether in fact there is something you can do about the issue – if so, do it, and if not, get on with those parts of your life that *are* working for you. Render order from chaos in some corner of your world, even if it is not the corner where your dilemma lurks.

5. Sitting with it

If your anxiety is the I'm-anxious-because-I-don't-know-if-this-will-work-out type, the sitting with uncertainty that is inherently part of the creative process, try these:

- Take small steps, baby steps, towards your destination.
- Be aware that you are not alone, anyone who has created something new for themselves has dealt with at least some of these issues.
- Find some like-minded souls – join a group, a business start-up course, a relevant club.
- Don't burn your bridges all at once – keep at least a foothold in your safe, known world.
- Find a mentor, someone who has been where you are now.

6. Breathe

Simple breathing can be very helpful in calming the physical symptoms of anxiety. Focus on deeply exhaling rather than on deeply inhaling, which can cause hyperventilation.

7. Relax

Relaxation techniques, such as progressive muscle relaxation, can be very useful. I am a great fan of meditation, and there are plenty of places where you can learn techniques ranging from relaxation to spiritual meditation.

8. Get help

If your anxiety is serious and affecting your quality of life, find a competent therapeutic practitioner to work with you.

Spend some time trying these strategies, but also think about things you already know that help you manage your anxieties, which may include planning your day properly, slowing down and doing less, prayer, getting enough sleep, eating properly or taking a good long walk every day.

Limiting beliefs

We all have a tape inside our heads that contains our beliefs about our world. Many of them were laid down long ago, and should be brought out and checked against the light of day from time to time, as they may no longer be useful to you.

Some of them were almost literally absorbed with your baby food, some from school, our society or early-life experience. How many people were told by their first teacher that they couldn't draw and still believe that today? Did your mother tell you that you shouldn't trust people, or your father explain that the only definition of success was a uni degree and a good salary? Did you absorb a message from the world around you that to be acceptable you needed a great body, a fast car or a big bank balance?

You may think that some of these aren't beliefs but are how the world really is. In fact, the more desperately we feel a need to defend a view like, 'Everyone knows that people can't be trusted', the more likely it is to be a belief, rather than an objective observation of reality.

Some beliefs are useful, such as, 'I can be really determined' or 'Life usually works out okay', but others like, 'I never finish things' or 'No one helps me' are not.

Tips for dealing with limiting beliefs
Here are some ideas for dealing with beliefs that are holding you back.

1. Get clear
The first step in changing beliefs is to get really clear on them – what actually are your perspectives and attitudes? Only then can you start changing those that no longer serve you. What are some of your beliefs about work? About success? About change? What do you believe about risk-taking? About the importance of

money? Think about your beliefs about work. Are they useful? Are they true?

2. Write about them

Take several sheets of paper and just write out all your beliefs on, say, getting older, for at least 10 minutes. If you run out of your own beliefs, write down things other people believe about age – the main thing is to keep going, no matter what. Read over the list and start to see that these are only concepts, some of which can easily be disproved and many of which are contradictory.

3. See things differently

Once you start reflecting on beliefs, you've started the process of detaching your beliefs from your sense of self, and started to see that they are only filters through which we see reality, not reality itself. If you can think of your belief systems like tinted glasses you can put on or take off, then you may start to see how much these attitudes colour your view of the world, rather than colouring the world itself.

4. Do a reality check

While beliefs are not reality, if you act as if they are, you'll create a life that fits with them. If you believe you're a loser, you are likely to behave as such, and it becomes a self-fulfilling prophecy. If you believe you're confident and attractive, you'll walk, talk and act that way and vastly increase the likelihood of others seeing you that way as well. Try it and see for yourself. Play the part for an hour or a day and see if anything in your world changes. Treat it as an adventure or an experiment – the results may surprise you.

5. What if the belief is true?

You may hold beliefs that have some objective truth, but which you would like to change. If you believe that you can't solve difficult problems, and on testing it seems that you really do lack this skill, then find a course, read a book or do whatever it takes to become more skilled at problem-solving, then test the belief again.

6. Sidestepping

One of the best ways to deal with ingrown beliefs is to sidestep them, to agree that this is your belief but go ahead with your plans anyway and thus slowly create a reality that challenges or even conflicts with the belief, so it loses some of its power over you.

It's quite possible to continue to hold beliefs that you know have no basis in fact. Alice may have wondered at the queen being able to believe six impossible things before breakfast, but we humans can easily believe plenty more than six contradictory things and, as long as you don't let this limit or paralyse you, all will be well. If somewhere deep inside you continue to believe you are not creative but still regularly let yourself do creative things in the world, then the belief is not controlling your life and will probably eventually starve for lack of oxygen.

A warning: for most of us, relying on affirmations just highlights the gap between the affirmation and our current state of belief and may also bring your inner critic sniffing around. If you do use them, it's much better to go with, 'I am moving in the direction of [my goal]' rather than 'I am fabulous'.

7. You don't have to go it alone

Beliefs can be very deeply held and difficult to change overnight or without help. Be patient with yourself, and if you find the going tough, talk to someone like a counsellor who is trained to distinguish between beliefs and reality and can support you.

As showstoppers can have serious effects on your life, I turned to psychologist Victoria Kasunic for her thoughts. She says that sometimes people who have made their decision to change and are ready to move suddenly become paralysed. It's usually a sign of fear and it can show up as fight, flight, freeze or fragment. People who are subject to a fight reaction will become argumentative; flight people will get out of a situation and avoid; freeze people will do the deer in the headlights, so they become immobile; and fragment people go to pieces, they fall apart in response to fear.

Kasunic says that 'for something like career change, where it's around identity, reputation, place in the world, connection with others, that social identity, some people will fight, but you're more likely to see people do the flight or the freeze'. She finds that young people are more prone to panic attacks, whereas in older people it becomes a more generalised worry or anxiety. It's not about what people think, but rather the risk that comes with letting go of the life you have spent years creating. 'You've established patterns of relating to your family, to your community, you've come so far, so it can seem like a bigger risk because, "I've created all of this, and so now if I fail, what will that mean for everything that I've already created?"'

It's also about identity, which we looked at in Chapter 8. As those of us who have been through it will appreciate, the midlife crisis is about, 'Who am I really and why am I here?' If you're in your 40s or 50s and think you're in the wrong job or the wrong life, this can become a real problem if you don't take steps to find some answers for yourself. The anxiety from midlife inaction can wake you up in the middle of the night.

As a psychologist, Kasunic knows that when we are children we develop our sense of who we are in relation to the rest of the world, and it's then that we build our negative core 'schema', our negative core belief system. As she says, 'it's like an operating system in a computer, it's unconscious, it's there in the background pressing all the buttons for you, emotionally and mentally. Its job is to protect you because it's a fear mechanism, but it's not very helpful when you're trying to do something.'

A very common core schema is 'I'm not good enough', says Kasunic. These people tend to become overachievers to compensate for the core schema. (It's just possible that I can relate to this one ...) When you get triggered emotionally, when you're tired, under a lot of stress or going through transitions and changes, it will come out. For someone with 'I'm not good enough', changing careers would really trigger this schema. Whereas, says Kasunic, if your core schema is around 'I'm not loveable', it wouldn't be such a problem in careers, it would come up more in relationships.

Kasunic summarises this in language that makes a great deal of sense to me. 'As human beings, we'll basically do anything to avoid feeling bad or scared, so we often use avoidance as a strategy to reduce fear. And we don't realise that if we keep avoiding things that make us fearful, we never learn that fear doesn't last. Fear moves in waves, and so we need to learn to surf the waves rather than getting our board and getting out of the water.'

This book is all about teaching you to surf the waves.

Victoria Kasunic's tips

1. Be mindful

It's helpful to notice when it's happening, and having some mechanism to self-reflect. Try meditation, mindfulness, yoga, tai chi, anything where you connect more with yourself, so you can be present and notice what's going on for you in a moment. The more you do this, the more you can catch those negative thoughts and reactions.

2. Try journalling

I recommend journalling because you start to make sense of yourself, to see a pattern – 'Oh, I did that again.' The fact that you can observe yourself says that it's not the entirety of you.

266

3. Get feedback

Ask close, trusted friends for feedback about your behaviour, your strengths and your weaknesses, because other people will see them. They'll see patterns of behaviour where you haven't supported yourself and can bring those blind spots into your awareness.

4. Get support

You may need professional support if the anxiety or stress or negative thinking is becoming debilitating, if you're not functioning as well as you could be with work and relationships. If you're dreading getting up in the morning, it's a very big indicator. If you're having trouble with sleep, you find you're drinking a bit more or eating a bit more to manage your anxiety, they're all signs that something is going on and you need more support.

Transitions

All change involves a transition from the old to the new. It's useful to embrace and accept this process as much as you can, though this is sometimes easier said than done. Each transition has its own pace, so if you find and respect that pace and be patient with yourself it will be a smoother trip. When we feel uncertain or uncomfortable, we may want to do something, anything, to ease the pressure or take away the feelings. Be wary about this; often the longer you can stay in uncertainty, the more likely your deepest needs and urges will bubble to the surface.

Talk it through with a trusted friend or a counsellor if the going gets rough. You may need to set up some temporary structures, like a journey job or extra support from friends. Are there people you need to clarify your situation with? Do you need more space to be alone at the moment? Take extra care of yourself and find what works for you, whether that's long walks, time with friends, a movie, even chocolate. Treat yourself as you would treat your best friend during a difficult time.

Realise you are in a cycle and the process will bring you out the other side. You may feel like the old you is dying, but a new you is being reborn at the same time – say farewell and grieve the old, but get ready to welcome the new.

I'm a fan of the rather marvellous *Transitions* by William Bridges.[1] I have used his approach personally and with clients since I first came across it in the early 1980s. It's a great resource when the ground under you shifts, as it demystifies the process, clarifies the difference between change and transition, and gives good practical advice alongside encouraging tales of fellow 'transitioners'. Bridges divides the transition process into three phases he calls 'endings', 'the neutral zone' and 'new beginnings'.

Endings

Periods of transition generally, though not always, start with an ending. You lose your job or realise you hate it. A relationship ends or someone dies. You wake up and realise your old life is no longer satisfying or that you can no longer live it the same way due to infirmity or other circumstances. Whatever the catalyst, it's important to acknowledge that something has gone, changed or been taken away. Until you do, you can't fully move on.

The neutral zone

As a longstanding *Star Trek* tragic I find the 'neutral zone' a powerful metaphor. It refers to the phase where you are between the old and the new. It's like the fallow field or the pause between sounds in music. You can't force this phase, but nor should you let yourself wallow or stall here.

Ideally, you'd go away during this time, do a retreat or some other form of contemplative practice. Given the constraints of modern life, this is not always possible, but if you can honour the need for time out, you'll be able to manage this process better.

Maybe make time to meditate, or take long walks or write in a journal. This is not a time where prescriptive processes or join-the-dots recommendations are of much use. It's messy, it's organic and it doesn't follow a formula, so just be authentic and go with it.

New beginnings

First signs here are subtle, so watch out for small outer or inner signs or clues. Whether in your career or personal life, this stage is a chance to really create your own new life. Make the most of it.

Victoria Kasunic shared two case studies of clients who have dealt with showstopper issues, and you'll see they both go through ending, neutral-zone and new-beginning stages.

Angela

Angela was a ballet dancer and had trained from quite a young age. She had gone over to Germany, was in a professional ballet company, and then had an injury so it wasn't going to be possible for her to be a dancer anymore. So she came back to life in Australia and started to have significant problems with anxiety; she basically struggled to travel on a train. She would just start to panic and have a lot of anxiety around doing anything new. She was a pretty controlled person anyway because as a dancer you need to be a disciplined and controlled person, but she became really controlling and obsessive around things being out of place. Even in my office, if the rug was skew-whiff, she would be bothered by that and would find it hard to stay in the moment with me.

We looked at what was underneath that, there was a lot of loss around her career ending and it being completely out of her control. Her core belief was, 'I'm not good enough' and it was like she wanted to retreat into herself and disappear from the world; she became so controlling about medical things that a sore throat meant she was dying.

We worked on discovering other things that she enjoyed. She was definitely very bright, she loved to knit, and she got back into knitting. Then a used-clothing store needed volunteers, so she started to volunteer there because she wasn't able to work due to her debilitation.

She started to feel good and she was bright and helpful and organised and started to get things into order in the store, and from there she was able to get paid work as a receptionist. From there she worked her way up until she was an executive assistant and she then went back to uni to study marketing. And that's what she's working in now.

Two things were key. One was creating a vision of something that was exciting. And the second thing was that the volunteering made her feel useful. She was feeling useless because her body was no longer useful as a dancer and that's what she'd been trained for and so was thinking, 'What am I good for?' And you feel so good when you help others and get that boost of positive energy. It's very hard if you don't have anything positive in your life that makes you feel good. So this was the fuel that got her buoyant and then she had the energy to take the other steps.

It was step by step. She got the first paid job and she did really well because in admin someone who's controlling and obsessive is an asset, so she kept getting acknowledged, promoted. That was important – she got a lot of positive acknowledgement and saw 'I am good at something else'.

When she first came to me she would have a panic attack on the way on the train and by the end she'd moved in with her partner, she was finishing her degree, she'd gone for another job. She's still a bit obsessive, but her life has expanded. She wouldn't have believed that was possible, I think, at the beginning.

Roger

Roger came to me just before he turned 60. He basically got shoved out of the company he started, and there was so much anger and resentment, he became poisoned by the experience. I notice that for men, particularly men who are made redundant or retrenched, it's a blow around this role of male as provider and the sense of self being very tied with work. For this client's generation, this is what you do for life, there is no 'I can do anything'. This is it, and then you retire and that's it. So it's quite a shift to suddenly have to say, 'That's not it and I have to adapt.' And it's harder as you get older. It's not fun.

Roger was an engineer, very systems- and process-oriented. It was really challenging for him because there were no rules, no principles anymore. He was an incredible man in terms of what he had done and achieved and his intelligence, and here he was thinking, 'I'll just get a job at a hardware store.'

We looked at all of his skills in mentoring and he had a lot of skills in training sales teams, so he started to do consulting work, which started to make him feel useful again. People who have been very results-oriented can have a tendency to be impatient, and so I'd say, 'Just let yourself integrate this bit, don't push.' Roger was like a master of the universe, he would say, 'I'm going to call everyone. If they haven't got back to me today I'm going to email them again.'

At the beginning his confidence had been zapped, but because he started with just a few hours at a time he could prepare, get himself together, and then rest afterwards. No one would have known the emotional upheaval that that took. It was about opening himself up, and also giving himself a little bit of time to sit with it and integrate it before he bit off the next bit.

CHAPTER 15

It's a wrap

May you have warmth in your igloo, oil in
your lamp, and peace in your heart.
Eskimo proverb

Be committed

I couldn't finish this book without talking about commitment –
and its close cousin, persistence. These days it's often considered
old-fashioned to be fully committed in work or in life. But a deep
commitment to your working life or your new identity may be
your most effective strategy to navigate rough waters, find that
next job or take the plunge and start your own business. For any
career step or project that involves going outside your known
universe, you'll need fierce commitment to yourself to get through
the obstacles – and if you don't champion yourself, who will?

It is important that this commitment is a conscious, full-
hearted and deliberate act. Only then can it form the bedrock of
your work. It involves making a deep decision to let go of what's
not working in your life and to move towards what you think
will work. You need to choose to be in charge of your life and to
be persistent in going after what you want. You need to choose
yourself.

Of course, there are times when you realise you're on a path
that's either not what you thought it would be or that doesn't
bring the satisfaction you hoped. The experiments and research

discussed in this book are intended to minimise the likelihood of this, as it did for Kylie in Chapter 10, who tried a number of things before finding her perfect combination. But sadly, even with the most careful planning, sometimes shit still happens. These can be painful realisations and may involve deep feelings of regret, betrayal and even despair. It takes courage to extract yourself from the wrong place, and even more courage to dare to try again.

I remember Barry, a participant in one of my workshops, telling us about his decision to retrain as an environmental scientist so he could work on climate change. He gave up his career as a radiographer in his late 40s and returned to university. His decision ticked all the boxes about using your strengths and finding a purpose, and his new field can only become more critical over the coming years. However, just when he graduated in 2013, our then prime minister announced significant job cuts to science positions, and so far in 2016 things haven't recovered. So for now, Barry is taking casual shifts in a hardware store instead of living his new working life. I really admire his attitude, his persistence and his refusal to fall into blame or bitterness. Barry is still committed to himself, even though his path isn't as straightforward as he had hoped.

Life is messy and there is no join-the-dots formula or guarantee of success. And as I tell every one of my clients, there is no magic pill here, no fortune-cookie paper with the name of your ideal career. You will need to dream big and really go for what you want, as well as considering a Plan B if it doesn't work out or it takes longer than you thought.

But a deep, fierce commitment to yourself, some persistence and ongoing courage will give you the best chance to create your new life. In this final chapter I share two stories with you, quite different on the surface but both about people who made that commitment to say 'Yes' to life, to create a plan and live it – and to create a Plan B for later, too.

Deb, 56, and Greg, 59

Deb and Greg changed their lives when they decided to travel around Australia with their son and his family. On their return, they realised that their attitudes to all sorts of things had changed, freeing them up to create a very personal mix of house-sitting, casual work and travel.

Greg: I'm an electrician and I've worked in many facets of that trade, mainly contract-based, and up until the last couple of years it's been pretty full on.

Deb: I did part-time work while our two children were little and when they were growing up I worked intermittently. I went to uni when they were at primary school and did a degree to increase my chances of a good job. Then we moved to Sydney from the NSW North Coast and I worked in human resources. Later we came to Brisbane and I worked for 10 years in a HR-related role.

By 2013 we had two small grandchildren in Sydney and we were travelling backwards and forwards a fair bit to have time with them.

My son called one day and said they were going to travel around Australia. After we got over the shock I said to Greg, 'Is that something we could do?' and Greg said, 'It's something I've always wanted to do.' So we went with them. We sold or gave away all of our furniture and things, put a few bits into storage and rented out the house.

Greg: We bought a 4WD and a caravan and we travelled around Australia. We've never been intrepid travellers, so although it wasn't a difficult decision, we certainly had reservations.

Deb: We started from Brisbane and headed south down the coast, then through Victoria, then South Australia. I almost cried on the Great Ocean Road. I always wanted to go there and it was amazing. In the end we were on the road for 13 months, we got right around Australia. The biggest thing was learning to work together, because we had a caravan that had to be put up and there were quite a few steps involved. It took us quite a while to learn to work with our very different approaches to things.

Greg: We're much more mates now than we used to be. And the relationship with our grandkids now is really solid because of that trip, because we spent so much time with them. It's also turned us into travellers and we've done two more big trips since.

It changed the direction of our lives. I certainly have a flexibility that I didn't possess and I'm happier, more excited about what's to come. And really we don't know what's to come. I'm a lot less stressed about what's just around the corner or what's five years away. While I was locked into that work cycle I felt quite trapped by that and thought it would be my life for the next however many years. Now I know that that's not the case, there're all sorts of things that we can do, so there's that whole flexibility and openness to change. I was quite resistant to change before that.

Deb: And you can have an awesome life without a lot of money, because we travelled very economically and we now live frugally because our priority is more travel. When we came back from the big trip we'd met a few house-sitters and we thought, 'Ooh, that's a good way to save some money.' We gave house-sitting a go, and it's worked out absolutely perfectly, we are doing it to this day.

I'm definitely more adventurous and every trip we push the boundary out a little bit more with where we'll drive to or the risks we'll take.

We're doing what we can for work at the moment. I went back to work and that didn't go so well, so I took a package and left. Greg did some work for a while and then we did more travel. We did a bit of house cleaning, we did a few Airtasker jobs and bits and pieces. I did some volunteer work and I've just started work in a friend's business, casual work for a few months, so we're just doing what comes up.

Greg: I've got this little 'Greg the Garden Gnome' idea sizzling along in my head, low-technology/high-impact garden clean-up, which actually goes hand-in-hand with Deb's idea of setting up a decluttering business. So that might work well for us. It's what I love to do. Even on all our housesits, I think we're up to number 12 or 14 now, we try to leave a little positive mark on the place. We make a little garden or do a little repair here and there, and Deb might organise a pantry and they love that.

Deb: Life has definitely changed. I love the uncertainty now, the fact that we don't know where we're going to be living. I understand now that there are so many possibilities and that we can make it work no matter what. We live in a fabulous country with lots of opportunities and lots of possibilities.

Greg: Before our trip I was always on the chase for success or to reach a higher pinnacle in my career, and now I realise that I may have actually reached that, may have succeeded in my career. That realisation gives me a whole bunch of other choices that I didn't feel as though I had before and we're both a lot more comfortable in our skins now.

Deb: I am completely satisfied. I feel completely content.

We still need income, but also I like going to work, I like having something to do and the decluttering business, I'm really looking forward to that, although it just has to wait. It'll be our own little business. We'll do it [house-sitting and travelling] for as long as we're physically able, which, for us, could easily be another 10 years, or until we get sick of it. There might come a time where we want to have our own veggie garden again and settle into a little minimalist cabin in the woods somewhere.

Greg: Final words? Don't die wondering, look outside the square, have a think about what your dreams are and look at being able to realise them in the here and now, not way off there in the airy-fairy future. Oh, and life's too short for shit wine. I learned on one of the trips, always drink your best wine first. You don't want to be dead the next day and have a nice bottle of wine in there that they're going to drink at your wake.

One of the big themes of this book has been about choice, about *you* deciding what will bring you satisfaction in your next stage and how you can make that happen. This is – and should be – a very personal thing. Despite the media frequently lumping all people over 50 into some homogeneous soup, generally in order to make a negative point about older Australians hogging big houses or costing too much in health care or pensions, we actually become more individual as we age – and so our life and work choices also become more individual. As we have seen in this book, for some this is a time to wind down their working lives in order to pursue other interests or to give back to the community. Others decide to start a small business or change careers. And some like Deb and Greg discover they can throw everything up in the air – where they live, how they live and what they do for work – and create a very personal and satisfying flexible new life.

There is an increasing number of Australians who see these years as a chance not only to change what they do but also to go for really big dreams. I often hear clients say to me, 'If not now, then when?' Equally often, I am the one saying this to a client who is hovering on the edge of a change that they have long dreamed of but continued to put off even starting, sometimes for decades. These new directions may involve lifestyle changes such as moving overseas to help their favourite charity on the ground, or to do a PhD, or to downsize so they can reduce their need for a regular income. Their dreams are always important to them but don't always look dramatic to other people; all that matters is the sense of personal satisfaction that results from realising your dreams.

Jane, 59

Jane has used the years since her children became adults to create some new and big work dreams and to start living them. A similar age to Deb and Greg, her decisions have taken her on a quite different trajectory.

I was the chairperson of a regional body of a presbytery and I was finishing as a congregational minister. I had come out of a very difficult ministry situation, which had taken its toll on me personally, and led me to questioning what I wanted to do next. I was at a hiatus point in terms of where I went in the Church and I wanted to be clear and make my own choices, rather than be driven by necessity to do something.

Doing an intensive assessment instrument with Joanna was absolutely revelatory. I've done a lot of personal exploration, development and reflective practice, but this was the first thing that identified abilities for me, and it gave me permission to claim my ability to generate ideas as something I bring that's very valuable in the context that I work in but I'd never been able to name before. It immediately opened my eyes to a different way of thinking about myself and it gave me a language for it, so it was really useful.

In a way, the most important thing was opening a door that I hadn't even known was there before and giving me the courage to walk through the door. There was a hiatus period when I was doing a project for the synod, which gave me a bit of breathing space to make a decision about applying for the position I'm in now, which is Associate Secretary of the Synod. So now, even though I'm still working in the Church, I'm working in the Church in a different way than I was before.

But I also have a Plan B, around doing mediation, which I didn't have before and I'm not afraid of what happens. The result is I feel much freer at work than I ever did before. I don't feel as trapped in the Church. I do what I do because I have something to contribute, it's rewarding and stimulating and exciting and all of those things, but once it stops being that then I've got other things that I can do.

If I knew how good the 50s were going to be I would have had them first. Menopause gets a bad press, but there was for me a huge upsurge of energy and capacity, and suddenly I'm not tied to kids and husband in the same way and I can look at the world differently and think, 'What do I want to do here?' and that was completely liberating. And I had the energy to go with it, that's what provoked the exploration. I stopped being afraid of the future and worried about being here for this child, that child or the other child. Actually, I'd quite like to go back to start the 50s all over again.

There's a sense of, 'Look, I'm happy for you to have your opinion, but this has nothing to do with you – I'm going to make my own choices.' I have boundless energy, much more than when I was 20. At 20 you're bound by hormones for goodness sake. Very boring. Hormones certainly drove my life more than I feel pleased about and I felt trapped by them. But I've got rid of the hormones.

I had a lunch with people I went to school with a few months ago now and they are retiring, some of them exactly my age have retired. I'm mystified. Why would you do that to yourself? They've not retired to do anything, they've retired to retire.

I'm so enjoying this period of my life, I think it's the best thing. I read a quote from Jared Diamond, the anthropologist, and he said that he's now 75 and he's doing his best work. And I think, 'Fantastic, I can do my best work, it's yet to come.'

I can't tell what the next decade will bring, and I'd be worried if I could. You don't even know yet what your best work will be and I think that's just totally liberating and exciting.

Last words

I find endings difficult. I avoid farewell parties. I hate fuss. I'm the one who just slips out the back. Maybe that's why, though I spent a lot of time thinking about the ending of this book, I left the writing of these final words until the very last days before the manuscript was due.

I've covered everything I wanted to cover about work reinvention. And if you're reading this, I hope you have done some reflection and some experimenting yourself, and are well on the way to changing your own working life. I wish you well.

I want to finish by saying something about intergenerational harmony. In August 2016, I went to an Ethics Centre debate in Sydney on the topic, 'Boomers owe a debt to the young'. It was part serious discussion, part entertaining performance, and as you'd expect, both sides argued with some passion. I left the debate with the same view I had before arriving – that all generations owe a debt to the others, that we must respect those who went before us and do our best to leave our world a better place for those who follow.

I went home feeling very sad, though, much affected by the feeling of conflict and outright antagonism I sensed on both sides.

I've never bought into the belief that we can or should blame others for our own situation and so I hadn't taken very seriously the whingeing in online forums and media articles about the grey tsunami ruining our country or the counter-polemic about lazy, narcissistic Gen Ys and millennials. But on the night of the debate I saw that many people do take these viewpoints seriously. I was quite upset and thought about it a lot in the following days – and I am now determined to advocate where possible for intergenerational harmony.

Pitting one side against the other isn't fair or useful. We need to grow up, to find a way to work and live together, to tap into all our strengths and harness them for the good of all generations alive today and for those who will follow us. I feel very strongly about this, so watch this space. (And if you can do whatever you can to bring harmony to our world, then that would be excellent, too.)

May you belong. And may you flourish.

Endnotes

Introduction

1. Australian Bureau of Statistics, Life tables 2011–2013, released 6 November 2014.
2. Department of Communities, Child Safety and Disability Services, *Ageing: Myths and reality*, 2012, qld.gov.au/seniors/documents/retirement/ageing-myth-reality.pdf, p. 12.
3. Laura Carstensen, 'Older People Are Happier', TEDxWomen talk, December 2011, ted.com/talks/laura_carstensen_older_people_are_happier.
4. abs.gov.au/ausstats/abs@.nsf/94713ad4forty-fiveff1425ca25682000192af2/8e72c forty-five26a94aaedca2569de00296978!OpenDocument.
5. abs.gov.au/AUSSTATS/abs@.nsf/2f762f958forty-five417aeca25706c00834efa/forty-fivefeea54e2403635ca2570ec000c46e1!OpenDocument.
6. smh.com.au/national/health/life-expectancy-will-we-just-keep-getting-older-20131107-2x4eh.html.
7. Australian Institute of Health and Welfare, aihw.gov.au/deaths/life-expectancy/.
8. abs.gov.au/ausstats/abs@.nsf/mf/3201.0.
9. abs.gov.au/ausstats/abs@.nsf/0/1CD2B1952AFC5E7ACA257298000F2E76?OpenDocument.
10. David J. Lowsky, S. Jay Olshansky, Jay Bhattacharya and Dana P. Goldman, 'Heterogeneity in Healthy Aging', *The Journals of Gerentology Series A: Biological Science and Medical Sciences*, June 2014, 69(6), pp. 640–9.
11. Axel H. Brösch-Supan, 'Aging, Labour Markets and Well-being', *Empirica*, vol. 40, issue 3, 2013, p. 397.
12. Australian Bureau of Statistics, *National Health Survey: Summary of Results*, 2007–2008.
13. Australian Institute of Management, 'Engaging and Retaining Older Workers', discussion paper, February 2013, p. 14.
14. smh.com.au/business/employment-up-as-australian-economy-improves-20140721-zvgus.html.
15. Alex Maritz, Roxanne Zolin, Anton De Waal and Rosemary Fisher, *Senior Entrepreneurship in Australia: Active Ageing and Extending Working Lives*, National Seniors Productive Ageing Centre, Melbourne, 2015.
16. See for example, Axel H. Börsch-Supan, 'Silver Economy: Pipe Dream or Realistic Possibility?', Max Planck Institute for Social Law and Social Policy Discussion Paper No. 26, 2014.
17. John Daley, *Game-changers: Economic Reform Priorities for Australia*, report for Grattan Institute, June 2012, p. 51.
18. Deloitte Access Economics, *Increasing Participation Among Older Workers: The Grey Army Advances*, report for the Australian Human Rights Commission, 2012, p. 4.
19. James C. Sarros, Andrew Pirola-Merlo and Robin Baker, *Research Report: The Impact of Age on Managerial Style*, report for the Department of Management, Monash University and the Australian Institute of Management QLD/NT, 2012.

20. Paul Rodgers, 'Do We Really Get Dumber As We Grow Older?', *Forbes*, 31 January 2014, forbes.com/sites/paulrodgers/2014/01/31/do-we-really-get-dumber-as-we-grow-older/#588212cf1f0c.

21. Sally Thompson, Julia Griffin and Kaye Bowman, *The Ageing Population: New Opportunities for Adult and Community Education*, report for Adult Learning Australia, February 2013, p. 10.

22. heraldsun.com.au/news/victoria/melbourne-grandma-millie-browne-98-is-worlds-oldest-app-store-game-developer/news-story/c69656b7aebc1328d2c3dde6d14be98a.

23. toknowinfo.hubpages.com/hub/Success-Stories-Never-Too-Old-Never-Too-Late-Late-Bloomers-Dreams-and-Achievements.

24. bbc.co.uk/history/historic_figures/roget_peter_mark.shtml.

25. 'Manufacturer Vita Needle Finds Investment in Older Workers Turns a Big Profit', *PBS NewsHour*, 2 January 2013, pbs.org/newshour/bb/business-jan-june13-makingsense_01-02/.

26. UK Department of Work and Pensions, *Employer Case Studies: Employing Older Workers for an Effective Multi-generational Workforce*, 2013, www.gov.uk/government/uploads/system/uploads/attachment_data/file/142752/employing-older-workers-case-studies.pdf.

27. SafeWork SA, *Age Friendly Workplaces: Case Studies – The Benefits of Employing Older Workers*, 2014, safework.sa.gov.au/uploaded_files/AgeFriendlyWorkplacesCaseStudies.pdf.

28. NRMA Living Well Navigator, *Trail Blazing Employers*, 26 June 2014.

29. ibid.

30. See Department of Communities, Child Safety and Disability Services, *Ageing: Myths and Reality*, 2012, for example, qld.gov.au/seniors/documents/retirement/ageing-myth-reality.pdf.

31. Marc Freedman, *Encore: Finding Work that Matters in the Second Half of Life*, Perseus Books Group, 2007.

Chapter 1

1. businessinsider.com.au/how-kfc-founder-colonel-sanders-achieved-success-in-his-60s-2015-6.

2. latimes.com/local/obituaries/la-me-frank-mccourt20-2009jul20-story.html.

3. juliachildfoundation.org/timeline.html.

4. britannica.com/biography/Paul-Cezanne.

5. Laura L. Carstensen, *A Long Bright Future*, Perseus Books, New York, 2011, p. 91.

6. Laura L. Carstensen, 'Older People Are Happier', op. cit.

7. Laura L. Carstensen, op. cit.

8. Australian Bureau of Statistics, *Australian Social Trends*, September 2010, abs.gov.au/AUSSTATS/abs@.nsf/Lookup/4102.0Main+Features30Sep+2010.

9. Merrill Lynch and Age Wave, *Work in Retirement, Myths and Motivations: Career Reinventions and the New Retirement Workscape*, 2014, p. 16.

10. Advisory Panel on the Economic Potential of Senior Australians, *Realising the Economic Potential of Senior Australians, Part 2: Enabling Opportunity*, 2011, p. 42.

11. Alex Maritz, 'Senior Entrepreneurship in Australia: An Exploratory Approach', *International Journal of Organizational Innovation*, vol. 7, issue 3, January 2015.

12. Katelijne Lenaerts, *Money for Jam: Enabling Women at Risk of Poverty to Create Financial Wellbeing through Micro-enterprise*, 2016, percapita.org.au/wp-content/uploads/2016/05/MoneyForJam_Final.pdf.

13. Sally Thompson, Julia Griffin and Kaye Bowman, *The Ageing Population: New Opportunities for Adult and Community Education*, report for Adult Learning Australia, February 2013, p. 11.

14. Such as the Commonwealth Department of Health and Ageing, Australian Human Rights Commission, Financial Services Council, National Seniors Productive Ageing Centre, the Commonwealth Department of Education, Employment and Workplace Relations, the Grattan Institute and Australian Institute of Management.

15. National Seniors Productive Ageing Centre, *Age Discrimination in the Labour Market: Experiences and Perceptions of Mature Age Australians*, report for the Department of Health and Ageing, 2013, p. 17.

16. Steve Straehly, 'Employers Mask Age Discrimination by Seeking "Digital Natives"', *AllGov*, 7 May 2015, allgov.com/news/top-stories/employers-mask-age-discrimination-by-seeking-digital-natives-150507?news=856426.

17. Australian Human Rights Commission, *Fact or Fiction? Stereotypes of Older Australians*, 2013, p. 27.

18. Ashton Applewhite, *This Chair Rocks: A Manifesto Against Ageism*, Networked Books, New York, 2016.

19. Becca Levy, 'Improving Memory in Old Age Through Implicit Self-stereotyping', *Journal of Personality and Social Psychology*, vol. 71, 1996, pp. 1092–1107.

20. Australian Institute of Management, op. cit., p. 15.

21. National Seniors Productive Ageing Centre, *Age Discrimination in the Labour Market: Experiences and Perceptions of Mature Age Australians*, report for the Department of Health and Ageing, 2013, p. 16.

22. To read more about these and other experiments, see Ellen J. Langer, *Counterclockwise: Mindful Health and the Power of Possibility*, Hodder & Stoughton, London, 2009.

23. Molly Andrews, 'The Seductiveness of Agelessness', *Ageing and Society*, vol. 19, 1999, pp. 301–18.

24. Australian Institute of Management, op. cit., p. 12.

25. Australian Human Rights Commission, *Willing to Work: National Inquiry into Employment Discrimination against Older Australians and Australians with Disability*, AHRC, Sydney, 2016.

26. Malcolm Gladwell, *What the Dog Saw*, Penguin Books Ltd, London, 2009.

27. collinsdictionary.com/dictionary/english/retirement.

28. sciencedaily.com/releases/2016/10/161005132823.htm.

Chapter 2

1. Jane Figgis, *Reskilling for Encore Careers for (What Were Once) Retirement Years*, Research Report, NCVER, Adelaide, 2012, p. 5.

2. ibid., p. 9.

3.   Australian Institute of Management, op. cit., p. 15.
4.   bloomberg.com/news/articles/2012-09-06/bmw-never-too-old-assembly-insures-against-lost-engineers (available to subscribers only).
5.   Alex Maritz et al., op. cit.
6.   ibid.
7.   ibid.
8.   ibid.
9.   Elizabeth Isele, personal communication, October 2014.
10. Volunteering Australia, *Key Facts and Statistics about Volunteering in Australia*, 16 April 2015, volunteeringaustralia.org/research-and-advocacy/the-latest-picture-of-volunteering-in-australia.
11. Benjamin H. Gottlieb and Alayna A. Gillespie, 'Volunteerism, Health, and Civic Engagement among Older Adults', *Canadian Journal on Aging*, vol. 27, no. 4, Winter 2008, p. 407.
12. Volunteering Australia, op. cit.
13. National Seniors Productive Ageing Centre, *Still Putting In*, 2009, p. 11, nationalseniors.com.au/system/files/200905_PACReport_Research_StillPuttingIn_0.pdf.
14. National Seniors Productive Ageing Centre, op. cit., p. 17.
15. nationalseniors.com.au/be-informed/news-articles/willing-work-inquiry-highlight-age-old-problem, 2015.

Chapter 3
1.   Adapted from Frederic M. Hudson, *The Adult Years*, Jossey-Bass, San Francisco, 1999, pp. 142–4.
2.   Deloitte Touche Tohmatsu, *Building the Lucky Country #3 Positioning for Prosperity?*, Catching the Next Wave Report, 2014.
3.   Lynda Gratton, *The Shift: The Future of Work is Already Here*, HarperCollins Publishers, London, 2011.
4.   smh.com.au/comment/brains-over-brawn-nearly-twothirds-of-jobs-will-be-for-knowledge-workers-by-2036-20160902-gr76fd.
5.   Frerich Frerichs, Robert Lindley, Paula Aleksandrowicz, Beate Baldauf and Sheila Galloway, 'Active Ageing in Organisations: A Case Study Approach', *International Journal of Manpower*, vol. 33, issue 6, 2015, p. 671; Brian Findsen and Marvin Formosa, *Lifelong Learning in Later Life*, Sense Publishers, The Netherlands, 2011, pp. 173–5.
6.   https://www.ted.com/talks/stefan_sagmeister_the_power_of_time_off?

Chapter 4
1.   Jerome Bruner, 'The Narrative Construction of Reality', *Critical Inquiry*, vol. 18, no. 1, Autumn 1991, pp. 1–21.
2.   Such as Joseph Campbell, *The Hero with a Thousand Faces* (Bollingen Series, no. 17), 2nd edition, Princeton University Press, 1972; and Dan P. McAdams, *The Stories We Live By*, Guildford Press, New York, 1993.
3.   Molly Andrews, *Narrative Imagination and Everyday Life*, Oxford University Press, Oxford, 2014, p. 62.
4.   ibid., p. 63.

5. Such as David Denborough, *Retelling the Stories of Our Lives: Everyday Narrative Therapy to Draw Inspiration and Transform Experience*, W.W. Norton and Company, New York, 2014.

Chapter 5
1. Patrick L. Hill and Nicholas A. Turiano, 'Purpose in Life as a Predictor of Mortality Across Adulthood', *Psychological Science*, vol. 25, no. 7, July 2014, pp. 1482–6.
2. Becca R. Levy, Martin D. Slade, Suzanne R. Kunkel and Stanislav V. Kasl, 'Longevity Increased by Positive Self-perceptions of Aging', *Journal of Personality and Social Psychology*, vol. 83(2), August 2002, pp. 261–70.
3. Mount Sinai Medical Center, 'Have a Sense of Purpose in Life? It May Protect Your Heart', *ScienceDaily*, 6 March 2015, http://www.sciencedaily.com/ releases/2015/03/150306132538.htm.
4. ibid.

Chapter 6
1. Marcus Buckingham, *Go Put Your Strengths to Work: 6 Powerful Steps to Achieve Outstanding Performance*, Simon & Schuster, New York, 2007.
2. Martin E.P. Seligman, *Authentic Happiness: Using the New Positive Psychology to Realize Your Potential for Lasting Fulfillment*, Simon & Schuster, New York, 2002.
3. Mihaly Csikszentmihalyi, *Finding Flow: The Psychology of Engagement with Everyday Life*, Perseus Books Group, New York, 1997.

Chapter 7
1. Marie Kondo, *The Life-changing Magic of Tidying Up*, Ten Speed Press, Berkeley, 2014.
2. Malcolm Gladwell, *Outliers: The Story of Success*, Back Bay Books, New York, 2011.

Chapter 8
1. Richard P. Johnson, *The New Retirement*, Retirement Options, North Carolina, 2001; and Richard P. Johnson, *What Colour is Your Retirement?*, Retirement Options, North Carolina, 2006.
2. afr.com/business/facing-irrelevance-after-life-on-the-corporate-treadmill-20130305-j126m.
3. Lynda Gratton and Andrew Scott, *The 100-Year Life*, Bloomsbury Publishing Plc, London, 2016.

Chapter 10
1. Department of Communities, Child Safety and Disability Services, *Ageing: Myths and Reality*, 2012, p. 30.
2. Norman Doidge, *The Brain That Changes Itself*, Penguin Books Limited, London, 2010.
3. Carol S. Dweck, *Mindset: How You Can Fulfil Your Potential*, Random House, New York, 2007.

4. ted.com/talks/carol_dweck_the_power_of_believing_that_you_can_
    improve?language=en.
5. Norman Doidge, op. cit., p. 258.
6. Tim Brown, 'Design Thinking', *Harvard Business Review*, June 2008, pp. 1–10,
    and ted.com/talks/tim_brown_on_creativity_and_play.

Chapter 11
1. Chip Heath and Dan Heath, *Decisive: How to Make Better Choices in Life and
    Work*, Random House, New York 2013.
2. Edward de Bono, *Six Thinking Hats*, Back Bay Books, New York, 1999.

Chapter 12
1. wbur.org/news/2014/06/09/long-term-unemployed-mit-mass.
2. Sehba Mahmood, 'Professional Preparation for Older Women: A View from New
    Zealand', *Educational Gerontology*, 34: 6, 2008, pp. 462–6.
3. Charles Handy, *The Age of Unreason*, Harvard Business School Press, Boston,
    1990.
4. Charles Handy, *The Second Curve: Thoughts on Reinventing Society*, Random
    House Books, London, 2015.
5. John English and Babette Moate, *Managing a Small Business in Australia:
    A Complete Handbook*, Allen & Unwin, Sydney, 2010.
6. Volunteering Australia, op. cit.
7. Australian Human Rights Commission, *Fact or Fiction?*, op. cit.

Chapter 13
1. Robert Fritz, *Path of Least Resistance: Learning to Become the Creative Force in
    Your Own Life*, Revised and expanded edition, Newfane Press, Newfane, 2010.

Chapter 14
1. William Bridges, *Transitions: Making Sense of Life's Changes: Revised 25th
    Anniversary Edition*, Perseus Books Group, Cambridge MA, 2004.

Resources

Books

Molly Andrews, *Narrative Imagination and Everyday Life*, Oxford University Press, Oxford, 2014.

Ashton Applewhite, *This Chair Rocks: A Manifesto Against Ageism*, Networked Books, New York, 2016.

William Bridges, *Transitions: Making Sense of Life's Changes: Revised 25th Anniversary Edition*, Perseus Books Group, New York, 2004.

Marcus Buckingham, *Go Put Your Strengths to Work: 6 Powerful Steps to Achieve Outstanding Performance*, Simon & Schuster, New York, 2007.

Susan Cain, *Quiet: The Power of Introverts in a World that Can't Stop Talking*, Penguin UK, 2012.

Joseph Campbell, *The Hero with a Thousand Faces* (Bollingen Series, No. 17), 2nd edition, Princeton University Press, 1972.

Laura Carstensen, *A Long Bright Future*, Public Affairs (Perseus Books), New York, 2011.

Mihaly Csikszentmihalyi, *Finding Flow: The Psychology of Engagement with Everyday Life*, Perseus Books Group, New York, 1997.

Edward de Bono, *Six Thinking Hats*, Back Bay Books, New York, 1999.

David Denborough, *Retelling the Stories of Our Lives: Everyday Narrative Therapy to Draw Inspiration and Transform Experience*, W.W. Norton and Company, New York, 2014.

Norman Doidge, *The Brain That Changes Itself*, Penguin Books Limited, London, 2007.

Carol S. Dweck, *Mindset: How You Can Fulfil Your Potential*, Random House, New York, 2007.

John English and Babette Moate, *Managing a Small Business in Australia: The Complete Handbook*, Allen & Unwin, Sydney, 2010.

Jonathon Fields, *Uncertainty: Turning Fear and Doubt into Fuel for Brilliance*, Penguin Group, New York, 2011.

Marc Freedman, *Encore: Finding Work that Matters in the Second Half of Life*, Perseus Books Group, New York, 2007.

Robert Fritz, *Path of Least Resistance: Learning to Become the Creative Force in Your Own Life*, Revised and expanded edition, Newfane Press, Newfane, 2010.

Malcolm Gladwell, *Outliers: The Story of Success*, Back Bay Books, New York, 2011.

Malcolm Gladwell, *What the Dog Saw*, Penguin Books Ltd, London, 2009.

Lynda Gratton, *The Shift: The Future of Work is Already Here*, HarperCollins Publishers, London, 2011.

Lynda Gratton and Andrew Scott, *The 100-Year Life*, Bloomsbury Publishing Plc, London, 2016.

Charles Handy, *The Age of Unreason*, Harvard Business School Press, Boston, 1990.

Charles Handy, *The Second Curve: Thoughts on Reinventing Society*, Random House Books, London, 2015.

Robert Pogue Harrison, *Juvenescence: A Cultural History of Our Age*, University of Chicago Press, Chicago, 2014.

Chip Heath and Dan Heath, *Decisive: How to Make Better Choices in Life and Work*, Random House, New York, 2013.

Frederic M. Hudson, *The Adult Years*, Jossey-Bass, San Francisco, 1999.

Don E. Hutcheson and Bob McDonald, *Don't Waste Your Talent: The 8 Critical Steps to Discovering What You Do Best*, The Highlands Company LLC, Larchmont, 2005.

Richard P. Johnson, *The New Retirement*, Retirement Options, North Carolina, 2001.

Anna Karpf, *How to Age: The School of Life*, MacMillan, London, 2014.

Marie Kondo, *The Life-changing Magic of Tidying Up*, Ten Speed Press, Berkeley, 2014.

Ellen J. Langer, *Counterclockwise: Mindful Health and the Power of Possibility*, Hodder & Stoughton, London, 2009.

John Lees, *The Interview Expert: How to get the job you want*, Pearson Business, United Kingdom, 2012.

Dan P. McAdams, *The Stories We Live By*, Guildford Press, New York, 1993.

Eric Ries, *The Lean Startup: How Constant Innovation Creates Radically Successful Businesses*, Penguin UK, London, 2011.

Richard Rohr, *Falling Upward: A Spirituality for the Two Halves of Life,* Jossey-Bass, San Francisco, 2011.

Lynne Segal, *Out of Time: The Pleasures and the Perils of Ageing*, New Left Books, London, 2013.

Martin E.P. Seligman, *Authentic Happiness: Using the New Positive Psychology to Realize Your Potential for Lasting Fulfillment*, Simon & Schuster, New York, 2002.

Hal Stone, *Embracing Your Inner Critic: Turning Self-Criticism into a Creative Asset*, HarperCollins Publishers, New York, 2011.

Michael J. Valenzuela, *Maintain Your Brain: The Latest Medical Thinking on What You Can Do to Avoid Dementia*, ABC Books, HarperCollins Publishers, Sydney, 2011.

Websites

australia.gov.au/information-and-services/business-and-industry/abn-acn-
business-management/small-business (good advice for small business)
cota.org.au/australia/ and nationalseniors.com.au (these both advocate for
older Australians and offer information and a membership program)
flyingsolo.com.au (community for small business owners)
highlandsco.com/ (home of the Highlands Ability Battery)
joannamaxwell.com.au (this is my site, and the place to download my
special report or sign up for my newsletter)
lifereimagined.aarp.org (Life Reimagined is a US site run by AARP and
has some nifty online workshops, life-mapping tools and more)
nationalseniors.com.au/be-informed/research/productive-ageing-centre
(National Seniors Productive Ageing Centre, produces some interesting
research)
nextavenue.org (Next Avenue, a US site with tip sheets and information)
oversixty.com.au (an Australian site with useful content and special deals
for the over 60s)
seniorpreneurs.org.au (for older entrepreneurs)
trello.com (simple planning software)

TED Talks

Stefan Sagmeister on the power of time off: ted.com/talks/stefan_
sagmeister_the_power_of_time_off?
Tim Brown on design thinking: ted.com/talks/tim_brown_on_creativity_
and_play
Carol Dweck on growth mindset: ted.com/talks/carol_dweck_the_power_
of_believing_that_you_can_improve?
Mihaly Csikszentmihalyi on flow and happiness: ted.com/talks/mihaly_
csikszentmihalyi_on_flow
Isabelle Allende on passionate ageing: ted.com/talks/isabelle_allende_
how_to_live_passionately_no_matter_your_age
Laura Carstensen on older people are happier: ted.com/talks/laura_
carstensen_older_people_are_happier
Michael Steger on what makes life meaningful: tedxtalks.ted.com/video/
What-Makes-Life-Meaningful-Mich
Jane Fonda on the third act: ted.com/talks/jane_fonda_life_s_third_act
For more, try these TED playlists: ted.com/topics/aging and ted.com/
topics/work

Acknowledgements

My first acknowledgement must be to all the people who so generously shared their stories with me for this book: Beth Barclay, Peter Bishop, Michelle Cairns, David A. Clark, Christie Cooper, Mark Denny, Jane Fry, Sandy Easterbrook, Jane Gavan, Nathalie Hazan, PJ, Joanne Lynch, David Michaelis, Jenny Morawska, John Moutsos, Maha Noore, Pauline O'Carolan, Jan Osmond, Julie Parkin, Robert Prinable, Yumiko Roberts, Michael Rosenthal, Paul Smith, Ross Smith, Jan Stuelcken, Deb Warren, Greg Warren, Conny Weyrich, Andy Zaple and those who wish to remain anonymous.

You have been my teachers and it has been a privilege to hear about your lives. The same goes for my many clients and workshop participants, who taught me at least as much as I (hopefully) taught them. Thank you all.

I owe a huge debt of gratitude to Brook Turner, Lisa Hresc and Claire Scobie, who all championed this book project in different ways, through all the days when I lost faith in it myself, or life threatened to crowd it out. You already know that without you this book would not exist. Now everyone knows.

I also want to acknowledge Jane Martin and the many other friends who continue to share rich and interesting conversations about what's next. Andrew Forester made it his mission to find interesting people for me to talk to and Stephanie Richards had an eagle eye for interesting snippets relating to the over 40s.

I have learned much from random conversations in taxis and Ubers, on planes, in shops and at parties and from people who make comments on my social media posts. These have been illuminating – and also serve to check I'm not just reflecting the worldview of people like me.

I acknowledge the brilliant opportunity to work with the people at Fremantle Media and Fairfax Digital and to have Ray

Martin as my mentor when I started doing radio work. *The Road Next Travelled* gave me the chance to work with Australians in their 50s and beyond who were reinventing their lives, it allowed me into new worlds and gave me confidence that people were interested in exploring the changing world of work and beyond.

I am truly grateful to the experts who have given of their time to talk to me, either as background or as interviews for this book: Susan Ryan AO, Elizabeth Isele, Ashton Applewhite, Bridget Brandon, Suzy Jacobs, Kate McCallum, Karynne Courts, Alex Roberts, Bambi Price, Claire Scobie, Anne-Marie Kane, Scarlett Vespa, Jane Figgis, Victoria Kasunic, Dori Stiles, Valerie Hoogstad and Judith Claire.

Thank you also to the people who have researched and written about these issues and who shone light into dark corners for me, most of whom I have never met but whose books I have devoured in gratitude.

Virginia Woolf was spot on when she said that 'A woman must have money and a room of her own if she is to write fiction.' The same is true for non-fiction, but in addition I relied heavily on help from the fabulous Bridie Jenner from Bridie's Typing Services, our cleaning service – and deliveries from my local Thai restaurant, whose fishcakes, chicken wings and drunken noodles got us through many dinner dilemmas.

And finally, to Katie Stackhouse, my publisher at ABC Books. I couldn't have asked for a more encouraging and supportive introduction to the world of book publishing.

Index